Key Concepts in
Health Psychology

Key Concepts in
Health Psychology

Ian P. Albery and Marcus Munafò

SAGE Publications
Los Angeles ▪ London ▪ New Delhi ▪ Singapore

SAGE Publications Ltd
1 Oliver's Yard
55 City Road
London EC1Y 1SP

SAGE Publications Inc.
2455 Teller Road
Thousand Oaks, California 91320

SAGE Publications India Pvt Ltd
B 1/I 1 Mohan Cooperative Industrial Area
Mathura Road
New Delhi 110 044

SAGE Publications Asia-Pacific Pte Ltd
33 Pekin Street #02-01
Far East Square
Singapore 048763

Library of Congress Control Number: 2007931848

British Library Cataloguing in Publication data

A catalogue record for this book is available from the British Library

ISBN 978-1-4129-1932-6
ISBN 978-1-4129-1933-3 (pbk)

Typeset by C&M Digitals (P) Ltd., Chennai, India
Printed and bound in Great Britain by TJ International Ltd, Padstow, Cornwall
Printed on paper from sustainable resources

For Mioara,
And also for Henry, Beth and Will.
And in memory of Rowland, the last of the Starkeys.

Ian P. Albery, June 2007

CONTENTS

1 DEFINING HEALTH PSYCHOLOGY   1

Defining Health Psychology
and: Bio-medical model
       Psychosomatic medicine
       Biopsychosocial model   2

Defining Health Psychology
and: Health psychology   4

Defining Health Psychology
and: Social inequalities in health   9

Defining Health Psychology
and: Epidemiology of health and illness   15

2 RESEARCH METHODS AND MEASUREMENT   19

Research Methods and Measurement
and: Study design   20

Research Methods and Measurement
and: Cross-sectional   23

Research Methods and Measurement
and: Longitudinal   26

Research Methods and Measurement
and: Experimental   28

Contents

LIST OF FIGURES

LIST OF TABLES

LIST OF BOXES

PREFACE

Background

Health psychology is one of the fastest growing disciplines in psychology but remains in its early years. Very few textbooks or journals, let alone societies devoted to the study of health psychology, existed prior to the late 1970s to early 1980s. By the twenty-first century, and our putting pen to paper for the production of this book, health psychology had matured significantly into its adolescence. Psychological societies and associations around the world have their own divisions or sections devoted to the discipline. For instance, in the UK the British Psychological Society established the Division of Health Psychology in 1997 from the Special Group in Health Psychology (see www.health-psychology.org.uk and www.bps.org.uk/dhp/dhp.home.cfm), and in the USA health psychology is represented as Division 38 of the American Psychological Association (see www.health-psych.org). There is also a burgeoning and active European Health Psychology Society (see www.ehps.net/1024/index.html) with membership and representation derived from across the whole of eastern and western Europe. Each of these societies have the general aim to study psychological processes of health, illness and well being in order to understand and implement the promotion and maintenance of health, to prevent illness and augment outcomes for those affected by illness, as well as to provide evidence that can be used to improve local and international healthcare systems and as such inform healthcare policy.

Major international journals have also been established to report specifically research related to the psychology of health (e.g. *Health Psychology* and *Psychology and Health*), many international and national conferences are organized so that researchers from around the world can converse about new and interesting findings and ideas, and it seems virtually infeasible to think that these days there are many universities around the world that do not offer courses or modules in health psychology.

From all this it would seem that academic health psychology is alive and kicking!

Health psychology as a profession

In parallel with the development of health psychology as an academic discipline providing applied empirical evidence for understanding psychological processes in health, there have also been significant moves in the maturity of health psychology as a profession. This has resulted in the development of health psychology competencies and professional skills to present the boundaries within which health psychologists should be expected to work and to which they should adhere. These include research competencies (e.g. familiarity with various research methods and research tools, and so on), teaching and training competencies (e.g. designing and delivering training about factors involved in the psychology of health to various consumer groups, and so on), consultancy (e.g. communication skills in the management of clients, and so on), as well as more general professional competencies (e.g. understanding and managing legal and ethical frameworks relevant to the professional environment).

An example of these competency requirements has been developed by the Division of Health Psychology within the British Psychological Society (BPS) and can been viewed at www.health-psychology.org.uk (see also Michie, 2004). Once a person has demonstrated these competencies to a governing body they can be approved as a professional health psychologist. In the UK achieving these competencies takes places via what is known as Stage 1 and Stage 2 training. Stage 1 training involves the postgraduate study of the core theories, models, methods and evidence in health psychology and as such provides core knowledge. This stage can be undertaken by successfully completing a BPS approved postgraduate qualification at a university. Stage 2 comprises supervised practice in which the individual is expected to show evidence of the core competencies (e.g. through written reports, assignments, supervisor's reports, and so on). Once a person has completed Stage 1 and Stage 2 training they can apply to become a full member of the Division of Health Psychology of the BPS and also a Chartered Health Psychologist.

But the story does not end there. Being an effective, competent, professional health psychologist, or indeed any other professional, means that you have to keep abreast of new information, new intervention techniques, contemporary legislation, and the like, in order to maintain the highest standards of professional practice. This means that registered health psychologists are expected to undertake and demonstrate what is called 'continuing professional development activities'.

So, I'm a chartered health psychologist but what kind of jobs can I do? Among many other examples health psychologists work as part of a multidisciplinary team in clinical and research practice. It is not uncommon to find a health psychologist in healthcare services such as in medical departments. They work in health promotion departments providing expert knowledge in the identification of core psychological factors that, for instance, lead people to behave in unhealthy ways, as well as having an important input into the design and evaluation of health promotion activities. You will also find them in university departments training aspiring health psychologists and undertaking health-related research which can be disseminated to the wider audience – just like us. Some even write books! A number of specific examples of the types of jobs chartered health psychologists undertake can be found at www.health-psychology.org.uk/menuItems/what_ is_health_psychology.php.

Aims of the book

Concepts are mental tools that we use when we are thinking about a subject. Conceptual thinking enables us to organize, catalogue, evaluate, interpret and explain the issue or topic we are interested in. While current textbooks in health psychology offer the reader some conceptual reasoning about different aspects of a discipline, there is no single source which provides a detailed conceptual analysis of current issues and debates, and theories and models, in health psychology. This book aims to provide the reader with a 'one stop', comprehensive and conceptual analysis of key issues in contemporary health psychology. This type of conceptual analysis also allows the learner to create meaningful relations among many related facts and ideas, which is essential for a full and critically discerning appreciation of an area of study.

In addition, health psychology concerns evidence and concepts drawn from a multitude of perspectives including those based on biological systems, cognitive or thinking systems, emotional systems and social systems. As such this book aims to offer the reader the opportunity to engage with a full range of approaches and methods in contemporary health psychology, and importantly, to be able to appreciate the relationships between each. We are trying to build 'a contemporary picture' of health psychology comprising many different interacting themes and concepts. Only when a person is able to appreciate the discipline in this way are they able to view the discipline of health psychology in its entirety.

Structure of the book

To achieve these aims we have included chapters in the book which can be thought of as cataloguing an overarching theme or unit of description in health psychology. In the first part of the book we have included chapters that detail concepts relevant for the understanding of how health psychology can be defined (Chapter 1) and also what sorts of research methods and measurement techniques are used to study psychology and health (Chapter 2). The next part of the book introduces key explanatory approaches in health psychology by examining social cognitive models and theories (Chapter 3), biologically based factors and models (Chapter 4) and approaches that have detailed factors that describe individual differences between people in their health behaviour and experience (Chapter 5). Chapter 6 identifies key concepts and approaches that have been used to study thinking processes and beliefs among people who are actually experiencing illness, whilst the following three chapters consider the psychology of long-term and short-term experience for a number of illnesses, and the health outcomes associated with those illnesses (Chapter 7 – acute and chronic illnesses; Chapter 8 – pain; Chapter 9 – addictive behaviours). In the final chapter we turn our attention to key concepts in health promotion interventions for people who are or who are not ill. We consider health promotion activities, adherence and persuasion processes, as well as the role of communication between the patient and care provider as fundamental concepts.

Within each of these chapters we have then identified a number of key concepts that have been the focus of debate, research and enquiry among those interested in the psychology of health. Each concept is presented and explored according to four key components. We first detail the contemporary *meaning* of a concept and then place it in its historical and applied position in the discipline by discussing the *origin* of the term. In effect we are asking the question what does the concept mean and where did it come from? Then we detail how the concept is *currently used* and understood by providing the reader with an analysis of current debates and empirical evidence in relation to the concept. Finally, we examine how relevant the concept is in the discipline per se by examining its *significance to health psychology*. In designing the structure of the book and in the identification and selection of the key concepts used we have made every attempt to be as inclusive as possible in the generation of themes and concepts relevant for contemporary health psychology.

Cross-referencing among concepts and a few examples of further reading for each concept is also provided so that the interested reader is able to identify and refer to related concepts and approaches, and explore the ideas presented in greater detail if they want to. In addition, we have included various figures, tables, images and text boxes which include further information designed to reinforce and make even clearer the meaning, development, current usage and significance of the concept to health psychology. The inclusion of a glossary of terms to provide a brief meaning of terms used in the text, and a complete reference section detailing all the published evidence cited for advanced study of primary reading material, completes the volume.

Happy reading!

Ian P. Albery and Marcus Munafò, June 2007

ACKNOWLEDGEMENTS

We would like to thank the staff at Sage Publications, London, for their extremely well organized and thorough approach to the production of this book. Our thanks go in particular to Michael Carmichael at Sage for his enthusiasm for the project which, we must say, rubbed off on us, 'the writers', at times when the book started to take second place to the many other things we have to deal with in our working lives. Thanks for the sustained encouragement and for motivating us by buying us lovely lunches. Also thanks to Emily Jenner at Sage for answering publication questions that, on the face of it, are obvious but perplexing for confused academics such as ourselves. Your patience is appreciated.

PUBLISHER'S ACKNOWLEDGEMENTS

The authors and publishers wish to thank the following for permission to use copyright material:

Department for Transport, United Kingdom, Think! Leaflet TINF/911a – *'Watch Out Even On Roads You Know'*.

Australian Government, Department of Health and Ageing, for reproduction of a leaflet from Grim Reaper campaign 1987

Cancer Research UK for permission to reproduce 'The Great Indoors' leaflet.

We thank Wiley-Blackwell Publishing for granting us permission to use extracts from the following articles:

Appendix A from Verplanken, B. & Orbell, S. (2003) "Reflections on past behaviour: a self-report index of habit strength" Journal of Applied Social Psychology, 33 (6), 1313–1330, Wiley-Blackwell

McKenna, F.P. & Albery, I.P (2001) "Does unrealistic optimism change following a negative experience", Journal of Applied Social Psychology, 31 (6), 1146–1157, Wiley-Blackwell

We thank Science AAAS for granting us permission to use extracts from the following articles:

Figure 2 from Caspi A et al, SCIENCE 301: 386-389 (2003) Reprinted with permission from Science AAAS

We thank The Open University Press Publishing Company for granting us permission to use extracts from the following articles:

Rutter, D. & Quine, L. (2002) (Eds.) *Changing Health Behaviour* Chapter 10, p 179, Figure 10.1 Persuasive Communication for the intervention condition. The Open University Press Publishing Company

Conner & Norman: *Predicting Health Behaviour 2e* (2005) p. 311, The Open University Press Publishing Company

Publisher's Acknowledgements

We thank McGraw Hill Publishers for granting us permission to use the following material:

Rutter, D. & Quine, L. (2002) (Eds.) Changing Health Behaviour.

Chapter 10, p 179, Figure 10.1 Persuasive Communication for the intervention condition.

While every effort has been made to trace the owners of copyright material, in a few cases this has proved difficult and we take this opportunity to offer our apologies to any copyright holder whose rights we have unwittingly infringed.

DEFINING HEALTH PSYCHOLOGY 1

ONE

DEFINING HEALTH PSYCHOLOGY
and: **bio-medical model**
        psychosomatic medicine
        biopsychosocial model
        health psychology
        social inequalities in health
        epidemiology of health and illness

What is this discipline we call 'health psychology'? Where did it originate and what was its developmental sequence? How is health psychology distinct from other areas that psychologists have submerged themselves in? This initial chapter focuses on these questions and details historically the approaches to health and illness which have contributed to the development of health psychology as a sub-discipline of psychology in general. In addition, we outline how health psychology is conceptualized and what the parameters of the discipline are, as well as the aims and objectives that underpin the area of study. Having examined approaches to health and illness and provided a definition of the area, a number of concepts are presented that detail terms that are of direct contextual relevance for the study of psychological processes in the aetiology and treatment of illness and the prevention of negative health outcomes. The first revolves around the question of what is the relationship between various social inputs on the one hand and the experience of negative health outcomes on the other? More importantly, what is the role of psychological factors in describing this relationship? The second draws on the concept of epidemiology in ascertaining the magnitude and nature of health and illness, and the role psychology plays in establishing reasons for figures related to numbers of people experiencing adverse health and/or undertaking maladaptive health behaviours.

DEFINING HEALTH PSYCHOLOGY
and: **BIO-MEDICAL MODEL**
and: **PSYCHOSOMATIC MEDICINE**
and: **BIOPSYCHOSOCIAL MODEL**

MEANING   The development of ideas about the origins and meaning of the terms 'health' and 'illness' has resulted in the emergence of a number of approaches designed to encapsulate the primary details of the concept and also provide parameters to its study. These approaches in many ways provide the conceptual pathway that has resulted in the discipline of health psychology. Think of these models as being formative in the historical development of health psychology as an independent level of enquiry. It is the parameters detailed in models and approaches developed to conceptualize health and illness that need to be considered, if the distinctiveness of a psychological approach to health is to be established.

ORIGINS   The study of health, illness and well being has a long history, dating back to the philosophical debates about the relationship between physical (bodily systems) and psychological systems found in the writings of the Greek philosophers Hippocrates (circa 460–circa 377 BC) and Galen (AD 129–circa 199). In so-called 'humoral' theory, these early writers argued that disease or illness arose when the four fluids argued to circulate the physical system (i.e. blood, black bile, yellow bile and phlegm) were out of balance. Importantly, however, these writers also proposed that there was a relationship between a preponderance of one of the bodily fluids and bodily temperaments or personality types. In other words, disease was associated with physical factors but these physical factors also affected the mind. The Middle Ages saw an obsession with demonology and mysticism and reinforced the view that illness was associated only with mental states. With the rise of modern medicine, however, dualism – the argument that the mind and body are independent and not causally related – became the favoured position, and as such physicians treated bodily ailments without the need to recognize the role of the mind in illness aetiology.

CURRENT USAGE   The **bio-medical model** adheres to this formulation. It considers that the mind cannot influence physical systems and vice versa and as such that the mind and body are completely separate entities. Illness is caused by external agents such as viruses or germs which create physical changes in the bodily system. Psychological processes are completely independent from any illness or disease process. The bio-medical model has provided the mainstay of descriptive parameters for the study of health and illness for over 300 years. During the last century, however, a number of perspectives have been developed which challenge the bio-medical perspective. These propose a greater role for psychological and social processes in the

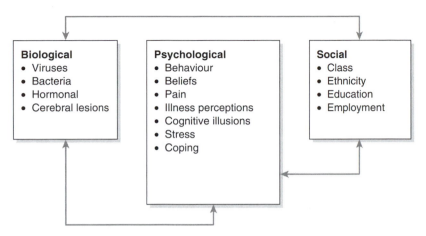

Figure 1.1   The biopsychosocial model of health and illness (after Engel, 1980)

aetiology and treatment of illness. **Psychosomatic medicine** grew as a branch of psychoanalysis and the study of hysteria developed by Freud and Breuer (Sulloway, 1980). It was observed that some people showed all the classic indications of neurological damage, such as paralysis of the legs or arms, when there was no underlying physical cause. Freud called this observation 'hysterical paralysis' and argued, on the basis of his famous work studying the patient Anna O, that the ailment was caused by mentalisms i.e. thoughts about experiences and feelings. While the arguments are intriguing, psychosomatic medicine suffers from its inability to provide sound empirical evidence to link causally mind matters and physical health (Holroyd and Coyne, 1987).

Probably the most influential contemporary model of health and illness is the **biopsychosocial model** which considers that biological, social and psychological factors interact as dynamic processes in determining the onset, progression and recovery from illness (see Engel, 1977, 1980; Anagnostopoulou, 2005; and also Figure 1.1).

As you can see in Figure 1.1, the biopsychosocial model proposes that factors ranging from the changing status of molecular structures (i.e. the biological), the presence of social support (i.e. the social factor) and thoughts and feelings (i.e. the psychological factors) co-vary with each other to produce illness or health. It therefore rejects the dualist philosophy of the bio-medical model. Donovan (1988) has proposed a biopsychosocial model of addiction which focuses on the interaction between the biological (e.g. neuroadaptation after the ingestion of an addictive substance), the social (e.g. submitting to peer pressure to use addictive substances or behaviours, socio-economic class, and so on) and the psychological (e.g. expectancies associated with undertaking a behaviour) to explain the multifaceted experience of 'addiction' (see also Marlatt et al., 1988). The biopsychosocial model also implies a more 'holist' approach for the study of health and illness, as well as interventions designed to prevent people from becoming unhealthy and making ill people well again. While, as a model, the biopsychosocial is inherently appealing by emphasizing the interplay between various forces and factors in the experience of health and illness, the complexity of these relationships means that the 'true' causal structure of the system may not be derived in a complete state (Armstrong, 1987).

SIGNIFICANCE TO HEALTH PSYCHOLOGY The bio-medical model, psychosomatic medicine and, in particular, the biopsychosocial model provide the history and parameters within which to view the development of the discipline called 'health psychology' (see health psychology concept – this chapter). These approaches have argued about the relationship between the mind and body either taking a dualist stance (biomedicine) or monist (biopsychosocial) stance, the later being adopted for the study of psychology and health.

Further reading

Donovan, D.M. (1988) Assessment of addictive behaviors: implications of an emerging *biopsychosocial* model. In D.M. Donovan and G.A. Marlatt (eds), *Assessment of Addictive Behaviors*. New York: Guilford Press. pp. 3–48.
This paper provides a useful introduction to the biopsychological model in the area of addictive behaviours.

Engel, G.L. (1980) The clinical application of the biopsychosocial model. *American Journal of Psychiatry*, 137, 535–544.
This work details how the biopsychosocial model may be applied in interventions in health-related problems.

See also **defining health psychology and health psychology**

DEFINING HEALTH PSYCHOLOGY
and: HEALTH PSYCHOLOGY

MEANING **Health psychology** is the term given for the academic discipline that seeks to understand the role of psychological processes in the experience of health and illness, the causes of health and illness, the progression of health and illness, and the consequences of health and illness. Health psychology is concerned with physical health as opposed to mental health – the latter being the focus of clinical psychology – although the

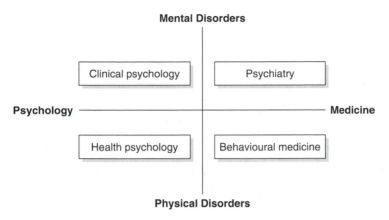

Figure 1.2   Where health psychology sits in relation to related areas of study (*Source*: Kaptein and Weinman, 2004)

differentiation between physical and mental health may be more arbitrary than real at times (Adler and Matthews, 1994). Kaptein and Weinman (2004) outlined a useful diagram to illustrate where health psychology is placed with near relatives in studying physical and mental disorders from psychological and medical viewpoints. This is reproduced in Figure 1.2.

Health psychology is an umbrella term for the study of those psychological processes that are important for understanding how health can be promoted and maintained, how illnesses can be treated and prevented in the first place, what psychology has to say about the aetiological and diagnostic basis of health and illness, and how an understanding of psychological processes is important for the development of healthcare and health policy systems. Based on Matarazzo's (1980, 1982) definition (see Box 1.1), Kaptein and Weinman (2004) call these 'the four core elements of health psychology' (p. 6).

Box 1.1   A definition of health psychology

Health psychology is the aggregate of the specific educational, scientific, and professional contributions of the discipline of psychology to the promotion and maintenance of health, the prevention and treatment of illness, the identification of aetiologic and diagnostic correlates of health, illness and related dysfunction and to the analysis and improvement of the health-care system and health policy formation. (Matarazzo, 1982: 4)

Matarazzo's definition of health psychology has been criticized for being over inclusive and allowing 'health psychology to inhabit all the domains of health-care delivery' (McDermott, 2002: 41). According to McDermott (2002) this is problematic because major parts of Matarazzo's conceptualization of health psychology actually refer to contemporary clinical psychology. Whether this assertion is accepted or not, McDermott argues for the reformulation of a definition of health psychology based on behavioural health. In other words, he proposes that health psychology should be about health maintenance and illness prevention in people that are already healthy. This includes a focus on health promotion and understanding processes of decision making in healthy people (including risk perception) rather than concentrating on treatment and recovery factors. In this way health psychology 'truly becomes a psychology of health, rather than a psychology of illness' (McDermott, 2002: 46).

ORIGINS Health psychology as a discipline is in its infancy. Very few textbooks or journals, let alone societies devoted to the study of health psychology, existed prior to the late 1970s to early 1980s. With the arrival of the twenty-first century we have seen health psychology grow significantly. Psychological societies and associations have their own divisions or sections devoted to the discipline, major international journals have been established to report health psychology research (e.g. *Health Psychology* and *Psychology and Health*) and there cannot be very many universities around the world that do not offer courses or modules in the area. In the UK, for example, you can even undertake professional training that leads to becoming a Chartered Health Psychologist (see www.bps.org for more information). However young, it is a discipline that is rooted in the historical and theoretical battle to understand the relationship between the mind (or thinking, emotions and so on) and physical change (that might be reflected in physical ill-health). We have already discussed this history in the previous key concept and have showed the development of the meaning of health from the ancient Greeks, through the bio-medical model and arriving at the biopsychosocial model which positioned psychological processes as one of the key determinants for determining the health status of the individual. The essential debate has developed from one in which the mind and body were seen to be independent (i.e. dualism) to a position taken nowadays that the mind and body are inherently connected and interact in a dynamic and regulatory way to create a healthy or unhealthy state. This conceptualization is best illustrated by the biopsychosocial model of health and illness (see Figure 1.1. and Engel, 1980). This integrates biological (e.g. viruses, genetics, and so on), psychological (e.g. health expectancies, belief sets, emotions, health behaviours, and so on) and social (e.g. normative values, and so on) factors into an interactive system which determines how illness can be caused as well as health restored. Health psychology has adopted this biopsychosocial perspective and emphasizes that health and illness are both the result of a complex system comprising biological, psychological and social causes.

Probably the most efficient way to detail contemporary health psychology is to utilize Matarazzo's definition (1982; see also Box 1.1) which identifies the core issues that health psychology seeks to provide evidence for understanding. In terms of the promotion and maintenance of health, health psychology plays a major role in understanding why, and importantly how, healthy people remain healthy. In this sense health psychologists are interested in understanding what predicts the adoption and maintenance of health protective behaviours in individuals who have not experienced a health problem directly. Here examples include the development of models that have identified health-related decision-making processes and the formation of an intention to behave in a health protective versus maladaptive health-related manner – the health belief model, protection motivation theory and the theory of planned behaviour is to name but a few (see Conner and Norman, 2005). Moreover, individual difference-based factors are also important for understanding why some people take protective decisions while others do not (see Contrada and Goyal, 2004).

CURRENT USAGE

The prevention and treatment of illness issue is concerned more with people who have been diagnosed with an acute or chronic illness. Health psychologists are concerned with understanding how people respond to the onset of illness, how they derive meaning for their illness and how they respond to the illness. Research has identified that certain treatment approaches, such as adherence to prescription regimes, are fundamental for both the prevention and/or successful treatment of medical conditions (see Myers and Midence, 1998) and that these health-related behaviours may be dependent on how an individual represents the meaning, cause, perceived consequences and severity of an illness (see Leventhal et al., 1997). A number of **meta-analyses** have showed that interventions based on psychological principles have been very successful in resulting in positive health effects in ill participants. Meyer and Mark (1995), for example, showed that across a number of interventions for cancer sufferers that had incorporated psychosocial factors in their design and implementation, participants were shown to derive beneficial effects in terms of well being, personal quality of life and psychological adjustment, as well as disease-related symptoms.

Matarazzo also proposes that another key theme in health psychology is attempting to understand the aetiology or causes of physical illness. We have also mentioned that behaviour has an impact on whether or not a person becomes ill in the first place and whether the illness progresses or can be treated effectively. In this sense behaviour, and those factors that guide behaviour (e.g. cognitive and emotional systems), may be seen as potential causes of an illness experience. On top of this there is other evidence that psychological states can manifest themselves in physical illness. For example, a reactivity to stressors in the environment has been shown to be related to the release of catecholamines during activation of the sympathetic nervous system, which in turn has been shown to be associated with the development of cardiac disease (see Henderson and Baum, 2004 for a review; see also Chapter 4 in this book).

Whereas the promotion and maintenance of health, the prevention and treatment of illness and the psychological basis of physical illness have all been subjects of psychological enquiry, little direct evidence exists to show that psychological knowledge has had an impact on the development of healthcare systems and health policy. However, given that many of the leading causes of death may have some behavioural component to them (e.g. smoking and cancer, food choice, obesity and heart problems, condom use and sexually transmitted diseases, and so on), international and national bodies concerned with the health of populations have adopted a more biopsychosocial approach to conceptualize illness and recognize the important role psychology has to play in the development of policy (see for example Department of Health, 1998; World Health Organization, 2002).

SIGNIFICANCE TO HEALTH PSYCHOLOGY

At first it may seem a little futile to ask what the significance of the definition of health psychology is to health psychology. However, definitions are important because they provide the basis for the parameters associated with an area of enquiry. With a discipline such as health psychology it is important to attempt to justify its distinctiveness because of the close relationship it has with other areas of study such as those related to clinical psychology and to behavioural medicine. As we have seen, health psychology is in fact cemented in certain key aims and objectives which, while sharing some overlapping with alternative fields of study, serve to emphasize the overall unique quality of the scheme.

Further reading

McDermott, M. (2002) Redefining health psychology: Matarazzo revisited. In D. Marks (ed.), *The Health Psychology Reader*. London: Sage. pp. 40–49.
An interesting reconceptualization of the defining characteristics of health psychology as a discipline in psychology.

Matarazzo, J.D. (1980) Behavioural health and behavioural medicine: frontiers for a new health psychology. *American Psychologist*, 35, 807–817.
The classic paper that introduces health psychology as a discipline of psychology and its defining characteristics.

Adler, N.E. and Matthews, K.A. (1994) Health psychology: why do some people get sick and some stay well? *Annual Review of Psychology*, 45, 229–259.
Reviews the main theoretical and applied aspects inherent in understanding individual differences in health behaviour and the experience of illness.

See also **defining health psychology and bio-medical model; defining health psychology and psychosomatic medicine; defining health psychology and biopsychosocial model**

DEFINING HEALTH PSYCHOLOGY
and: SOCIAL INEQUALITIES IN HEALTH

MEANING

Work in health psychology has played a major role in understanding the part played by invariant socio-economic and demographic factors in the experience of positive and negative health outcomes. The assumption which we as health psychologists make is that the relationship between social inputs (such as socio-demographic factors like education level or socio-economic status) and the experience of health outcomes is not best thought of as a *direct* link. It is proposed that the relationship is in some way mediated by more psychologically driven factors (see Adler et al., 1994). For example, assume that people from a lower socio-economic class are more likely to experience more heart-related health outcomes (e.g. Carroll et al., 2002). In this case health psychologists are interested in examining how such a relationship manifests itself through the operation of psychological processes. These people may experience more heart-based health-related issues because they are more likely to be overweight. Why are they overweight? Well it could be because they have a set of beliefs or attitudes about the consumption of unhealthy foods that are less negative and as such are more inclined to ignore warnings associated with unhealthy eating. Of course it could be that they are not particularly efficacious in their ability to select and choose healthy food alternatives, and so on. The point is that psychological processes are likely to be important in one's adoption or not of health-related behaviour and at times the nature of these psychological factors may vary by socio-demography.

ORIGINS

The debate about the link between social conditions and social demographic factors with health outcomes has a long history. In Victorian times descriptions of the appalling living and working conditions of sections of British society and their poor health status were not uncommon (e.g. Engels, 1845/1958). Seminal work on the study of particular **social inequalities** in health outcomes in the UK was reported in the so-called Black Report (Black, 1980; Townsend and Davidson, 1982). In this report Black demonstrated an increasing gradient characterizing the relationship between social class, based on occupational status, and **mortality rates**. Mortality rates are determined by dividing the number of deaths in a social class by the number of people in that social class. The report highlighted that for women the rate ranged from 2.15 for Class I (i.e. the professional class) to 5.31 for Class V (i.e. unskilled manual workers) and for men the figures were 3.98 and 9.88 respectively (see Figure 1.3).

In effect these analyses showed that people in lower social groups (unskilled and skilled manual work) are more likely to die than those in higher occupational groups (the professional and managerial classes). Similar findings were

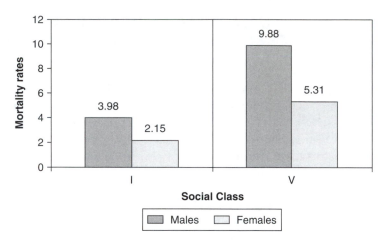

Figure 1.3   Mortality rates for males and females for two socio-economic groups
(*Source*: Black, 1980)

Note: Social Class I are professionals and Social Class V are unskilled manual workers.

also shown by Marmot et al. (1991) in the Whitehall studies. These showed the existence of the social gradient in a large sample of the UK's civil servants and provided some of the early evidence for the role of psychosocial factors in the social class, morbidity and mortality relationship. Marmot and McDowell (1986) also argued that the social gradient is in fact widening and becoming even more defined for many illnesses. Recent studies have added to the evidence base suggesting social inequalities in health status. In examining low birth weight for children born to mothers in Germany, Reime et al. (2006) showed that being unemployed, a single mother and over 39 years of age were associated with an increased risk of low birth weight babies. Myint et al. (2006) showed differences in cardiovascular risk factors for occupational class on the basis of gender and age. For instance, young women were shown to have increased smoking rates, and higher cholesterol levels, which were not found in men. In addition, for young people in manual social classes increased physical exercise was found. Still other evidence has shown that inequalities exist based on geographical location and an identity with the place one lives in (Bolam et al., 2006).

Various explanations have been given for the operation of the social (health) gradient. One argues that it is an artefact of the way 'social class' may be measured, or that people with a particular health status 'drift' or are 'selected' into certain occupations. The most influential explanation, and the one to which most contemporary researchers adhere, is that these social inequalities seem to operate because of an indirect relationship between social class and health status via behavioural

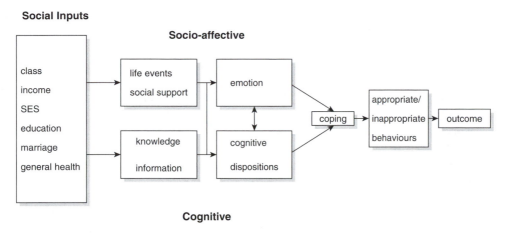

Figure 1.4 Rutter and Quine's (1996) model of social inputs, social psychological processes and health outcomes (*Source*: Rutter and Quine, 1996)

factors or psychosocial factors (Siegrist and Marmot, 2004). In other words, people in different social groups may or may not experience certain health outcomes because of the differing ways in which they behave in their social settings – **psychosocial risk factors**. Given the argument that social inputs like social class, gender, and the like, seem to have an indirect effect on health status and outcomes through more behavioural and potentially psychologically based factors and mechanisms, health psychologists may play an important role in unpicking these social inequalities in health.

CURRENT USAGE

The majority of work in health psychology has not been concerned with establishing the mediating role of psychological processes in understanding the relationship between social inequalities and health status, but has focused more on the link between, for example, belief sets and processes and health behaviour and health outcomes. In most contemporary models of health psychology, with the exception of the original formulation of the health belief model (see the health belief model concept in Chapter 3), socio-demographic factors are measured more as descriptive elements of the sample being studied and are not used primarily as predictive factors.

Nevertheless, some workers have provided us with a conceptualization of how social inputs (e.g. socio-economic status, education level, and so on) affect whether or not we experience negative or positive health outcomes based on differences in key psychological factors. For example, Rutter and Quine (1996) (see also Rutter et al., 1993) detailed a model which outlined the role of fundamental social psychological processes as mediating the effects of social inputs and health outcomes. Figure 1.4 is a diagrammatic representation of this model.

The argument shown in Figure 1.4 is that the means by which various social inputs (the left-most box in Figure 1.4) influence health outcomes (the right-most box in Figure 1.4) are through social psychological processes (the central boxes in Figure 1.4). In this way these social psychological processes act as mediators in the relationship. Rutter and Quine (1996) distinguish between socio-emotional psychological factors, such as the availability and perceived utility of social support, and psychological cognitive factors, such as cognitive dispositions – personal belief sets, perceived control, self-efficacy and so on. There is a plethora of evidence to link these types of factors with health behaviour and health outcomes (see Chapter 3 and Chapter 5 in this volume; see also Conner and Norman, 2005). The central component in the model of input, process and outcome is coping. It is argued that the cognitive and socio-emotional factors affect how people experience stressors in their environment and how they utilize and select strategies to apply to these stressors so as to alleviate the uncomfortable feelings associated with stress. For example, Schwarzer et al. (1994) showed in a longitudinal study that **social support** was fundamental in protecting people from negative health outcomes (in terms of physical symptoms) among those who were continuously unemployed over a prolonged period. In others words the use and access to social support was found to mediate the effect of unemployment on health outcome (see Box 1.2 and Figure 1.5).

Box 1.2   The role of social support in 'buffering' the effects of environmental stressors on health outcomes (after Schwarzer et al., 1994)

Basis of the research

In 1989 and after the fall of the Berlin Wall over 300,000 people left East Germany for West Germany, about 50,000 of them settling in Berlin. These people were invariably leaving behind them jobs and social support networks (such as that provided by employment) for a new and more uncertain life of possible unemployment. This exodus provided researchers with the opportunity to study the effects of coping mechanisms and the adaptation of migrants on health-related outcomes. More specifically, Schwarzer and his colleagues (1994) undertook a longitudinal study of the effects of factors that may provide mechanisms that curtail the experience of severe stressors on health outcomes. It was predicted that those individuals who found employment and/or were receiving social support would be healthier than those who were long-term unemployed and/or did not access social support structures.

Measures

Two-hundred and thirty migrants took part in the study. Self-report responses in terms of current employment status, perceived social support mechanisms (e.g. from friends and family, and so on) and self-reported physical symptoms in relation to a number of illnesses (e.g. heart complaints, exhaustion, stomach complaints, and so on) were all measured at three time points between 1989 and 1991.

Findings

For the main analyses employment status was recorded to create two main groups of individuals, those who had been unemployed throughout the period of the study and those who were employed. In addition, social support was categorized as those who reported receiving long-term social support and those who did not. Reported illness symptoms were examined to see how unemployment and social support affected them and also to see whether employment status and social support over time interacted to show differences in reported symptoms. Figure 1.5 shows the effect of employment,

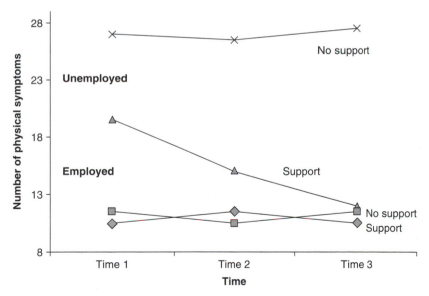

Figure 1.5 The effects of employment status and perceived social support on reported physical symptoms (*Source*: Schwarzer et al., 1994)

(Cont'd)

status and perceived social support on illness symptoms for the three study time points.

It is clear that the employed participants during the study period reported fewest symptoms and that this was not influenced by perceived social support at all. For the people who were always without work (permanently jobless) a different pattern was shown. While being jobless was associated with an increase in reported symptoms, those who were unemployed and who also did not perceive themselves as having social support consistently reported the highest number of symptoms across the time points. Contrast this with those jobless people who also received social support. These people showed a marked decrease in the symptoms reported over the three time points. In fact, by Time Point 3 they were not reporting significantly more symptoms than the employed participants.

Summary

Together this evidence is indicative of the developmental role social support plays over time in buffering the effects of major life stressors on physical health.

For Rutter and Quine the coping strategies applied lead to the adoption of appropriate or inappropriate behaviour. For instance, some people might undertake the inappropriate behaviour of smoking to alleviate a stressful encounter after having previously 'given up', and this behaviour and the preceding decision (coping response) have their roots in cognitions such as lowered self-efficacy as well as socio-emotive factors such as availability and the use of social support structures. As Rutter and Quine (1996) remark 'From dysfunctional coping styles come inappropriate behaviours, and from inappropriate behaviours it is a small step to negative health outcomes' (p. 10).

The model of the mediating effects of social psychological process on the relationship between social inputs and health outcomes is useful because it details parameters, or a representation, within which much of psychological research in health can be conceptualized. Although the model is generic, one strength of the model is in providing a generalized framework for reviewing research evidence and establishing broad parameters for future work.

SIGNIFICANCE TO HEALTH PSYCHOLOGY That there is a health gradient which describes the worsening health status of particular individuals because of their socio-economic status, education levels, and so on, is a robust and clearly defined observation. That this link is direct is more questionable. People interested in examining the indirect relationship between social inputs and health outcomes have argued that psychosocial, psychological and behavioural factors might provide mechanisms through which the health gradient manifests itself. In addition, if psychological processes are affecting the likelihood of experiencing decreased well being in health (given, for example, pre-existing socio-economic class), it might be possible to design treatments or interventions based on changeable psychological factors. In other words, the manipulation of key psychological factors and processes may serve to 'level out' the health gradient or at least decrease the health risks associated with being in, for example, a particular social grouping.

Further reading

Adler, N.E., Boyce, T., Chesney, M.A., Cohen, S., Folkman, S., Kahn, R. and Syme, S.L. (1994) Socioeconomic status and health: the challenge of the gradient. *American Psychologist*, 49, 15–24.
Offers the reader a good review of the relationship between socio-economic status and health status and the implications for health psychology research.

Rutter, D.R. and Quine, L. (1996) Social psychological mediators of the relationship between demographic factors and health outcomes: a theoretical model and some preliminary data. *Psychology and Health*, 11, 5–22.
Describes a useful generic model for conceptualizing the relationship between social inputs and health outcome mediated by core (social) psychological processes.

Siegrist, J. and Marmot, M.G. (2004) Health inequalities and the psychosocial environment – two scientific challenges. *Social Science and Medicine*, 58, 1463–1473.
Identifies and discusses the nature of social inequalities as being dependent upon the operation of psychological and behavioural processes.

See also **defining health psychology and epidemiology of health and illness; defining health psychology and health psychology**

DEFINING HEALTH PSYCHOLOGY
and: EPIDEMIOLOGY OF HEALTH AND ILLNESS

Why should health psychologists be interested in epidemiology? Because epidemiology as a discipline in its own right is the 'study of the distribution and determinants of health and illness in populations and of the action that is necessary to prevent disease and promote health' (Rugulies et al., 2004: 27). On the

MEANING

one hand, epidemiological research allows health psychologists to observe the magnitude and distribution of particular illnesses in certain populations. This serves the function of identifying whether an illness is of concern as a public health problem. On the other hand, epidemiological research provides evidence of possible causes for health and illness. These include, for example, societal-based, community-based or psychologically based causal factors. Epidemiologists are not, however, concerned with psychological processes. For instance, it is more common for this type of work to present evidence that is descriptive of the outcomes of psychological processes such as those which involve attitudinal research. The second part of Rugulies' quote is interesting because it specifically details that epidemiological research aims may involve the identification of methods for health promotion and studies designed to evaluate these interventions in given populations.

ORIGINS Epidemiological research has a long history – at least a few hundred years. Studies that can be seen as epidemiological in nature were undertaken as early as the eighteenth and nineteenth century and focused on both mortality figures attributed to environmental causes as well as more psychosocial issues. For instance, Durkheim (1897/1951) undertook work that sought to examine differences in suicide rates across a number of social groups including Protestants and Catholics, and married and unmarried people. Early epidemiological research was also fundamental in identifying factors associated with infectious disease such as the role of the consumption of dirty water on cholera rates, and the effect of better living conditions on **mortality** and **morbidity rates** associated with tuberculosis.

CURRENT USAGE More recent epidemiological research has taken the approach of examining **risk factors** associated with disease and illness. The basic idea here is to determine the association between the presence or absence of identified risk factors and the presence or absence of illness and mortality. For example, smoking is a risk factor for the development of, among other illnesses, heart disease. However, some people will smoke for their whole lives and never have any cardiac-related illnesses while some non smokers will develop heart disease. This example demonstrates that risk factors are not causal as such. Epidemiologists see risk factors as those variables that increase the probability that people who experience the risk factor will develop an illness compared to those who do not have experience with the risk factor. This comparative index is called the **relative risk ratio**. Relative risk is calculated by first dividing the number of cases of illness in a group of people who experience a risk factor by the total number of people who experience the risk factors – incidence exposed. Then by dividing the number of cases of illness in a group of people who do not experience a risk factor by the total number of people who do not experience the risk factor – incidence not exposed. Finally, the incidence exposed figure is divided by the incidence not exposed to give the relative risk.

Take the smoking and heart disease example we used earlier. The incidence exposed is equal to the number of cases of heart disease for smokers divided by the total number of smokers who do or do not get heart disease. The incidence not exposed is equal to the number of cases of heart disease for non smokers divided by the total number of non smokers who do or do not get heart disease, and the relative risk ratio is the incidence exposed divided by the incidence not exposed. A ratio of, for instance, 2.5 shows that smokers have a 2.5 times greater risk of getting heart disease than non smokers. A relative risk ratio of 1 indicates that there is no difference in relative risk. This type of approach has been used in many epidemiological studies including those associated with the link between smoking and heart problems (Doll and Peto, 1981), the relationship between alcohol and mortality rates (Doll et al., 1994) and the relationship between gender and many illnesses (e.g. cancer, accidents, coronary heart disease, stroke, and so on) (see Reddy et al., 1992), as well as studies that have examined the health gradient (e.g. Marmot et al., 1991; see the social inequalities concept in this chapter).

Epidemiological risk factor research is usually carried out using either cross-sectional studies (i.e. studying risk factors and illness prevalence at the same time in a single sample), case-control studies (i.e. comparing the numbers of risk factors in people with and without an illness) or prospective/longitudinal studies. Prospective studies are the most powerful option because they generate the initial identification of risk factors in samples who are then followed for a period of time to see who has and who has not become ill. In this sense some sort of causal relationship can be claimed because the risk factors were observed before the development of a disease.

SIGNIFICANCE TO HEALTH PSYCHOLOGY

Health psychology attempts to understand the relationship between various psychological and biopsychological mechanisms in health, illness and health behaviour. Epidemiology is about the incidence of illnesses, the determinants of illness and the incidence of risk factors being predictive of illness. The two are mutually complementary. Psychologists obtain useful information about the magnitude, nature and relative likelihood of illness experience from epidemiological investigation and epidemiologists utilize psychological and psychosocial factors in studying possible determinants of risk for health and illness outcomes. For example, a recent meta-analysis used published prospective studies to investigate the relationship between depression and anxiety and having a heart attack or suffering heart-related death (Rugulies, 2002). People with clinical depression were 2.7 times more likely to have a heart attack or die of coronary heart disease. The figure was slightly less at a 1.5 higher risk for people with a depressive mood.

Further reading

Rugulies, R., Aust, R. and Syme, S.L. (2004) Epidemiology of health and illness: a socio-psycho-physiological perspective. In S. Sutton, A. Baum and M. Johnston (eds), *The Sage Handbook of Health Psychology*. London: Sage. pp. 27–68.
An excellent review of the interface between the epidemiological study of health and psychological aspects of health behaviour.

Marmot, M.G., Davey Smith, G., Stansfeld, S., Patel, C., North, F., Head, J., White, I., Brunner, E. and Feenay, A. (1991) Health inequalities among British civil servants. *Lancet*, 337, 1387–1393.
The classic study that was one of the first to identify the role played by psychosocial factors in the operation of inequalities in a health outcome according to job status and role.

See also **defining health psychology and health psychology**

RESEARCH METHODS AND MEASUREMENT

2

TWO

RESEARCH METHODS AND MEASUREMENT
and: **study design**
     cross-sectional
     longitudinal
     experimental
     qualitative
     psychometrics

Good study design is essential if we are to be confident in our data and in the conclusions that we draw from them, and accurate measurement is an integral part of this. In this chapter we describe the importance of study design, and outline the various primary study designs which are used in health psychology and more widely, including cross-sectional, longitudinal and experimental designs. Each of these has its own strengths and weaknesses, and is ideally suited to specific kinds of research question. In addition, qualitative methods are discussed, which offer the potential to answer a completely different kind of research question to quantitative methods, and serve a complementary function. Many important research questions can only be answered meaningfully using qualitative techniques, and good research will know which study design is best suited to answering a specific question. Finally, we discuss the science of psychometrics, which is concerned with ensuring that measurements are accurate and do indeed measure what they are intended to measure.

RESEARCH METHODS AND MEASUREMENT
and: STUDY DESIGN

MEANING   The **design** of the study refers to the means by which the research question will be addressed, specifically in relation to the data that will be collected, the comparisons that will be made, the experimental conditions (if any) that will be manipulated, and so on. In many ways, the design of a study is more important than the analysis of the data resulting from that study; if data are poorly analysed it will always be possible to re-analyse them, but if a study is poorly designed in the first place then it may never be possible to meaningfully interpret the data which result from it. The design of a study will also have an impact on how data are subsequently analysed.

ORIGINS   Research can be defined as belonging to one of two primary categories: **observational** studies and **experimental** studies. As suggested by the name, in observational studies there is no direct manipulation of variables within the study, and data are simply collected on groups of participants. In an observational study, while the researcher collects information on the attributes or outcomes of interest, no effort is made to influence these. An example might be the prevalence of a particular health behaviour (e.g. cigarette smoking) in different groups defined by socio-economic status. In an experimental study, on the other hand, the experimenter directly influences events, in order to draw conclusions regarding the impact of that manipulation on the resulting observations. An example might be the impact of an intervention (e.g. an increase in self-efficacy beliefs) compared to a control condition on a particular health behaviour (e.g. giving up smoking).

A further sub-division which may apply to observational studies is between **prospective** studies, where information is collected about events subsequent to recruitment into the study, and **retrospective** studies, where information is collected about events in the past. Data regarding past events may be obtained from more objective sources (e.g. school records or patient notes) or, arguably, from more subjective sources (e.g. by self-report by the participant). Note that, in all cases, experimental studies are prospective (even if the period of prospective study may be very short!), whereas observational studies may be retrospective or prospective. It should also be noted that whereas different treatments can be assessed retrospectively, this would *not* count as an experimental study, since the delivery of different treatments would not be an element of a pre-specified study. In this case, the study would be a retrospective observational study.

Another sub-division is that studies may be classified as **longitudinal** studies or **cross-sectional** studies. In longitudinal studies, changes over time are investigated. Again, note that, in all cases, experimental studies are longitudinal (although once again, the period of longitudinal study may be very short), whereas

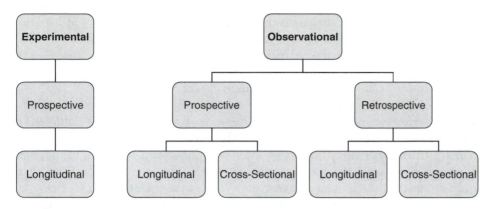

Figure 2.1   Study design

What are the basic categories of research design? The classifications that can be used include Observational versus Experimental, Prospective versus Retrospective, and Longitudinal versus Cross-sectional. The distinction between observational and experimental relates to the purpose of the study, and is the most important distinction. The other two distinctions relate to the way in which the data are collected. Most of the combinations of these terms are possible, although not all are. These are the basic types of research design. Some of these categories are described in more detail in subsequent sections.

observational studies may be longitudinal or cross-sectional. In a cross-sectional study participants are observed only once, offering a 'snapshot' of the characteristics of interest at that particular moment. Most surveys, for example, are cross-sectional, although a variant is the **pseudo-longitudinal** design, where data on participants are collected at only one point in time, but this is done, for example, on, participants of different ages in order to indirectly construct a distribution of changes in a population with age. This approach is usually less resource-intensive than a proper longitudinal design, although somewhat more prone to giving erroneous results.

Finally, some kind of comparison is desirable in observational studies, and essential in experimental studies. This comparison group or condition is called the **control** group, to which the experimental procedure is not applied in the case of an experimental study design, or against which the group of interest is compared in an observational study design. For example, if we want to evaluate whether or not a new treatment or intervention is effective, we would usually do this by means of a comparison of the group given the intervention against one *not* given the intervention (namely, a control group). The presence of a control group, in both experimental and observational studies, strengthens the inferences that can be made from the results of the study.

While more detailed distinctions can be made, these represent the main ways in which a study can be designed (see Figure 2.1).

CURRENT USAGE

The essence of statistical analysis is the understanding of likely causes of variation, which in the case of health psychology usually corresponds to variation in behavioural or psychological characteristics. Study design is important because it is the means by which we can be more (or less) confident that the apparent causes of variation in our study are in fact the genuine causes of variation.

For example, if we find that an intervention designed to improve self-efficacy beliefs is effective, we would need to know that those given the intervention demonstrated higher self-efficacy beliefs than those not given the intervention (namely, the control group), and that these two groups did not differ in their self-efficacy beliefs *before* the intervention was given. The strength of experimental study designs is that as long as participants are randomly allocated to either the experimental or control group, so that these groups do not differ at the outset of the study, any differences by the end of the study can be argued, with reasonable confidence, to be due to the experimental intervention. We would hope that there were no chance differences between the two groups *before* they received the intervention that might explain the difference observed after the intervention had been given.

Observational study designs, on the other hand, are more problematic as they require a comparison to be made where there is no active manipulation of events. For example, we may wish to investigate factors which it is impossible (or unethical) for us to manipulate directly (such as genetic variation). In this case, we would want to compare those with a particular characteristic (e.g. a particular genotype) to those with a different characteristic (e.g. a different genotype) on some measurement of interest (e.g. risk of a certain disease). Again, the more confident that we can be that our two groups do not differ in any other way, the more confident we can be that the difference of interest accounts for any observed differences in the measurement we take (in this example that having a particular genotype influences the risk of having a certain disease).

SIGNIFICANCE TO HEALTH PSYCHOLOGY

Health psychology is the application of psychological and behavioural theory and research to the understanding of health, illness and healthcare. In many cases the factors influencing health, illness and so on are not amenable to experimental manipulation, so that observational study designs are frequently necessary. It is therefore critically important to understand (a) how best to design an observational study in order to maximize the confidence that one may have in the conclusions drawn from the results of the study, and (b) what limitations may exist in the inferences that may be drawn.

For example, we might be interested in whether or not personality influences alcohol consumption. A cross-sectional observational study might indeed reveal that people with high levels of trait anxiety do indeed drink more alcohol. However, we would not be able to say from these data alone whether high levels of trait anxiety eventually lead to higher alcohol consumption, or high alcohol consumption eventually leads to higher levels of trait anxiety. The direction of **causation** would be impossible to infer from these results alone (although we might be able to speculate as to which alternative explanation was most plausible). Indeed, it might be the case that *both* effects are operating to give rise to our data (as a kind of positive feedback loop), but we would have no way of knowing.

Further reading

Altman, D.G. (1991) *Practical Statistics for Medical Research.* London: Chapman & Hall.
Chapter 5 discusses study design issues, while the rest of the book is an excellent introduction to medical statistics (which may be valuable to health psychologists who have covered statistics from the perspective of psychology only in the past).

Concato, J. (2004) Observational versus experimental studies: what's the evidence for a hierarchy? *NeuroRx, 1,* 341–347.
An interesting review which questions the widely held assumption that experimental study designs are necessarily superior to observational study designs. Focused on bio-medical research, but applicable much more widely.

Sterne, J.A. and Davey Smith, G. (2001) Sifting the evidence – what's wrong with significance tests? *British Medical Journal, 322,* 226–231.
Very informative review of the dangers of emphasizing p-values in research papers, and in particular the focus on so-called 'positive' findings. Also discusses the role of study design in the validity and veracity of research findings.

See also **research methods and measurement and cross-sectional; research methods and measurement and longitudinal; research methods and measurement and experimental**

RESEARCH METHODS AND MEASUREMENT
and: CROSS-SECTIONAL

One of the most common and well-known study designs is the cross-sectional study design. In a cross-sectional study participants are observed only once, offering a 'snapshot' of the characteristics of interest at that particular moment. In this study   **MEANING** design, a population, or a sample thereof, is studied in a single instance, either by examining a single well-defined group of individuals, or by comparing cases (namely, those with an identifiable clinical condition) versus controls (namely, healthy individuals).

ORIGINS

Cross-sectional study designs are widely employed in epidemiological research, where characteristics of individuals (e.g. those presenting with a particular disease) are related to potential risk factors, or characteristics of cases (e.g. those with a particular disease) compared to the characteristics of controls (usually healthy individuals drawn from the general population). An example might be that cholesterol levels are higher among patients with coronary heart disease compared to healthy controls. Cross-sectional studies tend to be faster and cheaper to conduct than **longitudinal** studies, for the obvious reason that participants need only be studied at a single time point, rather than repeatedly over several time points.

CURRENT USAGE

It may be tempting to interpret the results of a cross-sectional study as if they were drawn from a **longitudinal** study. For example, if we look at cholesterol levels and the proportion of dietary calories derived from saturated fat in a cross-sectional study of healthy individuals, we might expect to find a very strong correlation. In this case, one might be tempted to conclude that high levels of saturated fat in one's diet *cause* increased cholesterol levels. This would be an example of treating cross-sectional data as longitudinal data, because one cannot make inferences about **causation** from cross-sectional data, however tempting it might be to do so (and even if one turned out to be correct!). A trivial example illustrates this: height and weight are very highly correlated, but it doesn't make sense to suggest that height *causes* weight, or indeed vice versa. Certainly, you would not want to suggest (at least to adults) that they should eat more in order to grow taller.

In a **case-control** study, the characteristics of a set of cases (that is, those with some condition, such as a disease) are compared to the characteristics of a set of controls (namely, those without the condition). For example, we might look at the smoking habits of those with and without lung cancer. Since we start out with a predetermined number of cases, the rarity of the disease is no longer an issue. As with all cross-sectional studies, case-control studies do not allow inferences to be made regarding causation. Even in cases where the risk factor appears relatively fixed (e.g. the presence or absence of a particular genetic mutation related to disease), one must still be cautious, since this risk factor may be operating directly (namely, causing the disease via a relatively direct biological pathway) or indirectly (namely, via effects on behaviours which themselves are related to disease).

While case-control studies may be informative in principle, they may be limited by the extent to which cases and controls are matched on other variables which are not of interest. For example, if we are interested in comparing individuals with coronary heart disease to healthy controls, how do we go about selecting those controls? Do we simply randomly select individuals from the general population (who may, for example, have undiagnosed coronary heart disease)? Or do we select individuals from the general population who are *known* to not have coronary heart disease? Very slight differences between cases and controls may give rise to spurious results. For example, the rate of coronary heart disease is higher in males than in females, so that if the proportions of males among cases and controls differ slightly, we might see a difference that is independently related to sex (e.g. height) which *appears* to be related to coronary heart disease, but in fact is not in any meaningful sense.

A very large proportion of studies within health psychology are cross-sectional in nature. In essence, many do not differ in any important way from more traditional epidemiological studies which attempt to identify possible risk factors for disease. Whereas epidemiological studies generally focus on environmental risk factors (e.g. exposure to cigarette smoke), health psychology studies tend to focus on psychological and behavioural risk factors (e.g. self-efficacy beliefs, coping styles and so on).

The rationale behind the different studies is the same and, as a result, the limitations in interpretability are the same. For example, one might find a relationship between disease status and a particular coping style in a **cross-sectional** study, but one could still not be certain whether the coping style caused the disease, or vice versa. To do this, one would need to use a longitudinal study design and follow individuals with different coping styles over time, to see which of them subsequently developed the disease (and whether the development of the disease was linked to a change in coping style).

SIGNIFICANCE TO HEALTH PSYCHOLOGY

Further reading

Altman, D.G. (1991) *Practical Statistics for Medical Research.* London: Chapman & Hall.
Chapter 5 discusses study design issues, while the rest of the book is an excellent introduction to medical statistics (which may be valuable to health psychologists who have covered statistics only from the perspective of psychology in the past).

Biesheuvel, C.J., Grobbee, D.E. and Moons, K.G. (2006) Distraction from randomization in diagnostic research. *Annals of Epidemiology,* 16, 540–544.
Argues that experimental studies are not always necessary (in the context of diagnostic tests for disease), and that cross-sectional studies may be sufficient in some cases.

See also **research methods and measurement and study design**

RESEARCH METHODS AND MEASUREMENT
and: **LONGITUDINAL**

MEANING   Another broad class of study design is the longitudinal design. In a longitudinal study a group of participants (**cohort**) is observed more than once (in contrast to a **cross-sectional** study, where participants are observed only once), and progress over time is assessed (e.g. the development or onset of disease). This allows changes over time to be recorded, and these to be related to characteristics or factors that existed and were measured prior to the onset of a behaviour or disease, for example. This might give information about risk factors for the development of a disease in a cohort of participants, some of whom developed the disease over time and some of whom did not.

ORIGINS   **Longitudinal** study designs are widely employed in epidemiological research, and are generally regarded as being preferable to **cross-sectional** study designs as they are in principle less prone to potential problems of confounding arising from the inadequate matching of cases and controls in cross-sectional studies. Predictor variables are measured before the outcomes of interest occur, although it is also necessary to collect data on a large number of other variables to control for potential confounding. For example, depression levels at baseline may predict outcomes of interest, such as future illness, but may also be higher in females than in males, so that in order to identify the specific contribution of depression it would be necessary to measure and control for participant sex.

CURRENT USAGE   The most important advantage of **longitudinal** study designs over **case-control** designs is that they allow slightly more certainty that factors which predict the outcomes of interest (namely, factors measured before the onset of the outcome which are significantly associated with the likelihood of that outcome subsequently occurring) are genuinely associated with them. They do not allow inferences to be made regarding **causation** – this requires an **experimental** study design – but they do give stronger grounds for believing that the association between risk factor and outcomes is genuine as compared to case-control studies.

Nevertheless, there are still potential problems in longitudinal study designs. Not least, it can be difficult to determine whether a baseline factor which is associated with a particular outcome is in fact operating via some other, unmeasured, variable. For example, depression at baseline may predict the risk of future illness, but this may operate relatively directly (e.g. via effects on immune function) or indirectly (e.g. via effects on health behaviours such as diet and alcohol consumption). Although careful and comprehensive measurement of these potential confounding variables can help to exclude these possibilities, it will always remain the case that the association may be operating via some third, unmeasured variable. This is complicated further by the possibility that some unmeasured variable may be causing both variation in the baseline predictor and variation in the outcome with which it is associated (so that the baseline measure is not causally associated with outcome at all). For example, the same genetic factors may be linked to both depression and illness, giving the appearance of a relationship between depression and illness. The fact that the relevant illness outcomes have not yet developed at baseline may simply be because these take longer to be expressed.

At a practical level, these studies are time-consuming and expensive to conduct, in particular if the outcomes of interest take several years to develop and be expressed. This long-term follow-up also gives rise to potential problems of **attrition** within the cohort – participants may drop out, move, die, or otherwise be unavailable at follow-up, so that the final cohort for analysis may be considerably smaller than the one originally recruited. If the likelihood of dropping out of the study is related to the outcomes of interest, this may lead to biased results. For example, in a study of smoking cessation, individuals who are not successful in giving up smoking may be less motivated to remain in the study, resulting in successful quitters being over-represented in the final sample who complete the study.

Longitudinal studies are also not always an effective way to study associations, particularly when an outcome such as a particular disease is rare or takes a long time to develop. In the case of certain outcomes, there will simply not be enough individuals within a cohort who will develop the outcome of interest (or they will take a very long time to develop it). This will add to the cost and complexity of a longitudinal study design, as it will require an extremely large study (in order for a sufficient number of individuals to develop the outcome of interest) and/or a study which is continued for a very long period of time (in order to allow sufficient time for the outcomes of interest to develop). In situations such as these it is much more cost-effective and practical to run a case-control study instead.

SIGNIFICANCE TO HEALTH PSYCHOLOGY

A large number of studies in health psychology use longitudinal designs, although fewer than use case-control designs (primarily for reasons of cost and convenience). As with cross-sectional studies, these tend to be similar in many ways to traditional epidemiological studies of risk factors, but also tend to focus on psychological and behavioural risk factors (e.g. self-efficacy beliefs, coping styles and so on).

Longitudinal study designs in health psychology have a particular advantage over case-control designs because the psychological constructs of interest to many health psychologists are likely to be particularly affected by the onset of disease. For example, illness may result in a change in self-efficacy beliefs or coping styles, so that case-control studies will be very poorly suited to determining whether a particular copying style, for example, leads to illness, or vice versa. Of course, longitudinal study designs will still be limited, for the reasons described above, but will at least be able to show whether variation in coping style precedes and predicts the onset of illness, in this hypothetical example.

Further reading

Altman, D.G. (1991) *Practical Statistics for Medical Research.* London: Chapman & Hall.
Chapter 5 discusses study design issues, while the rest of the book is an excellent introduction to medical statistics (which may be valuable to health psychologists who have covered statistics only from the perspective of psychology in the past).

Manolio, T.A., Bailey-Wilson, J.E. and Collins, F.S. (2006) Genes, environment and the value of prospective cohort studies. *Nature Review Genetics*, 7, 812–820.
Highlights specific research questions (in the context of genetic risk factors for disease) which longitudinal study designs are better suited to answering than case-control designs (see also Molecular Genetics).

See also **research methods and measurement and study design**

RESEARCH METHODS AND MEASUREMENT
and: EXPERIMENTAL

MEANING Experimental study designs are the strongest of the available study designs in that they allow inferences regarding **causation** to be made. In these studies, participants are randomly assigned to one of two (or more) conditions. Since allocation is random, any differences between the groups after exposure to the conditions can be inferred to be a result of the effects of the conditions. An example is a **randomized clinical trial** (RCT) of a novel medication compared to a placebo – if outcome measures are improved in the medication group compared to the placebo group, we can infer that the benefit is the result of the medication.

ORIGINS Experimental study designs arose from two independent research traditions. In biomedical research, the rapid increase in the number of potentially effective medications and interventions available resulted in a need to be able to show experimentally that these interventions were more effective than simply a placebo. This resulted in the adoption of the randomized placebo-controlled trial as the gold standard of evidence that an intervention is an improvement over background effects such as spontaneous recovery and the **placebo effect**. The use of **randomization**, if done correctly, ensures that participants in the intervention and control groups are similar at the start of the trial.

At the same time, the development of psychology and other behavioural sciences which investigated human and animal behaviour, resulted in the use of experimental study designs in laboratory contexts. In principle, the rationale behind the adoption of experimental designs is the same as in bio-medicine: by allocating participants randomly to one of two (or more) groups, any resulting differences in behaviour can be inferred to have been caused by the experimental manipulation. For example, the impact of information on healthy eating (compared to a control condition which lacks this 'active ingredient', such as information on an unrelated topic) can be investigated in relation to the subsequent response to advertisements for food in an experimental, laboratory, setting.

An experimental study design is considered to provide the best level of evidence, both in the development of theory and understanding of mechanisms, and in the development of new or modified clinical practice guidelines. The principal reason for this is that only an experimental study design can demonstrate causality. A further advantage of experimental study designs is that data from these studies are the simplest to analyse statistically. Generally, any experimental design includes the following stages: recruitment of a sample from the relevant population, initial baseline assessment, randomization to the test or control condition, and follow-up assessment (see Figure 2.2).

CURRENT USAGE

Since the validity of the results from an experimental study depends on the randomization procedure not biasing the allocation of participants to either the test or control conditions, the quality of the randomization procedures used is critical. Simple methods may include the use of a coin toss or sealed envelopes (within which the condition allocation is given), while more sophisticated methods include the use of computer-generated randomization sequences and treatment allocation. The most important factor in randomization is that the method is not open to abuse. For example, if the experimenter can manipulate the allocation (perhaps to ensure that a patient he or she perceives to be in most need of treatment is not allocated to the placebo group) then the randomization procedure is subject to **bias** and the results of the study are invalid.

A further procedure which helps to ensure the validity of experimental study design is the **blinding** of experimenters and participants. Blinded means blind with respect to condition allocation. In a **single blind** study, participants do not know what condition they have been allocated to. This ensures that their responses will not be affected by prior expectations and that subsequent behaviour will not be affected by knowledge of the condition. In some rare instances, single blind refers to situations where participants know their condition allocation and only the person evaluating them is blinded. In a **double blind** study, participants and anyone who has contact with them or makes judgments about them is blinded to the assignment of condition. This ensures subjective judgments will not be affected by

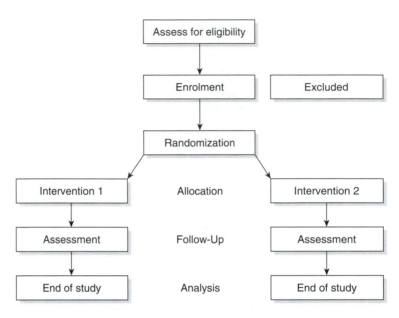

Figure 2.2   Experimental study design

Experimental study designs include initial assessment for eligibility, enrolment (at which point some participants may be excluded, for example because they decide that they no longer wish to take part) and randomization followed by allocation (on the basis of this randomization) to a particular experimental condition. After randomization there is a follow-up period where appropriate data are collected and analysed. Randomized controlled trials typically report the numbers of participants at each stage of this process in a diagram similar to that shown here.

knowledge of a participant's treatment. It is also possible to conduct **triple blind** studies where the individual responsible for data analysis is blinded to the relationship between the data for analysis and condition allocation within these data.

It is also important that the sample on which an experimental study is conducted is representative of the population about which one wishes to make inferences. In practice, this can be hard to achieve. For example, many laboratory studies recruit participants from the student population for convenience (because these studies are often conducted within a university's research environment), but the results of these studies may not generalize to the wider population. In RCTs, participants are often excluded if they have a pre-existing disease, or are on medication and so on. While this is done for reasons of safety when testing novel interventions, it once again means that the results may not generalize to the wider population on whom one might wish to implement the intervention in future.

A more complex experimental design is one which employs a **cross-over** design (see Figure 2.3), so that participants act as their own control. The basic elements of this variant are the same, but rather than being randomized to one condition

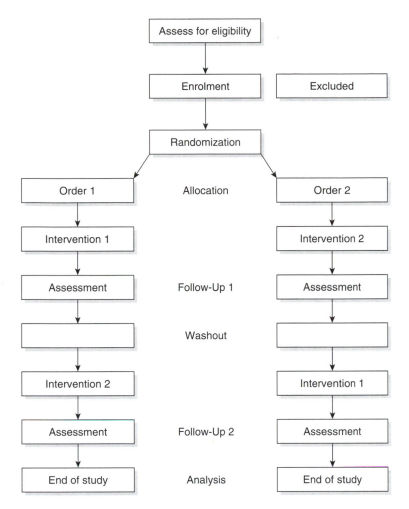

Figure 2.3 Cross-over study design

Cross-over study designs are the same as basic experimental study designs, except that each partic-ipant undergoes each intervention, usually with a washout period in between to allow the effects of the first intervention to dissipate. Participants are randomized to receive the two interventions in a partic-ular order.

only, each participant receives both conditions, in sequential order. Participants are still randomized, but in this case according to the order in which they will receive the two conditions. Since participants are acting as their own controls this method reduces the impact of chance differences between participants in each condition. However, since there may be carry-over or practice effects (namely, completing fol-low-up questionnaires twice rather than once may influence results on the second occasion, perhaps due to participants remembering how they responded the first time), the order in which conditions are administered to participants needs to be taken into account in the eventual statistical analysis. This means that this design is very complex in practice.

In the context of RCTs, there are, generally speaking, two types of intervention trials: **superiority** trials and **equivalence** trials. The purposes of the two types of trials are what their names suggest. Superiority trials are performed to show that one of the interventions is superior to the other. That is, they are carried out to establish a difference between the interventions. Equivalence trials are performed to show that the interventions are, according to some definition, the same or equivalent. The vast majority of RCTs are of the former kind, generally using some kind of appropriate placebo in order to show that a particular intervention is of some benefit. In health psychology, the choice of an appropriate placebo can be difficult, since the intervention is usually behavioural or psychological in nature, so that an analogue of a pharmaceutical placebo (namely, a sugar pill) is not readily available. Often some kind of minimally active intervention is used as a placebo in such instances (e.g. relaxation treatment).

SIGNIFICANCE TO HEALTH PSYCHOLOGY Experimental study designs contribute to both the development of theory within health psychology, and the establishment of evidence that health psychology interventions are efficacious (or not!). Laboratory studies on volunteers, for example, may provide the basis for confirming the role of specific psychological constructs in governing behaviour (e.g. the effects of mood on a desire for cigarettes), while RCTs may provide a basis for confirming that psychological interventions are effective (e.g. behavioural support for smoking cessation).

Further reading

Altman, D.G. (1991) *Practical Statistics for Medical Research.* London: Chapman & Hall.
Chapter 5 discusses study design issues, while the rest of the book is an excellent introduction to medical statistics (which may be valuable to health psychologists who have covered statistics only from the perspective of psychology in the past).

Jorgensen, A.W., Hilden, J. and Gotzsche, P.C. (2006) Cochrane reviews compared with industry supported meta-analyses and other meta-analyses of the same drugs: systematic review. *British Medical Journal*, 333, 782.
Interesting systematic review which suggests that the results of meta-analyses of randomized controlled trials sponsored by the pharmaceutical industry differ from those without this sponsorship. Discusses the role of bias in study design and reporting.

See also **research methods and measurement and study design**

RESEARCH METHODS AND MEASUREMENT
and: **QUALITATIVE**

Qualitative research attempts to provide a rich, descriptive account of the same psychological and behavioural phenomena, via analyses of **textual accounts** – either written or spoken – in order to produce detailed **narrative** reports. Quantitative research, by contrast, objectively measures psychological phenomena to enable statistical analysis, reducing phenomena to numerical values, and applying statistical operations to these to test hypotheses. While quantitative research attempts to be as objective as possible and to control experimental conditions, qualitative research accepts (even welcomes!) the subjective nature inherent in using a qualitative approach.

MEANING

Qualitative research has a long research tradition, which derives largely from a realist perspective, and focuses on **thematic methods**. That is, it attempts to identify themes within narratives, first-person accounts and so on which describe real-life phenomena without sacrificing the richness and detail of these phenomena. It uses qualitative methods to analyse qualitative data, although the exact nature of these data may be very different to those collected in a quantitative study.

ORIGINS

If language use is the phenomenon of interest, then text is regarded as the object of research, with the real-world operating as the background to this. This kind of approach is used, for example, in **Discourse Analysis**. If real-world phenomena, such as behaviours, are the object of research, then text is regarded as the lens or medium through which the real-world (as the object of interest) can be understood and investigated. This kind of approach is used in **Grounded Theory** and **Focus Groups**.

Describing qualitative research as a single kind of research does not do justice to the many conceptual and theoretical approaches which fall within this very broad category. One common theme, however, is that behaviour is not necessarily amenable to scientific study in the same way that physical matter is, for example, and that attempts to do this, while potentially valuable in some respects, will necessarily give rise to an impoverished understanding. **Constructivism** regards behaviour as a response to situational demands, rather than as a fixed attribute of an individual. This would mean that personality, for instance, may be located *between* people, rather than *within* people (Hampson, 1988). This clearly has important implications with respect to **psychometric** approaches to the measurement of personality traits. According to this view, behaviour is negotiated between participants in a social exchange, and operates as a function of the situational and intrapersonal requirements. Qualitative methods are valuable because they attempt to understand the nature of this exchange, rather than simply reduce it to single numbers

CURRENT USAGE

Table 2.1   Differences between quantitative and qualitative research

	Quantitative	*Qualitative*
	Requirement	
Question	Hypothesis	Interest
Method	Control and randomization	Curiosity and reflexivity
Data collection	Response	Viewpoint
Outcome	Dependent variable	Accounts
	Ideal	
Data	Numerical	Textual
Sample size	Large (power)	Small (saturation)
Context	Eliminated	Highlighted
Analysis	Rejection of null	Synthesis

There are various important differences between quantitative and qualitative research, both in terms of the requirements of the study and the ideal data, sample size and analytical methods. Most importantly, quantitative and qualitative methods address very different kinds of research question (see Table 2.3).

Table 2.2   Strengths and weaknesses of qualitative research

Strengths	*Weaknesses*
Low constraints of tradition or method	Poor internal reliability
Grounded hypotheses	Weak decisiveness
Contextualized hypotheses	Poor generalizability
Non-normative focus	Rarely integrated
Comprehensiveness	Seems easy
Detail	Seems harmless

There are a number of strengths and weaknesses to qualitative research, some of which are listed here. The most important strengths include the comprehensiveness of qualititative research, which embraces richness and depth. Unfortunately, it is relatively uncommon for qualitative research to be integrated with quantitative research, even though it has the potential to inform the design of quantitative studies.

(such as the score on a personality questionnaire). Quantitative research emphasizes replicability, reliability and validity, while qualitative research emphasizes contingency, situatedness and reflexivity (see Table 2.1).

Data collection methods in qualitative research are different from those in quantitative research in a number of important ways. Observation, either as a participant or non-participant, is critical (as opposed to measurement via instruments), with **interviews** (either of individuals or groups) and **documentary analysis** (of records, transcripts, and so on) forming the basis of data collection.

A variety of qualitative methods of data collection and data analysis exist, the most common of which include grounded theory and discourse analysis. **Grounded Theory** attempts to construct a theory based on qualitative data, without pre-existing hypotheses. The core feature of Grounded Theory is simultaneous data

Table 2.3 Different research questions and methods in quantitative and qualitative research

Quantitative question	Quantitative method	Qualitative question	Qualitative method
'By how much does thrombolytic therapy improve survival in acute myocardial infarction?'	Meta-analysis of randomized controlled trials	'Why do some patients delay seeking help when they have acute central chest pain?'	Individual (semi-structured) interviews, with cross-validation between interviewers
'What proportion of smokers will give up when advised to do so by their doctor?'	Prospective observational (cohort) study	'What sort of smoker responds to advice to quit, and how might we influence the remainder?'	Individual (semi-structured) interviews, with cross-validation between interviewers
'What features of acute febrile illness predict serious diseases such as bacterial meningitis?'	Retrospective (case-control) study	'What worries parents when their pre-school children are acutely ill, and why?'	Individual (semi-structured) interviews, or focus group discussions

Quantitative and qualitative methods each have their place in research, and are each best suited to answering specific kinds of research question. Some examples are given here, along with the specific methods or study designs which might be used to answer each question.

Table 2.4   Lay beliefs about hypertension (*Source*: Heurtin-Roberts, 1993)

High Blood	High Pertension
Physical disease of the heart and blood	Disease of the 'nerves' caused by stress, worry and personality
Blood too 'hot', 'rich' or 'thick' over extended periods	Believed to be volatile and episodic, rather than long lasting
Level of blood rose slowly and remained high	Levels of blood rise and fall rapidly at times of stress
Caused by diet, heredity and 'heat' in the environment	Treated by amelioration of stress and psychological symptoms

Heurtin-Roberts investigated lay beliefs about hypertension among African-American women in New Orleans. This research revealed a complex pattern of beliefs related in part to modern bio-medical conceptions of hypertension, but also to cultural beliefs and folk medicine. Health education campaigns which fail to take into account people's existing beliefs about disease may not succeed if the advice provided does not match these existing beliefs.

collection and analysis, with analytic categories developed from the data as data collection is ongoing. Comparisons of data and data, data and concept, and concept and concept allow these categories to be developed, and further theoretical sampling and data collection are used to confirm these categories. Discourse Analysis is concerned with the role of language in the construction of social reality, and emphasizes discourse as performance, and in particular the fluidity and variability of discourse. It asks what participants are doing with discourse (that is, what function it serves for them), and investigates the creation of meaning in language. Other methods exist, including phenomenological analysis (which explores how we make sense of the world), narrative psychology (which explores the role of narratives in understanding the world), conversation analysis (which explores spontaneously generated conversation), and cooperative enquiry (where the researcher is a participant in the research).

SIGNIFICANCE TO HEALTH PSYCHOLOGY

Qualitative methods can be argued to be of more importance in health psychology than in other areas of psychology, because the concepts which health psychologists deal with are intended to reflect the 'real world' in a very direct way, which has application in the understanding and treatment of physical health and illness. It is possible (indeed likely) that the concepts employed in bio-medicine may not be understood by the general public, so that interventions, health education campaigns and so on may fail because they are not understood by those they target.

One well-known example illustrates this potential problem. Heurtin-Roberts (1993) investigated folk beliefs regarding hypertension in African-American women in New Orleans. The study identified two distinct groups of individuals in this population, who could be characterized according to the differences in their beliefs regarding this disease. One group believed in the bio-medical definition of hypertension, while the other group believed in two distinct diseases (see Table 2.4).

From a bio-medical perspective, the two distinct 'diseases' identified by the second group of individuals each shares some features of the bio-medical concept of hypertension. Clearly, health education campaigns based on the bio-medical concept of hypertension which do not take into account these important and strongly held folk beliefs may be unsuccessful.

Further reading

Heurtin-Roberts, S. (1993) 'High-pertension' – the uses of a chronic folk illness for personal adaptation. *Social Science and Medicine*, 37, 285–294.
Investigation into lay beliefs around hypertension, and the extent to which chronic illness can be understood in a cultural context which emphasizes particular coping responses and behaviours.

Smith, J.A. (ed.) (2003) *Qualitative Psychology: A Practical Guide to Research Methods*. London: Sage.
An excellent introduction to qualitative methods, specifically as applied to psychology. Discusses a range of techniques and conceptual models and frameworks, including **Grounded Theory**, **Discourse Analysis** and so on in detail.

See also **research methods and measurement and study design**

RESEARCH METHODS AND MEASUREMENT
and: PSYCHOMETRICS

MEANING

Psychometrics is concerned with the measurement of psychological **traits** such as knowledge, abilities, attitudes and personality traits, typically although not necessarily using questionnaire-based methods. The study of psychometrics relates primarily to the investigation of differences between individuals and between groups of individuals. The principles of psychometrics guide the development and use of instruments and procedures used in the measurement of psychological traits.

ORIGINS

A number of prominent figures in the early days of psychological science contributed to the development of the field of psychometrics. The most well-known, at least with respect to their contribution to psychometrics, are Francis Galton and Charles Spearman, both of whom developed and refined psychometric approaches to the measurement of intelligence and general aptitude or cognitive ability. Their contribution also included the development of factor analysis (see Box 2.1), which continues to be used extensively in psychometrics and plays a central role in the development of questionnaire instruments.

Box 2.1 Factor analysis

Suppose a psychologist proposes a theory that there are two kinds of intelligence, 'verbal intelligence' and 'mathematical intelligence'. Behavioural traits such as these cannot be observed directly and have to be measured indirectly, for example using an intelligence test. Factor analysis is used to identify 'factors' that explain a variety of results on different tests. For example, in our hypothetical examples, factor analysis could be used to identify whether performance on intelligence tests was related to performance on two different kinds of question within these tests (for example, those relating to 'verbal intelligence' and those relating to 'mathematical intelligence'). If these factors exist, people who get a high score on one test of verbal ability will also get a high score on other tests of verbal ability. Factor analysis is the method by which these inter-relationships are identified.

Factor analysis has a long history in psychometrics, and has been used to identify personal traits (for example, what is the optimal number of traits which we need to describe a large proportion of the variability in human behaviour) and the structure of intelligence (for example, what are the different sub-types of intelligence which exist, and how do they relate to each other). It has the advantage of providing structure and simplicity to complex datasets, although it has the disadvantage of being a complex procedure, and is only as good as the data which are used in the factor analysis.

Psychometrics has been applied extensively to the measurement of personality, attitudes, mood, intelligence, cognitive ability, and so on. The inherent difficulty in measuring these constructs, which lack a tangible physical correlate, drives the use of psychometrics, which attempts to properly quantify and define these constructs. The earliest psychometric instruments were designed to measure intelligence, the best known of which is the Stanford-Binet IQ test developed originally by Alfred Binet, and psychometric instruments continue to be used widely within education and educational psychology. Another major area of study in psychometrics relates to personality, and a large number of personality measures and related models and theories exists.

There are three fundamental properties of any good test or instrument: **objectivity**, **reliability** and **validity**. The traditional and most important concepts in psychometrics are reliability and validity. Reliability refers to the extent to which a measurement is free from unsystematic error, and therefore measures something accurately. Validity is the extent to which a measurement indexes the underlying psychological construct which it is intended to. To illustrate this, a clock which is five minutes fast is reliable (it is measuring time), but invalid (it is not measuring the right time). Ideally, an instrument should also be free from systematic **error** (e.g. systematic biases, such as a ruler which includes 11 millimetres in each centimetre). However, it is unsystematic error which is the main concern, since a test cannot be valid if it is not reliable. It is, however, possible for a test to be reliable but not valid (as in the case of the fast clock, above).

In technical terms, reliability refers to the proportion of variance in the measurement which is due to unsystematic (that is, random) error. Unsystematic error may arise from a number of sources. For example, if people's responses to a questionnaire vary depending on their mood (when the questionnaire is not in fact intended to measure variation in mood but something conceptually unrelated, such as intelligence), then this variation is uninformative with respect to the intended measurement. Since this uninformative variation will vary unpredictably (namely, unsystematically) between participants, this will serve to reduce the overall reliability of the instrument. Various potential threats to reliability exist, which may be more or less relevant depending on exactly what the instrument in question is intended to measure. For example, instruments which are intended to measure stable, underlying traits (such as personality and intelligence) should be relatively unaffected by factors such as time of day, current mood and so on. Conversely, instruments which are intended to measure state factors (such as mood) are likely to be sensitive to these factors (given that mood varies from time to time).

Test-retest reliability refers to the extent to which the measurement taken on an instrument at one time point correlates with that taken at another time point, although this should only be high in cases where we do not expect the measure to change over time (e.g. intelligence). Other tests of reliability include inter-rater reliability (which assesses the extent to which different experimenters give the same rating, in cases where interview rather than questionnaire instruments are used) and alternate form reliability (which assesses the extent to which different versions of a test are correlated, in cases where one might want to use two versions of a test to avoid practice or learning effects).

One sense in which all instruments should be relatively free from unsystematic error is that they should be internally consistent. That is, all items on a questionnaire should tap into the same underlying construct. This is typically assessed using the split-half test, which calculates the correlation between one half of the items on a test with the other half. If all the items are measuring the same underlying construct, the two halves should be highly correlated. Cronbach's alpha is the mean of all possible split-half correlations, which is a more accurate measure of internal consistency.

The validity of psychometric instruments is difficult to assess in practice because the constructs so measured do not have tangible physical properties (unlike, say, blood pressure). The validity of such instruments, therefore, must be assessed indirectly, by correlating measures with a criterion measure known to be valid. Various forms of validity exist (unlike reliability, where there is only one kind, although *threats* to reliability may occur from different sources).

Concurrent validity is a sub-set of criterion validity, and refers to the extent to which the instrument correlates with an appropriate criterion which is measured at the same time (e.g. a new version of an intelligence test and an existing version). Predictive validity is another sub-set of criterion validity, and refers to the correlation with an appropriate criterion measured at a later time (e.g. intelligence and future examination performance). Content validity reflects the extent to which the instrument includes measures of all of the relevant features of the construct of interest (usually assessed by an appropriate panel of experts). Face validity reflects the extent to which the items of a test appear relevant and appropriate to (usually non-expert) participants who are likely to form the 'target audience' for the instrument. A measure has construct validity if it is related to other variables as required by the theory which underpins the instrument (e.g. intelligence and examination performance), and also unrelated to variables to which it should not be related (e.g. intelligence and personality). The former is sometimes known as convergent validity, and the latter as divergent validity, and the pattern of evidence from both provides evidence of construct validity. This is sometimes assessed using the Multi-Method Multi-Trait Approach.

SIGNIFICANCE TO HEALTH PSYCHOLOGY Health psychology relies heavily on psychometric instruments, including mainly questionnaire instruments but also interview instruments, to quantify the constructs which are central to many of the research questions studied. It is therefore important that these measures are both reliable and valid – we would want to be reasonably certain, for example, that a measure of health-related locus of control was in fact measuring what it purported to measure. For this reason, researchers generally use instruments which have undergone an extensive and stringent process of reliability and validity testing. The use of instruments which have not gone through this process (e.g. questionnaires developed quickly on the basis of a researcher's intuition and solely for the purposes of a single study) is discouraged.

Further reading
Kline, P. (1999) *A Psychometric Primer.* London: Free Association Books.
Gives an introduction to test theory and the principles of psychometrics, with a particular emphasis on the questionnaire measures typically used by psychologists.

See also **research methods and measurement and study design**

3

SOCIAL COGNITIVE MODELS

THREE

SOCIAL COGNITIVE MODELS
and: **social cognitive theory**
       theory of planned behaviour
       health belief model
       protection motivation theory
       implementation intentions
       health action process approach
       precaution adoption process model
       transtheoretical model of behaviour change

Broadly speaking social cognition is concerned with how people respond to and make sense of socially derived situations. This approach assumes that social behaviour is described best by people's perceptions of reality rather than some objective description of their social environment. Social cognitive approaches emphasize that individuals are information processors. Cognitions and thoughts are held to mediate the relationship between observable stimuli and responses in social settings (Fiske, 2004). This chapter is concerned with various key approaches, models and theories that have been developed, or applied from social psychology, to examine the role of various thinking processes in the decision to undertake health-related (the formation of behavioural intentions) and observed health behaviours (see Conner and Norman, 2005; Rutter and Quine, 2002). In addition, this chapter examines some of the key models and approaches that have been utilized to understand how people change from undertaking a maladaptive health behaviour to adopting a self-protective behaviour. The chapter also details a number of examples where the manipulation of key beliefs using theoretically driven change process models has resulted in the adoption of decisions to act and subsequently behave in a more healthy manner.

SOCIAL COGNITIVE MODELS
and: SOCIAL COGNITIVE THEORY

Social Cognitive Theory (SCT) is an approach that emphasizes the role social modelling, or vicarious learning, has on human motivation, thinking and behaviour (Bandura, 2000). According to SCT, motivation and behaviour are regulated through volitional pre-action thinking and behavioural change is determined by a sense of personal control over the environment. A number of key cognitive factors are important for understanding behaviour.

MEANING

Self-efficacy describes beliefs in the ability to undertake a particular action in order to realize a wanted or desired outcome. In other words, self-efficacy concerns beliefs that are specific to people's ability to control environmentally based or situationally based demands. Bandura argued that self-efficacy is expectancy-based cognitions about control and as such serves a self-regulatory function. It determines whether certain instrumental actions will be used to attain certain goals, how much effort a person will direct towards the acquisition of a goal and whether the action will be continued in the presence of obstacles to behaviour. In this way beliefs related to self-efficacy provide a major motivational source in the enactment of behaviour, and as such these beliefs predict motivation to act. Self-efficacy beliefs develop through vicarious experience. The observation of another person having successfully completed a given behaviour enhances personal self-efficacy in the observer. These beliefs also develop and change as a result of an individual experiencing the situational demands and acting in an appropriate way (called 'personal mastery'), as well as being the subject of persuasion process related to control by important others or through the influence of affective arousal. For instance, decreased emotional arousal or an optimistic belief set in response to a threatening situation should result in inflated perceptions of control over behavioural enactment (Bandura, 1997).

A second key concept inherent in SCT is that of perceived **outcome expectancies** which are the perceived consequences of planned action. In essence outcome expectancies take the form of if-then associations, such that 'in situation X, if I behave in way Y then outcome(s) X will result'. Anticipated outcome expectancies may be physical, social or self-evaluative in nature (Dijkstra et al., 1997). Physical outcome expectancies reflect changes in symptomology (e.g. a decrease in breathlessness after sustained physical exercise), social outcome expectancies refer to changes in social responses with the enactment of a behaviour (e.g. the response of important others to your behaviour – normative beliefs) and self-evaluative outcome expectancies concern beliefs about the self as a result of behaving in a certain way (e.g. increased feelings of self-esteem, self-worth). Both self-efficacy and outcome expectancies are held to be direct predictors of behaviours, although it has been argued that they have their effects in an indirect way via goal setting mechanisms.

Goals (or intentions) are direct predictors of behaviour. For SCT, outcome expectancies are used in the initial formation of the intention to undertake a particular behaviour. Self-efficacy appears to be important at the intentional phase as well as in the post-decisional phase when behavioural intention is translated into action (namely, behaviour) (DeVillis and DeVillis, 2000).

ORIGINS

SCT has its basis in the 1970s and a paradigm shift away from the study of behaviour as the unit of analysis to one encompassing thinking and cognition as underlying processes governing the enactment of observed behaviour. Until the advent of SCT (Bandura, 1986), psychology had assumed that learning was the result of stimulus-response relationships governed by reinforcement schedules with a particular focus on the consequences of responses. Bandura's (1977) **Social Learning Theory** argued that learning through trial and error was not the only way in which people learnt to behave in social situations. It was argued that individuals learn through the social modelling of knowledge and competencies by imitating other people, or through vicarious conditioning (or observational learning) such as seeing another person being punished or rewarded for their behaviour in a social situation. To learn in this way demands that observers create and recall a representation of the situation. In other words, Bandura proposed that learning processes were explained by how people cognitively represent the observed learning episode. People learn by initially observing another's behaviour, then represent the learning scene in their minds and subsequently perform the same behaviour. The cognitive representation is the necessary bridge between an individual's observation and their action.

CURRENT USAGE

As individuals progress from thinking about behaving in a certain way, forming a behavioural intention and setting a behavioural goal to actually enacting the behaviour, they utilize and develop expectations about the outcomes of their behaviour and their ability to perform said behaviour. It is for this reason that many of the models you encounter in the social psychology of health have their basis in SCT and the use of one or more of the core constructs in attempting to understand health-related behavioural intention, action or behavioural change (Conner and Norman, 2005). These include, among others, the theories of reasoned action and planned behaviour, the health action process approach, protection motivation theory, the health belief model and the transtheoretical model of behaviour change (see the appropriate key concepts in this chapter). Studies have detailed the contribution of SCT constructs in a number of health behaviours including sexual risk taking behaviours (e.g. Kok et al., 1992), physical exercise (Rodgers et al., 2002), adhering to medication (e.g. Williams and Bond, 2002), and addictive behaviours (e.g. Christiansen et al., 2002). This work has shown outcome expectancies and self-efficacy to have significant explanatory power in intention formation and behavioural enactment (see Luszczynska and Schwarzer, 2005). For instance, Dijkstra et al. (1999) showed that self-evaluative expectancies, like shame and regret, and positive outcome expectancies were important for predicting smokers' attempts to quit.

Table 3.1   Manipulating key factors in social cognitive theory: the percentage of participants making forward change stage transitions in a stage of change matched intervention study among smokers (*Source*: adapted from Dijkstra et al., 2006)

Stage of change	Information condition		
	Pros of quitting	**Cons of not quitting**	**Increase efficacy**
Precontemplation	*34.1%*	18.9%	10.8%
Contemplation	20.4%	*37.2%*	14.3%
Preparation	44.4%	*39.1%*	23.8%
Action	50%	61.1%	*72.7%*

Note: Italicized figures are the matched interventions for the stage of change. Information conditions were as follows. Pros of quitting – the intervention booklet provided for participants contained information to increase the negative outcome expectancies of smoking and the positive outcome expectancies of quitting. Cons of not quitting – the intervention was designed to decrease the negative outcome expectancies of quitting and the positive outcome expectancies of smoking. Increase efficacy – the intervention was designed to increase efficacy by preparing individuals with coping skills to deal with situations in which they would be at a high risk of relapse.

In addition, recent research has demonstrated the role of SCT constructs in the development and implementation of matched interventions. Dijkstra et al. (2006) studied the effectiveness of a matched intervention for smokers who were not thinking about changing their behaviour (precontemplation stage), those who were thinking about changing (contemplation stage), those preparing to change and as such forming a decision to do so (preparation stage), as well as a group of ex-smokers (action stage). Each of these groups received an intervention containing information that was matched to an individual's stage in the change process. Matched interventions involved the manipulation of the positive expectancies (namely, increase them) of stopping smoking for those in the precontemplation group, a decrease of the negative expectancies associated with stopping smoking for those in the contemplation stage group, or an increase in self-efficacy for those in the preparation and action stages. Results showed that after a two month period those who had received a stage matched intervention based on SCT were more likely to have made a forward transition in the change process. For example, a significant number of those who were originally thinking about stopping smoking formed an intention over time to stop or had actually managed to quit (see Table 3.1).

In addition, precontemplators benefitted most from increased expectancies related to the advantages of stopping smoking, contemplators benefitted from information designed to overcome the cons of stopping smoking, and those in the action stage benefitted most from information designed to increase self-efficacy. Those in the preparation stage appeared to benefit from changing positive and negative expectancies about quitting as well as from self-efficacy enhancement.

SIGNIFICANCE TO HEALTH PSYCHOLOGY SCT is of fundamental importance for health psychology because it has formed the basis from which models of health behaviour (e.g. the health belief model, protection motivation theory), health behaviour change (e.g. the transtheoretcial model, health action process approach) and general social cognition models applied to health-related decision making (e.g. the theory of reasoned action and theory of planned behaviour) have been derived. There is no single model which has been applied or developed for the study of health behaviour that does not make reference to the core constructs of self-efficacy or outcome expectancies in their schemes.

Further reading

Bandura, A. (1986) *Social Foundations of Thought and Action*. Englewood Cliffs, NJ: Prentice-Hall.
A classic text that provides the reader with a detailed exploration of the key components of social cognitive theory.

Luszczynska, A. and Schwarzer, R. (2005) Social cognitive theory. In M. Conner and P. Norman (eds), *Predicting Health Behaviour (2nd edition)*. Buckingham: Open University Press. pp. 127–169.
Provides a useful theoretical and applied review of how components of social cognitive theory have been utilized, tested and applied in the context of health-related decision making and health behaviour.

See also **social cognitive models and theory of planned behaviour; social cognitive models and health belief model; social cognitive models and protection motivation theory; social cognitive models and implementation intentions; social cognitive models and health action process approach; social cognitive models and precaution adoption process model; social cognitive models and transtheoretical model of behaviour change; individual differences and habit and self-efficacy**

SOCIAL COGNITIVE MODELS
and: THEORY OF PLANNED BEHAVIOUR

MEANING Many studies have looked at the so-called 'attitude-behaviour relationship'. One approach was Ajzen's (1991) **theory of planned behaviour** (TPB). He was interested in studying how the beliefs held by an individual are important for understanding how they decide to behave toward an attitude object and also how their

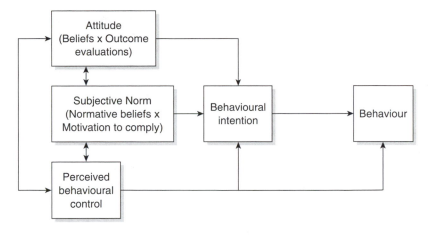

Figure 3.1 Theory of planned behaviour (Ajzen, 1991)

beliefs predict how they subsequently behave. Ajzen's TPB model was derived from the earlier **theory of reasoned action** (TRA) (Fishbein and Ajzen, 1975) and differs only in that the TPB is aimed at understanding types of behaviour that are not necessarily under a person's volitional control.

Figure 3.1 shows the structure of the TPB. Basically, beliefs are structured according to an **expectancy-value** framework. In other words, people hold expectancies about what outcomes they should get if they behave in a particular way. At the same time they also hold beliefs about the value of that outcome for themselves. So, for example, think about taking regular physical exercise. You may think that taking regular physical exercise will result in the outcome of making you feel healthier (outcome expectancy) and that feeling healthier is a good thing (value association) (see Conner and Sparks, 2005 for examples).

ORIGINS

The TPB argues that the immediate antecedent of actual behaviour is **behavioural intention** and that if we intend to take regular physical exercise there is an increased likelihood that we will do so. This intention to behave is predicted by three belief-based factors: attitude, subjective norm and perceived behavioural control. **Attitude** is made up of core beliefs about the outcomes of a behaviour and the value we hold about these outcomes (we've already come across an example of this earlier – taking regular physical exercise). **Subjective norm** encompasses those beliefs we have about how other people we perceive as being important to us would like us to behave (normative beliefs) and the value we hold about behaving in line with other's wishes (motivation to comply). So in taking regular physical exercise it may be that you perceive that health experts and/or friends want you to take exercise. This is a normative belief. The motivation to comply reflects the beliefs that you want to do what these important others wish you to do. If you believe that, for example, health experts want you to take regular physical exercise and that you like doing what health experts expect of you, you are likely to form the intention to take regular physical exercise and hence behave in this way.

The primary difference between the TPB and the TRA lies in the assumption made by the TRA that all behaviour is under volitional control. For many behaviours this may not be the case, such as addictions or other behaviours that have become more habitual over time. The TPB uses the concept of **perceived behavioural control** (PBC), which are beliefs that relate to how much control a person thinks they have over a certain behaviour, to explain the attitude-behaviour relationship in non-volitional behaviours. For instance, you are likely to form an intention to take regular physical exercise if you believe that it is under your own control, namely that you have the ability to do the behaviour (see also the concept of self-efficacy in social cognition theory and in Chapter 5). We hold many different attitudes, normative beliefs and control beliefs about single behaviours and it is the sum of these expectancy-value relations that predicts a person's intention to behave in a particular way, which subsequently predicts actual behaviour.

CURRENT USAGE   The TRA/TPB has been used in the prediction of a number of health behaviours including, among others, drug use (e.g. McMillan and Conner, 2003), physical activity (e.g. Hagger et al., 2002), sexually risky behaviours (Godin and Kok, 1996), adherence processes and screening (e.g. Steadman et al., 2002; Hunter et al., 2003), and dietary behaviours (e.g. Armitage and Conner, 1999). Evidence suggests that the TRA and the TPB accurately predict between 40 and 50 per cent of variance in behavioural intention and between 21 and 36 per cent in actual behaviour for either health or non health-related behaviours (e.g. Sutton, 1998; Armitage and Conner, 2001; Trafimow et al., 2002). While some have argued that the model as it is conceptualized provides a 'sufficient' account of factors predicting intention and/or behaviour, there has been some speculation about other factors that may be important as extensions to the TPB/TRA (Ajzen, 2002a). These include more affective factors, moral norms, and self-identity (see Conner and Armitage, 1998; Sheeran, 2002). For instance, rather than being predicted by subjective norms, intentions and behaviours may be predicted by more morally based normative values and beliefs. These are beliefs related to the moral legitimacy or illegitimacy of performing a behaviour (Evans and Norman, 2002). In addition, people's perception of the likelihood of regretting undertaking a behaviour in the future – anticipated regret – has been shown to contribute significant variance to the prediction of an intention to act (Richard et al., 1996). Another factor that has been the focus of some considerable research interest is the role of habit or past behaviour on future behaviour. It is hypothesized that the effect of past behaviour on future behaviour is direct and that this relationship is not necessarily dependent upon the working of other TPB components, namely subjective norms, attitude or perceived behavioural control (Sutton, 1994; Conner and Armitage, 1998; see the habit concept in Chapter 5).

It has been argued that past behaviour affects future behaviour because well-learned behaviours may occur repeatedly in the same context (e.g. wearing a seat-belt) such that cognitive control over this behaviour eventually becomes automatic and unconsciously activated (Ouellette and Wood, 1998; Verplanken, 2005). Behaviours that are not so well-learned, or those that occur in more unstable contexts, remain under conscious control. The effects of past behaviour are challenged if the predicted behaviour is realistic and precise implemental plans for translating intentions into behaviour have been developed (Ajzen, 2002b) (see implementation intentions). Relatedly, Fazio's (1990) MODE model (MODE stands for 'Motivation and Opportunities as Determinants') studied the conditions under which attitudes towards an object predicts behaviour automatically. Fazio proposes that when motivation and the opportunity to think consciously about a potential behaviour are low, attitudes towards the target will activate behaviour immediately and automatically, as long as these attitudes are accessible and easily retrievable from memory. When people can consciously deliberate about a behaviour and motivation is high, the automatic attitude-behaviour relationship will be overridden. In other words, the more we think about it, the more our behaviour will be characterized by deliberative processing. To date, little work has been undertaken in health psychology to assess implicit cognition – as opposed to explicit cognition as used in the operationalization of TRA/TPB constructs – involved in the generation and guidance of health behaviours (although see Stacy et al., 2000; Sheeran, Aarts et al., 2005). These processes emphasize the operation of automatic memory associations rather than the rational and explicit processing of behavioural beliefs for the prediction of health behaviours.

SIGNIFICANCE TO HEALTH PSYCHOLOGY

The TPB has identified a number of key factors that may be important for understanding how and why an individual makes a health-related decision. This model emphasized the role of expectancy-value judgments in the formation of a behavioural intention (or goal) for both general beliefs related to outcomes associated with adaptive or maladaptive behaviour, beliefs related to how social influence from important others is important for behavioural conformity, and how perceptions of control may be significant in forming an intention or decision to act. Where the model has been less successful is in explaining why the attitude-behaviour relationship is not perfectly correlated or predictive and as such how intentions are translated into actual behaviour (see implementation intentions key concept).

Further reading

Ajzen, I. (1991) The theory of planned behaviour. *Organizational Behavior and Human Decision Processes*, 50, 179–211.
The original conceptualization of the theory of planned behaviour, including a discussion of the development of its key concepts and predictions for decision making.

Armitage, C.J. and Conner, M. (2001) Efficacy of the theory of planned behaviour: a meta-analytic review. *British Journal of Social Psychology*, 40, 471–499.

An interesting review based on statistical inference of the effectiveness and efficacy of the theory of planned behaviour in predicting behavioural intention and actual behaviour.

Conner, M. and Sparks, P. (2005) Theory of planned behaviour and health behaviour. In M. Conner and P. Norman (eds), *Predicting Health Behaviour (2nd edition)*. Buckingham: Open University Press. pp. 170–222.

An extremely useful review of the key components of the theory of planned behaviour and how such components have been used in the exploration of health-related behaviour and decision making.

See also **social cognitive models and social cognitive theory; individual differences and habit and locus of control; individual differences and habit and self-efficacy**

SOCIAL COGNITIVE MODELS
and: HEALTH BELIEF MODEL

MEANING   Health psychologists are interested in what factors are important for understanding how people adopt and change adaptive or maladaptive health behaviours. Some of these factors are cognitively based (such as beliefs and attitudes) and relate to the thinking processes involved in a person making a decision to act in a particular way. The **health belief model** (HBM) is one such model that specifies how individuals cognitively represent health behaviours and which components are important for predicting self-protective health behaviour.

ORIGINS   In the mid-twentieth century health researchers in the USA began to address how health education interventions could be made most effective. These researchers were interested in identifying factors that both predicted the decision to adopt health behaviours and were also amenable to intervention, namely psychological factors that could be manipulated through health-related education and persuasive communication. It was not enough to show that individuals who differed on various demographic factors (e.g. age, gender and socio-economic status) made different decisions in adopting, or not adopting, health behaviours, since these factors cannot be changed. Work had to be undertaken to establish differences grounded in psychological factors important in the decision since these are more amenable to intervention. Originally conceptualized by Rosenstock (1974), and consolidated by Becker et al. (1974), the HBM was developed to account for the role of a number of belief-based psychological factors in health-related decision making and

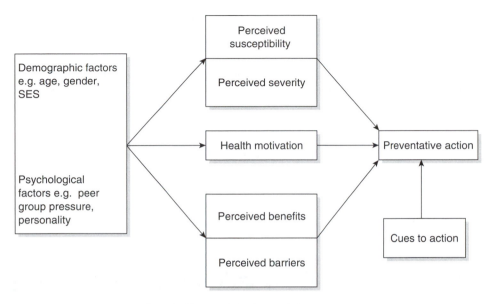

Figure 3.2   The health belief model (Janz and Becker, 1984)

health behaviour. Like other models (e.g. the theory of planned behaviour, the theory of reasoned action), the HBM is an expectancy-value model. The individual represents undertaking a behaviour in terms of core and predictable sets of beliefs, framed as expected outcomes associated with doing a behaviour as well as the value ascribed to the outcome of the behaviour. These core belief sets (or health-related cognitive representations) mediate the relationship between socio-demographic factors and actual health behaviour (see Abraham and Sheeran, 2005). It is to these six core sets of beliefs that we now turn (see Figure 3.2).

The HBM focuses specifically on threat perception and health-related behavioural evaluation as the primary aspects for understanding how a person represents health action (Strecher and Rosenstock, 1997). Threat perception is comprised of two primary belief types. **Perceived susceptibility** to health problems reflects that people believe that they are more or less likely to suffer a negative (or positive) health outcome – for example, 'My chances of getting breast cancer are great' (Champion, 1984). **Perceived severity** reflects cognitions about the consequences of such an illness – for example, 'If I had breast cancer my whole life would change', or 'The thought of breast cancer scares me' (Champion, 1984). Behavioural evaluation also comprises two sets of beliefs – **perceived benefits** (of change), or the perceived utility (efficacy) of undertaking a health-related behaviour, and the **perceived barriers**, or costs, in undertaking that behaviour.

According to Becker et al. (1977) to encapsulate the idea of perceived threat, perceived susceptibility and perceived severity are weighed-up against each other by the person 'thinking' about the health-related behaviour. Believing that one is likely to experience a negative health outcome and that the outcome will be severe should predict an increased likelihood of performing the health protective behaviour. Similarly, it is argued that the perceived benefits of undertaking a behaviour are weighed up against the perceived barriers while formulating a decision to take protective behaviour. No guidelines for specifying the relationship between variables in the HBM have been produced. Indeed studies that have included interactions between, for example, severity and susceptibility have shown that the interaction does not provide additional explanatory power for behavioural enactment in retrospective reports of behaviour, but may make a significant contribution when prospective behaviour is examined (see Abraham and Sheeran, 2005).

The model also proposes a fifth factor called 'cues to action', or 'triggers', that are likely to stimulate the activation of health behaviour when certain belief sets are held. These **cues to action** can be either internal (e.g. mood, symptom perception) or external to the individual (e.g. health promotion literature, media advertisements, social influence processes). For instance, health-related advice as a cue to action has been shown to be predictive of adherence behaviour (e.g. in vaccination programmes) (see Norman and Conner, 1993). The final key factor specified by the HBM refers to a person's readiness to be concerned with health-related matters for themselves. This is labelled 'health motivation' (Becker et al., 1977; Umeh and Rogan-Gibson, 2001).

CURRENT USAGE

The HBM has been utilized in the prediction of a large number of preventative and adherence health behaviours including screening (e.g. Rawl et al., 2001), risk-taking behaviours (e.g. Abraham et al., 1996) and adherence programmes (e.g. Wdowik et al., 2001) (see also Abraham and Sheeran, 2005 for a review). In general, perceived susceptibility, perceived severity, perceived benefits and perceived barriers have all been found to be significant predictors of a diverse range of health behaviours (Janz and Becker, 1984). Although significant, however, the effects of each factor on behaviour are relatively small (see Harrison et al., 1992). Other work has extended the HBM to include factors such as perceived control and self-efficacy as additional constructs in successfully predicting health protective behaviour alongside other HBM specific constructs (e.g. Norman and Brain, 2005). While this evidence is important, HBM theorists have not consistently specified the relationships between self-efficacy, perceived control and behavioural intention with the other HMB constructs. However, more recent work has shown the HBM constructs to have a greater distal impact on behavioural enactment via more proximal determinants such as perceived control, self-efficacy and behavioural intention (Abraham et al., 1999).

Like other social cognition models of health behaviour the HBM has potential utility because it has identified a number of key factors that are important in predicting whether a person will or will not undertake health protective behaviour. Because HBM constructs are predictive of health behaviour, changing these beliefs may lead to a change in behaviour. This is important because the HBM model was originally set up to guide health behaviour promotion initiatives in the USA and it is of little surprise that HBM constructs have been used in the design and evaluation of interventions in a number of health behaviours such as breast self-examination (Ludwick and Garczkowski, 2001), smoking cessation (Strecher et al., 1994) and eating a healthy diet (Abood et al., 2003). These studies have shown some success in changing individuals' perceptions of susceptibility, severity, benefits and barriers and these changes being reflected in actual health behaviour (Yabroff and Mandelblatt, 1999).

In addition the HBM belief constructs have been developed and applied for inclusion in other models seeking to examine the cognitive precursors of health behaviour, including the health action process approach and protection motivation theory (see key concepts in this chapter). Other approaches have shown that the inclusion of HBM constructs in addition to those specified by other models (e.g. TPB – Abraham et al., 1999) improved the predictive ability of the model and identified key health beliefs in behaviour.

The HBM is important in health psychology because it provides a description of a number of cognitively based factors thought significant in understanding decision-making processes in health behaviours and sick role behaviours. It recognized that in forming a decision to undertake health protective behaviour, people incorporate a form of rational thinking in weighing up a number of cognitively based factors simultaneously. This form of rational decision making includes a cost-benefit analysis of perceptions related to the threat of illness and also an analysis of how beneficial or disadvantageous a particular course of action could be for the individual. With such conceptual knowledge it should be possible hypothetically to change these types of thought processes in order to change behaviour through targeted interventions or health promotions activities.

SIGNIFICANCE TO HEALTH PSYCHOLOGY

Further reading

Abraham, C. and Sheeran, P. (2005) The health belief model. In M. Conner and P. Norman (eds), *Predicting Health Behaviour (2nd edition)*. Buckingham: Open University Press. pp. 28–80.
A useful and contemporary review that details the theoretical development of the health belief model and its utility in understanding and predicting health-related decision making and health behaviour.

Janz, N. and Becker, M.H. (1984) The health belief model: a decade later. *Health Education Quarterly*, 11, 1–47.
A classic review by the theory's founders of the state of play of the health belief model after 10 years of testing. Interesting when read in conjunction with the Abraham and Sheeran (2005) chapter.

See also **social cognitive models and social cognitive theory; social cognitive models and health action process approach; social cognitive models and protection motivation theory**

SOCIAL COGNITIVE MODELS
and: PROTECTION MOTIVATION THEORY

MEANING   One method by which psychologists have attempted to influence individuals' attitudes and subsequently their behaviour towards an attitude object is through the use of fear appeals. We are bombarded with media images and health promotion campaigns that have as their basis the objective of eliciting in the reader or viewer a negative emotional state, by making the person 'feel' at risk of experiencing a negative health outcome. This experienced emotional state is based in the fear of experiencing the negative outcomes of maladaptive health behaviour.

Early work argued that fear may have a persuasive impact on attitudes and behaviour because experienced fear, and the emotional arousal evoked, act as a motivational source for the appraisal of current beliefs and attitudes. In other words, if a persuasive communication evokes fear the individual will be motivated to reduce this unpleasant psychological state by altering their beliefs and/or their behaviour towards some attitude object (Sutton, 1982). There is a relationship between fear and a drive to reduce this experienced fear through belief or behavioural modification.

The relationship between the level of fear experienced (or arousal) and the likelihood of observing behavioural change is not linear with increasing fear resulting in increasing levels of belief or behavioural change. What appears to account for the relationship is an inverted U-shaped relationship (Janis, 1967). As well as facilitating or motivating a person to search out ways of reducing the fear or threat through following behavioural advice, arousal or fear may also lead to more deliberative processing of the recommended action and as such act as interference for change. Up to an optimal level of fear arousal, as the level of fear increases facilitation effects are hypothesized to increase at a greater rate than interference effects. Once this optimal level is reached interference effects created by fear increase at a greater velocity than facilitation effects. This early interest in the role of fear and threat experience in attitude change, belief acceptance and behavioural modification through persuasive communication was developed further in **protection motivation theory** (Rogers, 1975).

ORIGINS   Protection motivation theory (PMT) is a conceptual framework for the study of the impact of **fear appeals** (or emotional arousal) on behavioural modification. Rogers (1975, 1983) produced a model that sought to describe the relationship between the experience of fear and behaviour enactment. More importantly, PMT provided an account of the fear-behaviour relationship by identifying key cognitive factors that mediated the experience of fear arousal on behaviour (see Norman et al., 2005 for a review). Figure 3.3 provides a schematic representation of PMT.

PMT identified the degree of severity of an event, the likelihood of an event happening if no adaptive response is made to the threat event, and how efficacious the response is to reduce the threat of the event, as three primary stimulus variables.

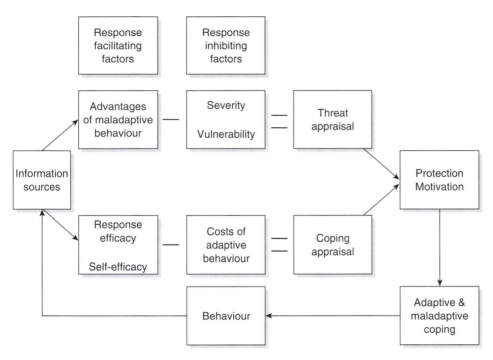

Figure 3.3   Protection motivation theory (Maddux and Rogers, 1983)

A number of environmentally based (e.g. fear appeals) or intrapersonal (e.g. personality) factors act as sources of information. These sources activate two independent cognitively based appraisal processes called 'threat appraisal' and 'coping appraisal', which operate in parallel and contain factors that act as cognitive mediators in the relationship between the experience of threat and behavioural enactment. Threat appraisal concerns factors that are important for understanding the basis of the threat being experienced and which increase or decrease the chances of making a maladaptive response, such as denying the reality of the threat. Perceived severity of threat and also vulnerability to the threat are central components in **threat appraisal** and are thought to inhibit maladaptive responses. For instance, a person may be motivated to take self-protective action and thus inhibit otherwise maladaptive responses if it is perceived that they are vulnerable to a severe or subjectively perceived serious health threat. At the same time, PMT also specifies that there may be rewards that are intrinsic (e.g. expectancies of a positive mood or the relief of negative mood) or extrinsic (e.g. expectancies related to social approval) to individuals that can operate to promote or facilitate the adoption of maladaptive behaviour.

Coping appraisal comprises three psychological factors that are important for coping efficiently with a perceived threat or fear appeal and which affect the likelihood of an individual making an adaptive response. **Response efficacy** refers to beliefs that a recommended self-protective action would decrease the health threat and self-efficacy concerns beliefs associated with whether this behaviour can be performed by the individual (see the social cognition theory concept in this chapter). A high level of response efficacy and self-efficacy increases the likelihood of an adaptive behaviour being undertaken. The third coping appraisal factor reflects the idea that there may be response costs that inhibit the likely performance of a self-protective action. Think of these as perceived barriers to behaviours (see the health belief model) such as a drug user associating 'giving up' with experiencing severe craving or even the loss of a defined social network.

The final core factor in PMT refers to an individual's intention to perform a recommended action to reduce the health threat. This is called protection motivation. Protection motivation is the result of the thinking processes a person engages in during threat appraisal and coping appraisal. It is related positively to perceptions of severity and vulnerability, response efficacy and self-efficacy, and related negatively to rewards for maladaptive responses and the perceived costs of adaptive responses. In addition, protection motivation results when severity and vulnerability to a health threat are greater than the rewards for acting in an unhealthy way, and when response and self-efficacy outweigh the costs associated with taking the recommended health protective action.

CURRENT USAGE

PMT has been used to predict a large range of health behaviours such as exercise (e.g. Plotnikoff and Higgenbottom, 2002), drinking (e.g. Murgraff et al., 1999), sexual risk behaviours (Sheeran and Orbell, 1996) and adherence (Norman et al., 2003). The model components have also been the subject of meta-analyses, in which the statistical findings for a number of studies are combined to give an overall picture of the power of factors on behavioural outcome (Floyd et al., 2000; Milne et al., 2000). In general, these studies showed that the core PMT factors significantly predicted intention or protection motivation and concurrent behaviour, with self-efficacy and response costs showing the greatest predictive power. In addition, future behaviour – the prospective measurement of actual health behaviour adoption – was also shown to be predicted by vulnerability, self-efficacy, response costs and protection motivation (intention).

Intervention studies have also been used to study the predictions made by PMT for a number of health-related cognitions and behaviours including those for exercise adoption, smoking, sexual risk behaviours and breast self-examination (see Norman et al., 2005 for a review). These studies have either manipulated experimentally one or more PMT core factors and measured relevant intention and behaviour change, or have measured changes in related cognitions alone. In a recent meta-analysis Milne et al. (2000) showed that intervening with specific PMT-related constructs was successful in displaying the changes in all threat appraisal factors (severity and vulnerability), as well the coping appraisal factors of response efficacy and self-efficacy.

No effect for response costs was shown in this analysis although the limited evidence base when manipulating this concept may simply not be sufficient to conclude either effectiveness or non-effectiveness. This analysis also showed that the manipulation of threat appraisal factors is more powerful than for coping appraisal factors. Remember, this is only for measured changes in these cognitions after manipulation. So what is the effect of manipulating PMT-related cognitions on intention to behave (namely, protection motivation as specified in the model) and actual health-related behaviour? It has been shown that in general changing a person's perceived self-efficacy or response efficacy (that is, coping appraisal components) is more important in predicting intention than the other PMT constructs (e.g. Stanley and Maddux, 1986; Yzer et al., 1998).

SIGNIFICANCE TO HEALTH PSYCHOLOGY

One of the most common vehicles through which belief-based behavioural change is manipulated is by using fear appeals. PMT is important because it has provided an account of the relationship between the experience of arousal through fear evocation and a person's propensity to be motivated to take self-protective action. The model identified two appraisal processes, threat-related and coping-related, that each individual undergoes in forming a response to a threatening message or experience. Each of the processes comprises a number of cognitive or cognitive-emotional factors that interact in a dynamic fashion with each other when forming a protection-related behavioural decision. These types of factors, and how they interact with each other in forming behavioural intentions, allow for the planning of interventions aimed to change these perceptions such that participants become more likely to be motivated to protect themselves.

Further reading

Milne, S., Sheeran, P. and Orbell, S. (2000) Protection and intervention in health-related behaviour: a meta-analytic review of protection motivation theory. *Journal of Applied Social Psychology*, 30, 106–143.

A useful paper detailing the effectiveness of components of the model across a number of studies looking at health-related decision making and behaviour.

Norman, P., Boer, H. and Seydel, E.R. (2005) Protection motivation theory. In M. Conner and P. Norman (eds), *Predicting Health Behaviour (2nd edition)*. Buckingham: Open University Press. pp. 81–126.

A contemporary and useful review of the status of protection motivation theory, its components and predictions, in understanding how people may or may not process health-related information and behave accordingly.

See also **social cognitive models and social cognitive theory; social cognitive models and health belief model**

SOCIAL COGNITIVE MODELS
and: **IMPLEMENTATION INTENTIONS**

MEANING One of the perennial issues of debate in health and social psychology is the relationship between the formation of an intention to act in a particular way, also known as goal setting, and enacted behaviour. Many social cognitive models of health behaviour propose that the immediate precursor of behavioural enactment is intention (see concepts of theory of reasoned action/theory of planned behaviour, protection motivation theory, health action process approach, precaution adoption process model). In a meta-analyses of studies that have presented evidence for the relationship between intention and behaviour, Sheeran (2002) showed that nearly 50 per cent of participants who intended to behave in a certain way did not subsequently go on to perform the behaviour, and only 7 per cent of those who had not formed an intention ended up undertaking the behaviour. It seems that the intention behaviour gap is accounted for by those people who originally form an intention but do not act. Intentions may not necessarily be translated into behaviour. In another recent meta-analysis of evidence in which changes in intention were experimentally manipulated and the effects on behaviour measured, Webb and Sheeran (2006) showed that a medium to high change in intention lead to a small to medium change in behaviour.

Sheeran, Webb et al. (2005) and Sheeran, Milne et al. (2005) argue that three processes may account for this failure in translation from intention to action. The first concerns intention viability. This is the idea that some behaviours are dependent upon how much actual (not perceived) control people have over undertaking a behaviour in the future (e.g. Sheeran et al., 2003). The second process is called 'intention activation'. This describes the observation that situational demands will change how salient or intense the activation of an intention or goal is for an individual, relative to other goals activated simultaneously. Goals will only be achieved or implemented if they are salient (or cognitively obvious) and have been activated. Finally, intention elaboration argues that behaviour may be dependent on how fully engaged or how far a person elaborates on the situational factors (internal or external cues) that would make the intention possible.

In essence, the operation of any behaviour requires the elaboration of a number of individual actions, each of which has been performed in a particular situation or context (Abraham and Sheeran, 2004). If such elaboration has not taken place it is likely that intention will not be realized in behaviour. For example, the intention to use a condom in sexual encounters will only translate into behaviour if a person has thought about, or elaborated upon, individual actions related to the intention. In this case these actions might include the simple purchase of condoms, or that an individual has negotiated condom use with a sexual partner. If goal intentions are not sufficiently activated or elaborated upon, the probability of intentions translating into actions is decreased.

The process of **implementation intentions** describes one method by which effective activation and elaboration of goal intentions can be achieved (see Gollwitzer et al., 2005). This concept derived from the model of action phases (Gollwitzer, 1990) which states that achieving a behavioural goal is dependent upon a motivational phase (a pre-decisional phase), in which intentions are formed, and a volitional phase, in which these intentions are realized (a post-decisional phase). The former motivational phase comprises beliefs about how desirable or possible a potential action is (e.g. assessing the pros and cons), whereas the latter volitional phase comprises processes that enhance the initiation of this action by emphasizing the production of action plans. Most social cognition models applied to health behaviour have only emphasized motivational factors that lead to the formation of intention (see theories of reasoned action and planned behaviour, and protection motivation theory). Although these models state that intentions will lead to behaviour, they do not adequately address how this will occur. Implementation intentions work provides a framework to conceptualize how intentions are translated into actions.

Implementation intentions are formed when an individual recognizes a response that will lead to the successful completion of a goal, and also identifies a situation in which that response would be possible. In effect a person is planning where, when and how to undertake a behaviour – 'If situation X happens, I will do Y'. This is different from goal intentions which only specify what behaviour a person intends to do, not when, where and how they will undertake this behaviour. In this sense, implementation intentions can be seen as being subordinate to behavioural intentions. They are the basis of behavioural intentions but also link intention with actual behaviour. Forming an implementation intention creates a cognitive or mental connection between a particular situation and a particular response in that situation (Gollwitzer and Branstätter, 1997). It is also agued that this link operates in such a way that behaviour is automatic – implicit cognitive representations are activated without an individual's awareness or control of the process (Sheeran, Webb et al., 2005).

By developing a cognitive representation of a critical situation in which a behaviour occurs, this implies that implementation intentions have their effect because this representation becomes highly accessible – such that the situation becomes more easy to detect, more salient and is more easily attended to (see Webb and Sheeran, 2004). After having formed an implementation intention the person becomes cognitively 'committed' to a behaviour if a particular stimulus is encountered. It is argued that control of action passes from the self to the environment and the situation automatically triggers the activation of the implementation intention representation. This behaviour occurs very quickly and does not require much cognitive effort or attention. Implementation intentions are immediate and efficient processes (Gollwitzer, 1993).

A body of research has now accumulated showing both the effectiveness and the dimensions of implementation intentions in health behaviours. This has included work on diet (e.g. Armitage, 2004), exercise behaviour (e.g. Milne et al., 2002), smoking and binge drinking (e.g. Murgraff et al., 1996; Higgins and Conner, 2003), and screening for breast cancer and cervical cancer (e.g. Orbell and Sheeran, 1998).

These studies have reliably confirmed that the formation of an implementation intention has the effect of making the probability that a person will undertake a behaviour, and implement their goal intentions when a situation arises, significantly greater than with control participants (see Koestner et al., 2002; Sheeran, 2002). For example, Steadman and Quine (2004) showed that the formation of an implementation intention, focused on testicular self-examination, resulted in 65 per cent of the experimental group (implementation intention formation group) performing the behaviour after a three week period as compared to about 40 per cent of the non-experimental group (non-implementation intention group). See Box 3.1 for an example of an implementation intention study.

Box 3.1   The power of implementation intentions in translating health intentions into health behaviour: the case of testicular self-examination (after Steadman and Quine, 2004)

Basis of the research

Testicular cancer accounts for approximately 1 per cent of all known cancers in males and is particularly prevalent among the young and middle-aged. When detected early and appropriate intervention is given, survival rates are very good at about 95 per cent (Peate, 1999). However, as with other forms of cancer successful intervention is dependent upon the early identification of the disease and of the problem (namely, a lump in the testes), and not delaying medical advice by the males themselves. In other words, testicular self-examination provides one mechanism which should increase the likelihood of the identification of a problem which should then be acted on by approaching medical services. Steadman and Quine (2004) examined the effect of requiring a group of young males under 35 years of age to plan where, when and how they would perform testicular self-examination in the following three weeks. In other words, 93 participants were required to form an implementation intention and a further 66 acted as a control (non intervention) group. Allocation to each of the groups was randomized.

Measures

At Time 1 participants were each given a health promotion leaflet that focused on how to perform testicular self-examination (TSE). In addition, they

---

were asked questions related to their knowledge about TSE, their past behaviour in undertaking TSE, as well as their intention to undertake TSE in the next three weeks. After filling in these questionnaires the experimental group was asked to form an implementation about where, when and how they would perform TSE during the following three weeks, to then write this down and also to visualize themselves performing TSE under these conditions (see Steadman and Quine, 2004 for the precise wording of the implementation intention intervention). Those in the control group were not asked to form an implementation intention. Three weeks later all of the participants were asked whether or not they had performed TSE.

Findings

The initial findings showed no difference between the experimental and control groups in terms of their age, their previous TSE experience, their knowledge about TSE or their intentions to perform TSE in the future. Therefore any effect of the implementation intention intervention could not be accounted for by pre-existing differences between groups. The main findings of the study concerned the proportion of males undertaking TSE at least once during the preceding three weeks. Figure 3.4 presents these findings.

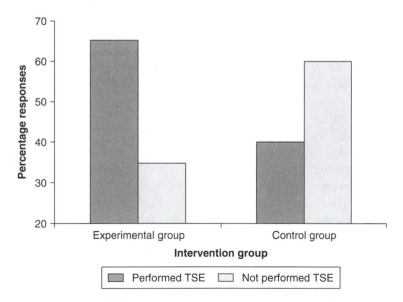

Figure 3.4   Percentage of TSE for experimental and control groups (after Steadman and Quine, 2004)

(Cont'd)

This graph shows that significantly more males performed TSE in the implementation intention (experimental group) than in the control group; 65 per cent and 40 per cent respectively. Interestingly, Steadman and Quine also reported that behavioural intention did not change over the course of the intervention period. In other words, implementation intentions seemed to have an effect on behaviour while leaving the intention to act undisturbed. This suggested the intervention did not appear to have its effect through changing behavioural motivation, but acted directly on goal-directed behaviour.

Summary

While this study can be questioned in terms of using self-report behaviour as a completely reliable measure of behaviour, it nevertheless demonstrates the use of goal-directed planning procedures, such as the development of implementation intentions, as an effective tool in promoting the adoption of new behaviours or to change existing behaviour in favour of a healthy alternative.

SIGNIFICANCE TO HEALTH PSYCHOLOGY

The work on implementation intentions has made a major contribution to health psychology because it provides a framework to study how and under what conditions behavioural intentions can be translated into actual health behaviour. This has been a failing with a number of the social cognition models identified in this chapter (e.g. theory of reasoned action, theory of planned behaviour, protection motivation theory, health belief model). Implementation intentions have offered insight into the factors that are important in the intention behaviour relationship. In applied terms, the concept is important because in theory implementation intentions can be used to take motivational factors in intention planning and goal setting and link them to behavioural enactment, thus maximizing the likelihood of completing the motivation-intention-behaviour sequence.

Indeed, work has shown that combining a motivational intervention based on core components from other health behaviour models with an implementation intention intervention will lead to significantly greater cognition realignment (motivational change), intention formation and, importantly, behavioural enactment. For example, Sheeran, Milne et al. (2005) report an increased likelihood of future testicular self-examination among males who had received both a tailored intervention based on the core components of protection motivation theory (e.g. self-efficacy and response efficacy, perceived costs, perceived severity and vulnerability), as well as an implementation intention to perform the behaviour. The PMT beliefs were manipulated by requiring participants to read and engage with a health education leaflet. After this they read the implementation intentions instruction which are reproduced in Box 3.2.

Box 3.2   An example of an intervention using implementation intentions (*Source*: Sheeran, Milne et al., 2005: 311)

Many people find that when they intend to adopt a new health behaviour such as testicular self-examination (TSE), they then forget to do it or 'never get round to it'. It has been found that when you form a specific plan of exactly how, when and where you will carry out the behaviour you are less likely to forget about it or find that you don't get around to doing it. It would be useful for you to make such a plan of when and where you intend to conduct TSE over the next month. Fill in the following statement providing as much contextual information as you can, e.g. on Monday next week, at 8.00 in the morning, in my bathroom, after I have had a shower.

> During the next month I will perform TSE on .... (day) at................ (time) at/in .... (place). Add any further contextual information, e.g. after a shower, after breakfast, etc..

To ensure you have made the necessary link in your mind between the situation you have outlined above and performing TSE, imagine the situation and tell yourself 'If I find myself *in this situation*, then I will perform TSE'.

Further reading

Gollwitzer, P.M. (1999) Implementation intentions: strong effects of simple plans. *American Psychologist*, 54, 493–503.

Describes how implementation intentions can be conceptualized and their role in the translation of beliefs about intentions to behave in a certain way into actual behaviour.

Sheeran, P. (2002) Intention-behavior relations: a conceptual and empirical review. In W. Strobe and M. Hewstone (eds), *European Review of Social Psychology, Volume 12*. Chichester: Wiley. pp. 1–30.

Provides a useful review of the importance of implementation intentions in understanding when and how an intention to act results in the planned action.

Sheeran, P., Milne, S., Webb, T.L. and Gollwitzer, P. (2005) Implementation intentions and health behaviour. In M. Conner and P. Norman (eds), *Predicting Health Behaviour (2nd edition)*. Buckingham: Open University Press. pp. 276–323.

Specifically focuses and reviews literature that has utilized and tested the conceptual premises of implementation intentions in understanding the adoption (or not) of health behaviour and how these intentions can be manipulated to change health behaviour.

See also **individual differences and habit and habit; social cognitive models and health action process approach; social cognitive models and precaution adoption process model**

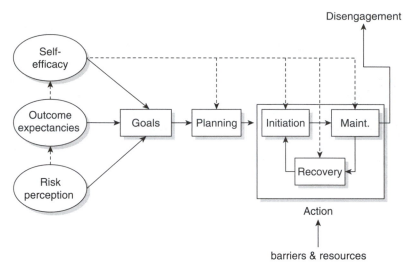

Figure 3.5   The health action process approach (Schwarzer, 2004)

SOCIAL COGNITIVE MODELS
and: HEALTH ACTION PROCESS APPROACH

MEANING   The **health action process approach** (HAPA) is conceptualized as a stage-based model (see also the transtheoretcial model and the precaution adoption process model concepts in this chapter), in the sense that it specifies two distinct phases that must be passed through in order for a person to adopt, initiate and maintain a health protective or compromising behaviour (see Sutton, 2005, for an overview). Moreover, the HAPA provides an account of the psychological components of each of these phases and how each of these components interacts with others to influence either an intention to behave or action (see Figure 3.5).

ORIGINS   Developed by Schwarzer (1992), the HAPA states that the first stage or phase in the adoption of health behaviour is characterized by being pre-intentional and motivational in nature – referred to as the **motivational phase**. This phase predicts that the intention to act, or the behavioural goal, is predicted directly by perceived self-efficacy, outcome expectancies and risk perception processes. Intention here is thought of as a goal intention – intending to do something in order to reach a required state, such as intending to take regular exercise to feel healthier. In addition, self-efficacy in this motivational phase is concerned with pre-action beliefs, sometimes called 'task self-efficacy' – 'I can take regular physical exercise even if I have to change my lifestyle in some way'. The model also makes predictions about how each of these factors influences the others. Risk perception (or threat) is viewed as being a more distal antecedent of intention, having its effects on outcome expectancies which in turn influence perceived self-efficacy. In other words, increased self-efficacy for adopting a health behaviour is generated from the development of more health beneficial outcome expectancies, which are seen as being the result of increased risk perception for the health threat. In essence, a person thinks about the threat posed and then thinks about the consequences of their behaviour before thinking about whether they can do what is required to remove the threat.

Once a person has formed the intention to take self-protective action they then enter the second phase called the **volition phase**. To translate intention into action, the HAPA proposes that people have to undertake a planning process and focuses on those factors that are important for the initiation and control of action. One such factor is implementation intentions (see the implementation intentions concept) in which requiring people to formulate a plan for future behaviour based on where, when and how they will undertake the behaviour is particularly effective (Gollwitzer, 1999). Initiative self-efficacy is also important at this stage. This is the belief that people are able to initiate the planned action when the planned circumstances occur, such as believing that you can implement a plan to stop smoking when your 'quit day' arrives.

Having translated the intention into action, the HAPA states that maintenance self-efficacy is important for the continuation of behavioural change. Fundamental to these efficacious beliefs are perceptions that you can surmount any barriers that may challenge your current behaviour. This type of efficacy is really about coping, in that it emphasizes adaptive responses such as the use of social support in reinforcing the belief that you can continue with your current changed behaviour. For instance, some individuals might use social support networks to enhance maintenance self-efficacy. Indeed, it could be argued that the enhancement of maintenance self-efficacy is fundamental in the operation of support groups such as those used in smoking cessation programmes. Finally, recovery self-efficacy refers to the idea that there may well be slips in behaviour such that people may return briefly to the 'old', maladaptive, behaviour. During these times people have to believe that they have the ability to return to behaving in the recommended way and reaping any perceived benefits (Renner and Schwarzer, 2003).

A number of studies have tested the predictions made by the HAPA model for a number of health-related behaviours. These have included breast self-examination (e.g. Luszczynska and Schwarzer, 2003), dieting (e.g. Renner and Schwarzer, 2005), binge drinking (Murgraff et al., 2003) and taking exercise (Sniehotta et al., 2005). The majority of these have focused on the motivational or pre-intentional phase, although more recent longitudinal work has begun to address the post-intentional or volition phase. In general each of the core constructs of the HAPA has had the predicted effect on behavioural intention, the translation of intention into action and the maintenance of behaviour. Across a number of studies intention has been

CURRENT USAGE

predicted by risk perception, outcome expectancies and task self-efficacy (e.g. Renner and Schwarzer, 2003), planning (post-intention but pre-action) has been predicted by either maintenance and task self-efficacy (e.g. Luszczynska and Schwarzer, 2003) and health behaviour has been predicted by maintenance and recovery self-efficacy (e.g. Sniehotta et al., 2005). Other studies have utilized HAPA components to develop interventions to change individuals' behavioural intentions and actual behaviour. For example, Luszczynska (2004) showed that a brief intervention aimed at increasing maintenance and task self-efficacy, as well as positive outcome expectancies for breast self-examination (BSE), resulted in both the predicted effects in these variables and importantly an increase in BSE measured about 15 weeks after intervention.

SIGNIFICANCE TO HEALTH PSYCHOLOGY

The HAPA is a stage model of health behaviour. It is important because it has identified two key phases (motivation and volition) that together describe the process by which (1) an individual becomes motivated to act in a health protective manner, (2) how an intention to form in that way is realized, (3) how that intention is translated through action planning into behavioural enactment, and (4) how that behaviour is maintained. Central to the model is self-efficacy having an important influence at pre-action motivation phases and post-action volition phases that include action planning and behavioural self-regulation and management. The HAPA is a very good alternative to the theory of planned behaviour, the health belief model, and protection motivation theory, because it explicitly makes predictions about how intentions may be translated into behaviour through action plans and the use of processes such as implementation intentions.

Further reading

Schwarzer, R. (1992) Self-efficacy in the adoption and maintenance of health behaviours: theoretical approaches and a new model. In R. Schwarzer (ed.), *Self-efficacy: Though Control of Action*. Washington, DC: Hemisphere. pp. 217–243.
Provides a very useful overview of key components of the health action process, its predictions and its relationship to the psychological processes in health behaviour.

Sutton, S. (2005) Stage theories of health behaviour. In M. Conner and P. Norman (eds), *Predicting Health Behaviour (2nd edition)*. Buckingham: Open University Press. pp. 223–275.
Provides an extremely useful review and critique of a number of stage-based models including the health action process approach.

See also **social cognitive models and social cognitive theory; social cognitive models and implementation intentions; individual differences and habit and self-efficacy**

SOCIAL COGNITIVE MODELS
and: PRECAUTION ADOPTION PROCESS MODEL

Like the transtheorteical model of behaviour change and the health action process **MEANING**
approach (the TTM and the HAPA respectively; see TTM and HAPA concepts),
the **precaution adoption process model** (PAPM) identifies a number of stages that
people progress through in a defined sequence, from being unaware of a potential
health threat to the maintenance of behaviour designed to remove this threat (see
Sutton, 2005 for a review). Time to progress through these stages is unlimited as
is the time spent on each of the stages (see the transtheoretical model concept for
a different approach). The PAPM also provides a description of qualitatively different psychological factors that predict movement from one stage to the next, which
is a requirement to demonstrate a stage-based approach.

The PAPM was developed initially to identify those psychological processes that **ORIGINS**
were important for people in their decision to undertake health protective action and
the enactment of this decision into behaviour. The model derives and was developed
from Weinstein and colleagues' work which explored how and why people undertook (or not) home radon detecting. Radon is a naturally occurring carcinogenic gas
produced by the decay of uranium in the soil. From their early work Weinstein and
colleagues identified seven distinct stages that people pass through in sequence and
also the psychological factors that are fundamental for an individual to move from
one stage to the next (Weinstein, 1988; Weinstein and Sandman, 1992). These are
called 'stage transitions' and Figure 3.6 presents these seven stages.

In Stage 1 people are unaware of a health threat in that they have no knowledge
about the risks posed by the threat. This is likely when there has been little health
promotion about the issue or when the threat is very uncommon. Transition to
Stage 2 occurs when a person is made aware of the threat though the media or
other mechanisms. Stage 2 describes the idea that people have become aware of
the risk posed by a health threat, but have not thought about adopting the recommended action and as such remain unengaged. For example, they might think that
their level of behaviour is insufficient to pose a real threat to their health (see the
optimistic bias concept in Chapter 5). Transition to Stage 3 may be dependent
upon personal experience with the threat or hazard. For instance, a person who
smokes and who has previously thought that they are at a decreased risk because
they do not smoke as much as other stereotypical smokers (comparative appraisal)
might become engaged with the threat posed by their smoking if they start to
become more breathless and attribute this to their behaviour – a personal experience of outcomes related to the hazard.

In Stage 3 people consider whether to adopt the precaution or not. In effect they
are undecided. From Stage 3 a person can move on to Stage 4 or to Stage 5. Stage 4

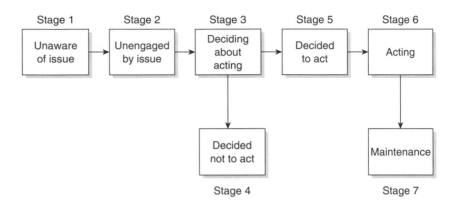

Figure 3.6   Precaution adoption process model (Weinstein and Sandman, 1992)

is important because it recognizes that some people make the active decision not to behave in a protective way, while Stage 5 reflects that the decision to act in a healthy way has been made – and as such an intention has been formed. Movement between Stage 3 to Stage 4 or Stage 5 is dependent on perceived susceptibility and the severity of an outcome, perceived social norms for the behaviour, and beliefs about how effective a behavioural precaution might be (see response efficacy in the protection motivation theory concept in this chapter).

Stages 6 and 7 are post-intentional stages and are about behavioural adoption per se. Stage 6 is the action stage – behaviour to reduce the risk has begun – while Stage 7 (maintenance) reflects the idea that behaviours are long lasting and have to be maintained over time (e.g. smoking cessation). However, not all health behaviours have to have a maintenance stage: some are one-offs such as immunisation behaviour. Transitions between Stage 5 and Stage 6 are predicted by factors that reflect the maximization of perceived self-efficacy, such as the removal of barriers to action or possibly the adoption of implementation intentions.

The PAPM also proposes that people can move backwards in the stage sequence without going through all the intermediate stages. However, it is not possible to go from stages 3, 4, 5, 6 or 7 to either stages 1 or 2 – for example, you cannot go from a state of intention or action to a state of being unaware or unengaged with a health threat (Weinstein and Sandman, 2002).

CURRENT USAGE   Applications of the PAPM have been limited to a small number of studies and behaviours including home radon testing (e.g. Weinstein and Sandman, 2002), mammography screening (Clemow et al., 2000), and osteoporosis prevention (Blalock et al., 1996). Compare this to the huge number of studies that have utilized the transtheroetcial model for application (see the TTM concept in this chapter). One study by Weinstein et al. (1998) used an experimental intervention study to examine the predictions made by the PAPM by matching or mismatching those who had decided to use a radon testing kit (but had not purchased it), or those who were undecided, to stage specific interventions. The idea was that particular interventions using stage-specific psychological factors should cause people to move from one stage to the next depending on which stage they were currently at. To do this people received information, in the form of a video, designed either to increase the perceived likelihood of possible radon contamination or designed to make it less effortful to buy a testing kit (namely, to increase efficacious beliefs about buying a kit). So the likelihood condition should influence those in the undecided group and move them on to later stages, and the low-effort manipulation should move those who are decided on to action-based stages.

Weinstein et al. (1998) found that, in general, stage matched and mismatched conditions were more effective in comparison to the control group (see Figure 3.7). In addition, the high likelihood condition was much more effective in moving undecided people rather than the decided people to later stages, while the low effort video proved more useful in moving decided individuals to a test group compared to other interventions. The combination condition was most effective, although the intervention itself was much more time consuming and potentially extremely expensive. Interventions based on the PAPM stage-specific transition factors showed the predicted specificity in terms of forward movement between stages. In other words, to influence the transition from the having made a decision stage to an action stage is best served by manipulating perceived efficacy, while emphasizing risk, vulnerability or susceptibility is appropriately applied to those in a more pre-intentional stage. Such evidence is useful for providing validation evidence of the PAPM as a stage-based model.

SIGNIFICANCE TO HEALTH PSYCHOLOGY

The PAPM emphasizes the role of both pre-action factors and also post-action implemental factors in the planning and execution of health protective behaviours. Like the transtheoretical model (TTM) and the health action process approach, the PAPM also incorporates a stage-based approach for understanding progress in behavioural change. These all include stages in which a person is either unaware of a threat or a health relevant issue or is totally unengaged by the threat. These stages together comprise what the TTM calls the 'pre-contemplation stage'. The PAPM thus has the advantage of specifying more fully that people will move from having little, if any, knowledge of an issue to having some knowledge but remaining unengaged. In addition, the PAPM includes a stage that defines people in terms of their decision not to act in the recommended fashion and as such explicitly recognizes that there are motivational reasons for the non-enactment of recommended behavioural intentions. Limited evidence to date of testing the predictions set by the PAPM is theoretically encouraging. Longitudinal and experimental studies provide broadly supportive evidence of the PAPM concepts and processes, and recent PAPM matched interventions have been successful in stimulating the forward movement of participants through the specified stages.

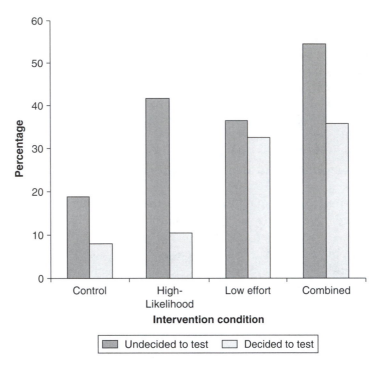

Figure 3.7   Percentage of participants progressing one or more stages in the PAPM towards using home radon testing by pre-intervention stage and matched/mismatched intervention condition (*Source*: Weinstein et al., 1998)

Note: After an initial telephone interview participants were classified into Stage 2 to 5 of the PAPM, but specifically into those people who were undecided whether to test (pre-intentional) and those who had decided to test (actional). Stage 1 people who had never heard of home radon testing were not included in the study. Information conditions were as follows.

High likelihood – a short video was sent to participants that contained information designed to make them feel at risk of radon exposure in their houses and mentioned that they could order test kits from a supplier. This was aimed at the undecided group. Low effort – a short video was sent to participants that contained information about how to select, purchase and conduct a test. An order form was enclosed. The information also emphasized how simple and cheap it is to get and use a radon test kit. This was aimed at the decided to test (action) group. Combination – a longer video that emphasized information given in the high likelihood and low effort conditions. Control – no intervention given.

Further reading

Sutton, S. (2005) Stage theories of health behaviour. In M. Conner and P. Norman (eds), *Predicting Health Behaviour (2nd edition)*. Buckingham: Open University Press. pp. 223–275.

Provides a useful review and critique of the key characteristics of all stage models and includes an analysis of the precaution adoption process model according to these dimensions.

Weinstein, N.D. and Sandman, P.M. (1992) A model for the precaution adoption process: evidence from home radon testing. *Health Psychology*, 11, 170–180. Provides evidence for the precaution adoption process model as a stage-based approach in health-related decision making and behaviour.

See also **social cognitive models and social cognitive theory; individual differences and habit and dispositional optimism; individual differences and habit and unrealistic optimism**

SOCIAL COGNITIVE MODELS
and: TRANSTHEORETICAL MODEL OF BEHAVIOUR CHANGE

MEANING

The **transtheoretical model** of behaviour change (the TTM; also known as the **stages of change model**) is a stage-based model (see the health action process approach and the precaution adoption process model concepts as other examples of stage-based models in this chapter). Stage-based models view behaviour change as the progress of an individual from a starting point in which they may not be thinking about changing their maladaptive behaviour to a state in which they have changed their behaviour in the desired direction. On the journey of behaviour change a person is thought to pass through a number of distinct stages in which their behaviour, or psychological state, can be well defined. The stages are ordered in a particular way and it is assumed that people will pass through these in that order, with every stage visited in sequence. In addition, to progress from one stage to the next requires different processes. For instance, a stage model would predict that motivational factors, such as weighing up the pros and cons of an action, will be important for describing the conditions under which a person will move from stage X to stage Y, but not for explaining the movement from stage Y to stage Z.

ORIGINS

The TTM was originally developed by Prochaska, DiClemente and colleagues during the 1980s (e.g. DiClemente and Prochaska, 1982; Prochaska and DiClemente, 1983) to provide an analysis of how people change their behaviour. Their early work was based on observing factors that were important when a person appears to change their behaviour without any external sources of help (called 'spontaneous remission'). These analyses led to the suggestion that people seem to pass through a series of distinct and predictable stages in a specified order during the process of behaviour change (see Sutton, 2005 for a recent review of TTM research).

This reliance on the concept of stages has led to the use of an alternative name for this approach, namely the stages of change model. However, it should be emphasized that the stages of change is but one characteristic of the TTM model. As the name suggests the TTM is an amalgamation of a number of key psychological and psychotherapeutic theories, constructs and concepts that together describe the processes that are important for understanding the psychology of behavioural change. In addition to the stages, the TTM emphasizes the role of evaluating the perceived pros and cons of changing behaviour (known as **decisional balance**), confidence and temptation and the (so-called) processes of change (Prochaska and Velicer, 1997). These core factors were developed and applied from psychotherapy and behaviour change approaches, then amalgamated and integrated to create an approach that was truly transtheoretcial in nature.

These stages of change are the fundamental organizing standard of the TTM. Five stages have been proposed to describe those people who have no intention of changing behaviour up to those who have changed their behaviour and have maintained this behaviour change for a period of time. Figure 3.8 shows the stages of change in the TTM.

The first three stages of the TTM are pre-actional in that they involve different levels of goal intention without any actual behavioural modification having taken place. The stages in this pre-actional phase are precontemplation, contemplation and preparation. Precontemplation is characterized by no current thoughts about the problems associated with a maladaptive behaviour and any necessary changes that may be necessary to decrease the chances of experiencing a negative outcome in the future. There is no intention to change a behaviour within the next six months. Contemplation is characterized by a behavioural intention to make a change within the next six months. At this stage people are thought to consider the changes that may be necessary if they are to avoid negative outcomes and maximize health-related benefit. For instance, they may become aware of risk factors associated with their current behaviour. The third pre-actional stage is called 'preparation' in which the individual has made action plans (processes in intention implementation) to make a change in the next 30 days. Effectively, the stages describe people in different motivational stages of readiness to change a specific behaviour.

Action and maintenance are post-actional in that they describe stages in which people have made the desired behavioural modification. In the action stage the change has occurred for less than six months, whereas a person is said to be in the maintenance stage when their change in behaviour has lasted for more than six months. While this five stage model has been the most commonly cited interpretation of the TTM, other authors have identified two further stages called 'termination' and 'relapse'. The former describes a stage in which an individual has overcome all temptation to reinstate a previously undesirable behaviour – they are high in behavioural self-efficacy. The latter is viewed as the state which results when a person returns to a previous way of acting (e.g. having a cigarette when in a social situation one night). This return to a previous behavioural or thinking pattern

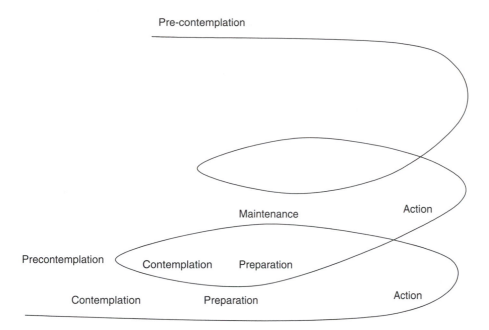

Figure 3.8   Stages of change in the transtheoretical model (*Source*: Prochaska et al., 1992)

Note: This version of the stages of change model is called the spiral model. Prochaska et al. (1992) proposed that the spiral pattern more effectively describes how a person progresses through each of the stages. It recognizes that people may well relapse after they have attempted to change a behaviour. For example, it is argued that the vast majority of people do not revert to the precontemplation stage but are more likely to find themselves in the contemplation or preparation stages. This spiral model proposes that people do not go round in an endless circle of precontemplation, contemplation, preparation, action and maintenance, and that after a relapse do not end up back where they started the change process. People learn from relapse episodes and make action plans accordingly.

may not be long lasting and can occur at any stage in the sequence, that is, pre-actional or post-actional (Prochaska and Velicer, 1997).

The TTM suggests that although people move through these stages in the defined sequence, there may be occasions when some move backwards from one stage to the previous one (e.g. from preparation to contemplation, and so on), staying at that stage for a while before making the onward journey to the stage which they had originally visited. In effect, the TTM allows a kind of recycling effect in which people can move between stages in a more cyclical manner. The best known example of this conceptualization is the spiral model of the stages of change (Prochaska et al., 1992).

Factors that influence the transition from one stage to the adjacent stage are also outlined in the TTM. The first is called 'decisional balance' which describes the weighing up of the pros and cons or benefits and barriers in behaviour change (see the health belief model for another use of the benefits/barriers principle). Transitions between different stages are predicted by differences in decisional balance characteristics. For instance, in comparison to the contemplation stage, thinking in the preparation stage may comprise greater emphasis on benefits of change over barriers.

Consistent with almost every social cognitive account of health behaviour and behaviour change, Prochaska, DiClemente and colleagues propose self-efficacy to be a very important factor in understanding stage transitions. They conceptualized self-efficacy as the balance between a confidence in one's ability to undertake health protective behaviour against the temptation to behave in an unhealthy manner. Think of these processes as the independent variables in predicting stage transitions. In other words, advocates of the TTM propose that these processes are the causes of movement between adjacent stages. The final set of proposals for describing factors important in predicting movement through the stages in the pre-defined sequence is called the 'processes of change'. These 10 processes of change include five experiential processes, or cognitive-affective factors, as well as five behavioural processes. They are listed and described in Box 3.3.

Box 3.3 Processes of change in the transtheoretical model

1. **Consciousness-raising** – identifying new facts, information sources and suggestions in support of a behavioural change (e.g. through health promotion campaigns, social interaction with significant others). Incorporating this information as part of the learning process.
2. **Dramatic relief** – experiencing negative emotions about related issues (e.g. worry or fear) and expressing these with significant others (e.g. with a friend, partner, or counsellor).
3. **Self re-evaluation** – realizing that there is a link between the behavioural change and one's own identity (e.g. viewing oneself as a non smoker, fit person or a healthy eater).
4. **Environmental re-evaluation** – appraising how the behavioural problem influences the physical environment and the experience of others in that environment (e.g. recognition of the bad effects on other important people of one's behaviour, such as in the case of passive smoking).
5. **Self liberation** – making a decision and committing oneself to act on the belief that changing a behaviour is possible and accepting personal responsibility for the change.
6. **Social liberation** – an understanding of societal support for the need for healthy behaviours as being fundamental in influencing social communities.
7. **Counter-conditioning** – identifying healthier behaviours and substituting them for the maladaptive behaviours (e.g. utilizing relaxation techniques or nicotine replacement as a means of overcoming the link between feeling 'stressed' and having a cigarette).

8. **Stimulus control** – identifying and avoiding triggers or cues to the problem behaviour.
9. **Contingency management** – increasing the rewards associated with positive behaviour change, as well as decreasing the rewards associated with unhealthy behaviours (e.g. putting aside the money saved as a result of not smoking for a month and buying something new with that money).
10. **Helping relationships** – identifying personal social support systems and networks (e.g. family, friends and professionals) to provide reassurance and reinforcement of the positive aspects of behaviour change and the negative aspects of not changing.

CURRENT USAGE

The TTM has been applied and studied in a vast array of health behaviours including smoking (e.g. Aveyard et al., 2003), exercise (e.g. Cox et al., 2003), condom use (e.g. Brown-Peterside et al., 2000) and drinking (e.g. Budd and Rollnick, 1996). In a number of meta-analyses studying the validity of TTM as a stage model, and the various processes of change factors identified by the model, there is some support for the utility of the model and its constructs (e.g. Marshall and Biddle, 2001). However, critics have suggested that behaviour change is not necessarily reflected in differences in processes between distinct stages, but is more likely to be about the same processes varying across the whole change-related span (e.g. Rosen, 2000).

Other work has tested the TTM components by incorporating stage matched and stage mismatched interventions to test the applicability of the model. For instance, only interventions matched to the factors thought to move a person from contemplation to preparation, and so on, should show such an effect. The manipulation of other factors relevant for later or earlier stage transition should not affect the focus transition. Evidence from such intervention studies has not been conclusive in their support of the TTM (e.g. Cox et al., 2003), nor has it been wholly supported by relevant meta-analyses (e.g. Bridle et al., 2005). Sutton (2005) argues that the inconclusive nature of these findings is not aided by researchers not directly testing the tenets of the TTM in the first place, and this leads him to conclude that ' … there have been no process analyses published to date demonstrating that TTM-based interventions do indeed influence the variables they target in particular stages and that forward stage movement can be explained by these variables' (p. 247) (see also Sutton, 1996).

SIGNIFICANCE TO HEALTH PSYCHOLOGY

The TTM was the first stage-based model presented in an attempt to understand the processes involved in how people change their behaviour and in particular their health behaviour. In this way it is similar to other stage theories including the precaution adoption process model and the health action process approach. The TTM proposes not only the stages through which a person travels in sequence while changing behaviour, but also identifies a number of core processes that instigate and motivate the change processes. In other words, these processes identify how people change and are important because they imply that change is a predictable behavioural process grounded in observable and measurable psychological factors. If this is the case, then theoretically interventions, based on knowledge about which factors are fundamental in ensuring the transition of a person in stage X to stage Y, could be designed. As the literature stands there is both support and contradictory evidence for the TTM as being a stage-based model at all, and also as to how valid each of the change processes are in describing and predicting stage transitions.

Further reading

Marshall, S.J. and Biddle, S. (2001) The transtheoretical model of behaviour change: a meta-analysis of applications to physical activity and exercise. *Annals of Behavioral Medicine*, 23, 229–246.
A useful statistically based review of a large number of studies that have utilized the transtheoretical model in understanding changes in behaviour related to exercise.

Prochaska, J.O. and Velicer, W.F. (1997) The transtheoretical model of health behavior change. *American Journal of Health Promotion*, 12, 38–48.
A detailed account of the key theoretical characteristics, components and predictions inherent in the transtheoretical model.

Sutton, S. (2005) Stage theories of health behaviour. In M. Conner and P. Norman (eds), *Predicting Health Behaviour (2nd edition)*. Buckingham: Open University Press. pp. 223–275.
A useful review of the key components of any stage-based model and includes a detailed analysis of the transtheoretical model in these terms.

Sutton, S.R. (1996) Can 'stages of change' provide guidance in the treatment of addictions? A critical examination of Prochaska and DiClemente's model. In G. Edwards and C. Dare (eds), *Psychotheraphy, Psychological Treatments and the Addictions*. Cambridge: Cambridge University Press. pp. 189–205.
A useful critique of stage-based approaches in the study and treatment of addictive behaviours, including a detailed critical account of the transtheoretical model.

See also **social cognitive models and social cognitive theory; social cognitive models and precaution adoption process model**

BIOLOGICAL AND PHYSIOLOGICAL MODELS

4

FOUR

BIOLOGICAL AND PHYSIOLOGICAL MODELS
and: **biological basis of behaviour**
> **twin, family and adoption studies**
> **molecular genetics**
> **psychoneuroimmunology**
> **psychophysiology**

Health psychologists typically use a **biopsychosocial model** to understand and explain health, illness and disease, and this relies strongly on biological and physiological models to explain certain aspects of behaviour and health. In this chapter we describe many of the approaches which can be taken to understand the biological basis of behaviour and health. Genetic approaches, for example, using both twin and related study designs and, more recently, molecular genetic designs, have consistently indicated a genetic influence on both health (including the risk of illness and disease) and health behaviours (including personality traits related to the risk of particular illnesses). Other approaches, such as psychoneuroimmunology and psychophysiology, explicitly attempt to link psychological phenomena with mechanisms related to the biological causes of illness and disease, such as the relationship between psychological stress and health. Rather than being viewed in isolation, biological and physiological approaches demonstrate the links between the social, psychological and physical components of the biopsychosocial model.

BIOLOGICAL AND PHYSIOLOGICAL MODELS
and: BIOLOGICAL BASIS OF BEHAVIOUR

MEANING Traditionally, medicine has employed a predominantly biological approach to understanding health, disease and illness. The **bio-medical model** proposes that all disease and physical disorders (as well as psychiatric disorders) can be explained by disturbances in physiological processes. These may result from injury, biochemical imbalances (either induced or inherent), infection, and so on. The bio-medical model assumes that disease is a result of these physiological processes, and largely separate from psychological and social processes. More recently, a growing acceptance of the biopsychosocial model, which attempts to incorporate psychological and social processes into our understanding of health, disease and illness, has resulted in a more prominent role for related disciplines such as health psychology. Nevertheless, biological and physiological models remain important in understanding health, disease and illness.

ORIGINS Although biological and physiological models of health can be traced back to antiquity, it was in the eighteenth and nineteenth centuries that knowledge in science and medicine grew rapidly. This was mirrored by a growing assumption that the body could be understood as a complex machine, and therefore was amenable to repair in the same way as any other machine. The Enlightenment, which emphasized the pursuit of truth and led to the development of the scientific method, also helped to establish the bio-medical model on a firm scientific basis. Despite the limitations of an exclusively biological model of health, it is undeniable that the bio-medical model resulted in substantial advances in the treatment of illness, and contributed positively to the improvement of human well being.

CURRENT USAGE Once psychological and social factors are incorporated into the bio-medical model a far broader model of how health and illness arise is generated. In particular, the biopsychosocial model rests on the central premise that biological, psychological and social factors all *affect* and are *affected by* health, disease and illness. The role of the biological and physiological nevertheless remains central in the biopsychosocial model.   Relevant biological processes are varied, and those which are of particular relevance to health psychology include **genetics** (including both twin studies and molecular genetic studies), **psychoneuroimmunology** and **psychophysiology**.

Genetics investigates the role of inherited variation in determining behaviour and, in the specific context of health psychology, in determining health, disease and illness. Although it is relatively easy to determine whether or not a particular disease, for example, runs in families, this may be due to either social factors or genetic factors (or both). Twin studies and molecular genetic studies provide methodologies which allow the specific contribution of inherited factors to be investigated. The role of genetics in health psychology is further complicated by the influence of genetic factors on personality traits and health behaviours. Indeed, Hans Eysenck (1988) once claimed that the link between cigarette smoking and lung cancer was due to a common genetic basis which independently increased the likelihood of each, so that cigarette smoking could not be said to directly cause lung cancer. While this view has since been discredited, the more general argument that genetic factors may influence health and illness via effects on behaviour remains a valid area of investigation. Although genetics plays a role in determining behaviour, it is the interaction of genetics with the environment that determines the ultimate outcome. Thus, while identical twins have the same DNA and genes, differences in their experiences during development and childhood results in different personalities, health outcomes, and so on.

Psychophysiology refers to the relationship between psychology and physiology. For example, if we are interested in the fear response, evidence from physiology would suggest that the amygdala is the region of the brain implicated in this group of behaviours. Psychophysiology, therefore, attempts to understand the relationship between behavioural inputs and outputs (e.g. environmental stimuli and the subjective feeling of fear) and physiological inputs and outputs (e.g. amygdala reactivity). It is this perspective of studying the interface of psychological and physiological mechanisms which makes psychophysiology potentially an extremely powerful explanatory framework. Historically, psychophysiology research has focused on the autonomic nervous system, although more recently technological advances have increased the potential to investigate the central nervous system, in particular using various brain imaging technologies such as **event-related potentials** (ERP), **functional magnetic resonance imaging** (fMRI), **positron emission tomography** (PET), and so on.

Psychoneuroimmunology may be regarded as a specific example of psychophysiological research, and investigates the relations between the psychological, physiological and immunological dimensions of health and illness, bringing together researchers from multiple disciplines, including psychology, neuroscience, immunology, physiology, and so on. For this reason, it is often regarded as an excellent example of the importance of the biopsychosocial model. Psychoneuroimmunology specifically focuses on the interactions between the nervous and immune systems, and the relation between behaviour and health. It deals with, among other things, the physiological functioning of the **neuroimmune system** in states of both health and disease and malfunctions of the neuroimmune system in specific disorders (e.g. autoimmune diseases, hypersensitivities, immune deficiency). For example, psychological stress is thought to influence immune function through emotional and behavioural manifestations such as anxiety, fear, tension, anger and sadness, and through physiological changes such as heart rate, blood pressure and sweating. While these changes may be beneficial if they are of limited duration (for example by increasing the readiness or preparedness of the individual to respond to the causes of stress), when the stress is chronic the system becomes unable to maintain equilibrium and may break down, potentially leading to illness and disease.

In addition, however, it is valuable to understand the broader context within which health and illness are investigated. **Epidemiology** is the study of the distribution and frequency of disease, and the factors (including environmental and social factors) which are related to this. Mortality refers to death, generally on a large scale, while morbidity means illness, injury or disability, essentially the meaningful departure from health or wellness. **Prevalence** refers to the number of identifiable cases, such as those with a particular disease, while incidence refers to the number of *new* cases reported during a specific period of time.

SIGNIFICANCE TO HEALTH PSYCHOLOGY

Given the importance of the biopsychosocial model in modern medicine and in health psychology, the various techniques described above offer potentially excellent means by which the inter-relationship between biological, psychological and social factors may contribute to health, disease and illness. For example, psychophysiological and psychoneuroimmunological methods may allow us to look at how exposure to a stressful situation will produce a response in the cardiovascular system, such as a change in heart rate or vasoconstriction. Larger-scale epidemiological studies, grounded in these methods, may allow us to investigate the extent to which the mechanisms may relate to larger-scale associations between psychological and social stressors (e.g. unemployment) and morbidity. Genetic studies may add to this knowledge by identifying sub-groups of individuals who are more (or less) likely to suffer adverse consequences resulting from exposure to psychological and social stressors.

Further reading

Carlson, N.R. (2006) *Physiology of Behavior (9th edition)*. Needham Heights: Allyn and Bacon.
A comprehensive introductory textbook which outlines the fundamentals of the biological basis of behaviour. Includes detailed coverage of the basic physiological sciences relevant to understanding behaviour.

Goetz, A.T. and Shackelford, T.K. (2006) Modern application of evolutionary theory to psychology: key concepts and clarifications. *American Journal of Psychology*, 119, 567–584.
Introduction to evolutionary psychology, which attempts to explain human behaviour with reference to why these behaviours evolved and were maintained due to survival pressures in our evolutionary past.

See also **biological and physiological models and biological basis of behaviour; biological and physiological models and twin, family and adoption studies; biological and physiological models and molecular genetics; biological and physiological models and psychoneuroimmunology; biological and physiological models and psychophysiology**

BIOLOGICAL AND PHYSIOLOGICAL MODELS
and: TWIN, FAMILY AND ADOPTION STUDIES

MEANING

For some time, we have known that development results from the dynamic interplay of nature and nurture. From birth onwards we grow and learn because our biology has programmed us to do so, because our social and physical environment provides stimulation, and because these factors interact with each other in what is increasingly being understood to be a subtle and complex way. Among the various human characteristics that are under both genetic and environmental influences are behaviours that may directly or indirectly relate to health, such as personality, smoking, drinking, and so on. **Behaviour genetics** refers to the study of the role of genetic influences on variation in behavioural traits such as these. Of course, by quantifying the genetic influence on these traits we also, indirectly, quantify the environmental influence, so behaviour genetics research gives us as much information about environmental influences as it does about genetic influences. Until relatively recently the only means by which the relative contribution of genetic and environmental variability in behavioural traits could be studied was by means of twin, family and adoption studies. Recent advances in **molecular genetics**, however, have meant that behaviour genetics now encompasses traditional twin, family and adoption studies, as well as molecular genetic studies.

ORIGINS

Sir Francis Galton in the nineteenth century was the first scientist to study heredity and human behaviour systematically. The term 'genetics' did not even appear until 1909, only two years before Galton's death. With or without a formal name, the study of heredity always has been, at its core, the study of biological variation. Human behavioural genetics, a relatively new field, seeks to understand both the genetic and environmental contributions to individual variations in human behaviour. There are several indications that a behavioural trait has biological (and therefore possibly genetic) origins, such as observing that a behavioural trait changes following a biological change (e.g. a personality change following a traumatic brain injury), or that the trait tends to run in families (e.g. the familial aggregation of psychiatric illness).

In order to separate the relative contribution of biological (that is, genetic) and environmental influences, traditional research strategies in behavioural genetics include studies of families, twins and adoptees. Galton studied the families of outstanding men of his day and concluded that 'mental powers' run in families. Galton became the first to use twins in genetic research and pioneered many of the statistical methods that remain in use today. Although Galton did not use the term, genetics offers considerable explanatory power in understanding heredity, with variation in the **genotype** (namely, the combination of different alternative forms, or **alleles**, of specific genes possessed by individuals) explaining variation in the **phenotype** (that is, the totality of observable characteristics and traits of an individual).

CURRENT USAGE

Modern behaviour genetics still depends heavily on the use of twin, family and adoption studies, with the cornerstone being the 'natural experiment' of twinning. Approximately 1 in 85 live births are twin births, and of these approximately two-thirds will be identical (**monozygotic** or MZ) twins and the remaining one-third non-identical or fraternal (**dizygotic** or DZ) twins. Since MZ twins have identical genotypes, whereas DZ twins share only 50 per cent of their variegated genotype, and yet in both cases twins will be raised in (presumably) identical environments, the logic of twin studies is that if a behavioural trait is more similar in pairs of MZ twins than it is in pairs of DZ twins, then that trait must presumably be under a degree of genetic influence. Family and adoption studies provide other means by which natural variation in genotypic similarity and environmental similarity can be associated with phenotypic variability to calculate the proportion of variation in the phenotype that can be accounted for by variation in the genotype.

We express the proportion of variation in phenotype that is due to variation in genotype as the **heritability** of a trait, sometimes expressed as h^2. A heritability coefficient of 0.50 means that 50 per cent of the variation in that trait is due to genotypic variation. When we talk about the relative influence of genotype and environment on phenotype, we are talking about the relative influence of *variability* in the former on *variability* in the latter. An informative example is the heritability of the number of digits on hands. Since the blueprint for a hand is clearly biological we might expect the heritability to be high in this case. We would be wrong! Since we are talking about *variation*, and the most common cause of having an unusual number of digits is typically due to *environmental* effects (e.g. industrial accidents), the heritability of *number* of digits is actually very low.

Accurate estimates of h^2 can be arrived at using structural equation modelling, which assumes that there are three distinct influences on phenotypic variation, comprising additive genetic effects (A), common or shared environmental effects (C), and unique or non-shared environmental effects (E). Such models are often referred to as **ACE models**.

The calculation of the heritability coefficient rests on several assumptions, such as that genes influence phenotypes in an additive (rather than multiplicative) way, and that the genotype is not correlated with, and does not interact with, the environment. In fact, it is likely that these assumptions do not always hold, and that gene x gene interactions (also known as epistatic genetic influences), gene x environment interactions, and gene-environment correlations do in fact occur. More complex statistical and methodological techniques exist for teasing apart these effects. Evidence for such effects comes from some surprising findings. Common environmental factors that children in the same family are exposed to tend to promote differences between these children, rather than similarities; also, measures of environmental factors seem to be genetically influenced, suggesting they are somehow *selected*; finally, genetic sensitivity to environments suggests interactions between genotype and environment.

Scarr and McCartney (1983) suggested that gene-environment correlations may be due to three distinct effects, which they term passive, evocative and active. Passive effects are due to the parents of children creating their environment for them; since the parents and children will be genetically related, there will be a correlation between the environment that the parents create and the children's genotype. Evocative effects are due to the effect that the children's genotype has on their environment; for example, physical attractiveness is often perceived to be associated with high levels of intelligence, so that two twins with a similar level of physical attractiveness may be *treated* in a similar way by those around them because of this perception. Active effects, finally, are due to the ability of children to *select* the environments to which they are best suited; for example, since physical strength is a necessary pre-requisite for certain sports, children with this attribute will tend to gravitate towards these sports, corresponding social groups, and so on. All this means that children who are genetically similar will probably find themselves in more similar environments than children who are genetically different. These environments will, in turn, influence development. This might, at first glance, look like a genetic influence on development, but may in fact be driven by environmental mechanisms that simply *correlate* with the genotype.

SIGNIFICANCE TO HEALTH PSYCHOLOGY

What can behaviour genetic research tell health psychologists? Most importantly, just because a behaviour or trait is found to be highly heritable does not mean that it is impervious to intervention or change (see Figure 4.1). It does allow some insight, however, into the relative contribution of genes and environment to that particular behaviour or trait in *this population* and at *this point in time*. The finding that a behaviour or trait is heritable is increasingly regarded as a starting point that may subsequently lead to the study of **molecular genetic** influences on that trait (namely, the influence of *specific* genes).

A range of behaviours and traits that are relevant to health psychology have been found to be heritable. First, the majority of common diseases are, to a greater or lesser degree, heritable. Heart disease, for example, is known to be heritable, and family history of heart disease is an important predictor of future risk. In addition to providing insight into the aetiology of this disease, health psychologists have studied the impact that the knowledge that one might be at increased genetic risk of the disease has on individuals. As well as diseases, behaviours and behavioural traits, such as personality, have been shown to be heritable. This may be relevant as certain personality traits are known to influence health-related behaviours such as risk-taking, which may include, for example, sexual behaviour. Finally, more specific health-related behaviours, such as cigarette smoking and alcohol consumption, are known to be highly heritable. This has lead to the emergence of the

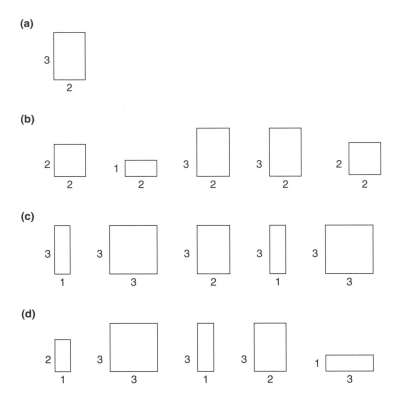

Figure 4.1   Heritability (*Source*: Sesardic, 2005)

Note: It is helpful to think of the role of genetic and environmental influences on behaviour as representing two sides of a rectangle. In example (a), the total phenotype of interest (e.g. intelligence) is represented by the effects of both genotype (say, height) and environment (say, width). Heritability, however, refers to the *proportion* of *variability* in phenotype due to genetic variability. In population (b), all of the *variability* in the area of rectangles is 100 per cent due to variability in height (all the widths are the same, but the areas differ). In population (c), on the other hand, all of the *variability* in area is due to variability in width. In population (d), the variability in area is due to variability in both height and width. It does not make sense, however, to say that the area of any single rectangle in population (b) or (c) is due 100 per cent to either height or width (despite the contribution of these to *variability* in area being 100 per cent respectively). Similarly, while the heritability statistic tells us how much variation in phenotype is due to genetic variation, it does not tell us anything about an individual. Also, even if the heritability of a phenotype is 100 per cent, that does not mean that we cannot change things. For example, if we changed the width of *all* the rectangles in population (b) from 2 to 4, the area of all the rectangles would double, but the contribution of height to *variability* in area would remain 100 per cent.

possibility of treatments for, for example, smoking cessation being tailored to the genotype of individuals.

Clearly, an understanding of health and health-related behaviours requires some knowledge of the role of genetic variation on these phenotypes. Moreover, as public awareness of the role that genes play increases health psychologists will need to be able to communicate genetic risk information to individuals, to address any questions that they may have, and also be aware of the potential impact that such information may have on individuals' sense of self-efficacy, control beliefs, and so on, which may be affected by such knowledge.

Further reading

Bartels, M., Van den Berg, M., Sluyter, F., Boomsma, D.I. and de Geus, E.J. (2003) Heritability of cortisol levels: review and simultaneous analysis of twin studies. *Psychoneuroendocrinology*, 28, 121–137.
Cortisol plays a key role in both physical and mental health, and is critical to psychoneuroimmunological studies of stress and health (see Psychoneuroimmunology). This paper reviews the evidence for genetic and environmental contributions to variations in basal cortisol levels.

Heath, A.C., Martin, N.G., Lynskey, M.T., Todorov, A.A. and Madden, P.A. (2002) Estimating two-stage models for genetic influences on alcohol, tobacco or drug use initiation and dependence vulnerability in twin and family data. *Twin Research*, 5, 113–124.
Addictive behaviours (see Addictive Behaviours) appear to share certain characteristics in common, suggesting a possible shared genetic influence. This paper presents two stage models suggesting distinct influences on drug use initiation and subsequent dependence.

Kendler, K.S. (2005) Psychiatric genetics: a methodologic critique. *American Journal of Psychiatry*, 162, 3–11.
This paper reviews various methodologies for studying the influence of genes on behavioural traits, including twin, family and adoption studies as well as molecular genetic techniques.

See also **biological and physiological models and molecular genetics**

BIOLOGICAL AND PHYSIOLOGICAL MODELS
and: MOLECULAR GENETICS

Until relatively recently the only means by which the relative contribution of genetic and environmental variability to variability in behavioural traits could be studied was by means of twin, family and adoption studies. New advances in molecular genetics, however, have meant that genetics research in humans now

MEANING

encompasses **molecular genetic** studies as well as traditional twin, family and adoption studies. These allow specific genetic variations (using **association** techniques), or regions of the genome (using **linkage** techniques), related to behaviour and disease to be identified.

ORIGINS   While twin studies consistently indicate that human personality traits and other complex behaviours, as well as susceptibility to disease and illness, are under a substantial degree of genetic influence, in the 10 years since the first publication of studies reporting an association between specific genetic variants and human behavioural traits (in this case, anxiety-related personality traits) a substantial literature has developed reporting data on the role of a variety of genetic variants, although only modest progress has been made in identifying molecular loci which robustly demonstrate association. One possible reason for this is the small magnitude of effect sizes which are likely to be typical of single gene effects on complex behavioural phenotypes, so that the majority of studies conducted to date may be under-powered. Certainly it is likely that genetic effects are likely to be modest (in other words, it will probably never be possible to accurately predict the behaviour of an individual on the basis of genetic information), and will probably operate interactively with environmental effects, serving to modify the effects of environmental stressors and the like (known as gene x environment interactions).

CURRENT USAGE   The term **genotype** refers to the entire genetic identity of an individual, while the term **phenotype** refers to observable, measurable characteristics of an individual (e.g. eye colour). In molecular genetic studies, specific physical variations in genotype are related to phenotypes of interest. The term **genome** refers to the entire sequence of the genetic code, which is made up of a genetic 'alphabet' consisting of the letters A, G, C and T. Half of the genome is inherited from the father, and half from the mother, and variation can occur in the exact genetic code, for example if a specific 'letter' differs.

A **gene** is a functional physical unit of heredity that can be passed from parent to child. All genes in humans are pieces of deoxyribonucleic acid (**DNA**), and usually contain information for making a specific protein. Genes may be **polymorphic** (namely, they exist in two or more forms) due to variation in the genetic code within the gene. For example, a C may be substituted by a T at a specific location within the gene. Since each individual possesses two copies of each gene (one from each parent), individuals may be grouped according to their specific genotype (in this case either CC, CT or TT). The different forms of a gene are known as **alleles**.

The term **genetic marker** is broader, and refers to a segment of DNA with an identifiable physical location on a chromosome whose inheritance can be followed (but is not necessarily a gene – it may or may not have any functional consequence). Since DNA segments that lie near each other on a chromosome tend to be inherited together, markers are often used as tools for tracking the inheritance pattern of a gene that has not yet been identified but whose approximate location is known.

Genetic **linkage** refers to the fact that certain genes tend to be inherited together, because they are on the same chromosome. Linkage is measured by the percentage recombination between loci, with unlinked genes showing 50 per cent recombination. Therefore, if we are interested in identifying regions of the human genome which may harbour a specific genetic variation related to a phenotype of interest, but don't have any a priori reasons for focusing on a particular region of the genome, linkage analysis may be appropriate. By using genetic markers spaced along the genome, we can identify *broad regions* which show linkage with the phenotype of interest (namely, they occur more frequently in individuals with the characteristic of interest than in those without the characteristic). Doing this allows more intensive study of the region of potential interest which is identified by linkage analysis, for example using genetic association techniques.

Genetic **association** studies aim to test whether single-locus alleles or genotype frequencies are different between two groups (where the phenotype is categorical, such as patients with a specific disease and healthy controls), or whether the mean of a continuous measurement differs between genotype groups (such as in the case of personality traits). Genetic association studies are based on the principle that genotypes can be measured directly by sequencing the actual genetic code. Unlike linkage analysis, association techniques offer the ability to localize any genetic effect very accurately to a specific region on the genome, but it is generally not practical (since it would be very expensive) to use association techniques across a wide region of the genome, since it requires very high-density genotyping (namely, the identification of a large number of very tightly spaced genetic markers).

A specific version of association analysis, which is common in human studies, is the **candidate gene** study. In such studies, specific candidate genes which are of a priori relevance to the phenotype of interest (for example, because of their known or supposed biological function, and the theoretical importance of this biological pathway in the development of the phenotype of interest) are investigated. Ideally, specific variants within this candidate gene which are known to influence the function of the gene are investigated, so that any relationship between these variants and the phenotype of interest is more likely to be causal (although such conclusions will always be inferential, since molecular genetic studies are correlational in nature).

Recently, a number of studies in the psychiatric genetics literature have investigated the interaction of genetic and environmental risk factors in determining the risk of disease (known as **gene x environment interactions**). These have generally focused on psychiatric outcomes, such as depression and antisocial behaviour, but have potential application in other fields, such as substance use and other health behaviours. For example, Caspi and colleagues found that different versions of the serotonin transporter gene moderated the impact of stressful life events on the risk of depression. Those individuals with one or more copies of the 'short' version of the gene who also experienced a number of stressful life events were more likely to develop depression subsequently, while those with two copies of the 'long' version of the gene were not (see Box 4.1). Given the centrality of the biopsychosocial model to health psychology, studies of this kind are likely to be of increasing importance in understanding the effects of the interplay of biological, psychological and social factors in health and disease.

Box 4.1   Example of a gene x environment interaction (*Source*: Caspi et al., 2003)

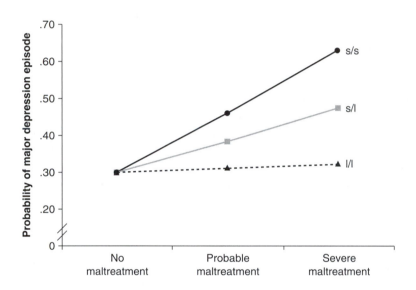

Caspi and colleagues reported evidence from a large cohort of children followed longitudinally from childhood through to early adulthood. They were genotype for the serotonin transporter gene, which exists in two forms (l: long, and s: short). The short version of the gene has been associated with a slightly increased risk of depression. Stressful life events, such as childhood maltreatment, have also been shown to increase the risk of depression. Caspi's study showed that among individuals who had not experienced childhood maltreatment, there was no association of the serotonin transporter gene with a risk of depression later in life. However, as the degree of stress experienced increased, genotype began to play a role. Those with two copies of the long allele did not show an increased risk of depression, while those with one or more copies of the short allele showed an increased risk of depression as the degree of stress experienced in childhood increased.

As well as offering an insight into the biological mechanisms of health, disease and illness, molecular genetic methods have been successful in identifying the genetic antecedents of complex behaviours, such as personality traits, which may influence relevant health behaviours. For example, cigarette smoking and alcohol consumption have both been shown to be under a degree of genetic influence. These effects may be relatively direct (e.g. by influencing the rate at which nicotine is metabolized) or indirect (e.g. by influencing personality traits such as impulsivity which themselves are related to the likelihood of smoking). Molecular genetic methods allow for the detailed investigation of the inter-relationships between biological, psychological and environmental (namely, social) factors and their impact on health and illness.

Molecular genetic technologies have also been successful in identifying rare mutations which increase the risk of specific physical diseases. Increasingly, information on risk status based on molecular genetic profile is offered to individuals in order to initiate or promote changes in relevant health behaviours, in order to reduce the increased risk arising from the possession of a specific genetic variant. There are high expectations regarding the potential for DNA-based risk information to motivate behaviour change more strongly than other types of risk information. Such expectations are consistent with theories of attitude change which predict that the greater the personal salience of information, such as information regarding one's own DNA, the greater the impact. Such research remains in its infancy but promises to be a fruitful and important area within health psychology, although there are also concerns that there may be negative effects of feeding back genetic information to patients, since this might engender a sense of helplessness and reduce feelings of self-efficacy, given (somewhat incorrect) public perceptions of the deterministic nature of genetic associations.

SIGNIFICANCE TO HEALTH PSYCHOLOGY

Further reading

Caspi, A., Sugden, K., Moffitt, T.E., Taylor, A., Craig, I.W., Harrington, H., McClay, J., Mill, J., Martin, J., Braithwaite, A. and Poulton, R. (2003) Influence of life stress on depression: moderation by a polymorphism in the 5-HTT gene. *Science*, 301, 386–389.
One of the first studies to suggest that genetic factors may modify the impact of environmental stressors. Although the focus was on depression as an outcome, the methodology has a wide potential application, and fits well with biopsychosocial conceptions of disease and illness.

Kendler, K.S. (2005) Psychiatric genetics: a methodologic critique. *American Journal of Psychiatry*, 162, 3–11.
This paper reviews various methodologies for studying the influence of genes on behavioural traits, including twin, family and adoption studies as well as molecular genetic techniques.

Munafò, M.R., Clark, T.G., Johnstone, E.C., Murphy, M.F.G. and Walton, R. (2004) The genetic basis for smoking behaviour: a systematic review and meta-analysis. *Nicotine and Tobacco Research*, 6, 583–597.
Reviews the evidence from a number of studies for the association of various candidate genes with smoking behaviour. Concludes that there is limited convincing evidence for a strong role for any of the genes investigated to date.

See also **biological and physiological models and twin, family and adoption studies**

BIOLOGICAL AND PHYSIOLOGICAL MODELS
and: PSYCHONEUROIMMUNOLOGY

MEANING   **Psychoneuroimmunology** (PNI) is based on the ability of the psychological state of an individual to influence his or her immune system, via the nervous system. Although it has both positive (that is, a positive mental state can promote wellness) and negative (that is, a negative mental state can promote illness) connotations, in practice the majority of PNI research investigates the **stress–health relationship** – in other words, the extent to which environmental stressors and their psychological appraisal can negatively impact upon an individual's health.

ORIGINS   Early conceptions of the immune system assumed that it was independent of other systems, including the central nervous system. Seminal early studies by Ader and Cohen in the 1970s, however, demonstrated that immune responses (e.g. a response to an immunosuppressive drug) could be classically conditioned, so that a distinctive taste paired with the drug could eventually bring about the immune response by itself, as a conditioned stimulus. This relationship between the central and peripheral nervous systems is crucial to the science of PNI, as it allows the possibility that psychological factors, via the **central nervous system**, can influence the peripheral nervous systems and other systems related to disease and health. Hans Selye (1946) described the **General Adaptation Syndrome** (GAS), the 'nonspecific (biologic) reaction of the body to any demand made upon it', which he argued was elicited by both physical and psychological demands (namely, stressors). The GAS includes three stages: the alarm reaction, resistance, and exhaustion (see Figure 4.2).

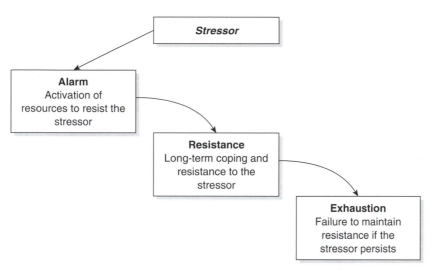

Figure 4.2   The General Adaptation Syndrome

Note: Selye's General Adaptation Syndrome describes three stages in the stress process. The initial stage is called the 'alarm stage', and reflects an increase in activity and autonomic arousal in response to a perceived threat. The second stage is called the 'resistance stage', and reflects longer-term arousal and coping in order to resist the effects of the stressor which has triggered the GAS. The third stage is called 'exhaustion' and reflects the situation which arises if the resistance stage fails to eliminate the stressor, when coping responses are exhausted and breakdown begins to occur. In evolutionary terms, the GAS provides an appropriate response to short-term physical threat (leading to, for example, a **fight or flight response**), but is inappropriate in the modern world as a response to psychological stressors which tend to be persistent (e.g. workplace stress).

CURRENT USAGE

The relationship between stress and health is complicated by the various definitions of 'stress' that exist: it can variously mean external factors leading to subjective distress, the psychological evaluation of those factors, or the subjective distress itself. A psychological stress process model includes the following terms: **stressors** (events or conditions which may give rise to a stress reaction), **appraisal** (the subjective response to or interpretation of potential stressor), **stress reactions** (short term reactions to stressors, sometimes called 'strains'), and long-term health outcomes. In terms of process, stressors may be understood as antecedents, appraisal and other features of the individual such as coping strategies and social support as moderators, and short- and long-term reactions and outcomes as consequences. Stress reactions can be conceptualized at a number of levels, all of which are relevant to the study of PNI: the physiological, emotional, cognitive and behavioural.

The physiological level describes the so-called 'fight-or-flight response', which occurs in response to a threatening or potentially threatening situation and is characterized by increased heart rate, elevated blood pressure, a redistribution of blood flow from internal organs to muscles, and the release of stress hormones such as adrenaline.

Emotional responses to stressors include feelings of helplessness, depression, anxiety, anger, and so on. A wide range of complex emotions can be elicited by stressful situations, and there is substantial variability across individuals in the exact emotions elicited by a given stressor (due in large part to the moderating influence of other factors such as coping strategies). Somewhat paradoxically, extreme stressors can often lead to a markedly blunted (that is, reduced) emotional reaction and expression.

At a cognitive level, biased and obsessional thoughts (including rumination, obtrusive thoughts about the event, and so on) may be a consequence of exposure to a stressful event, in particular including worry about the event or the consequences of the event. There is also evidence that stressful events may negatively influence executive function, including memory, although this effect may operate indirectly via other cognitive effects such as worry.

Behaviourally, a wide range of reactions to stressful events is possible, including the use of psychoactive substances (e.g. tobacco and alcohol, as well as illegal drugs – see Addictive Behaviours), sleep disturbance, changes in eating behaviour, social withdrawal, short temper, and so on. As well as the direct effects of stress reactions on physical health, these behavioural changes may themselves have marked negative effects on physical health.

Unfortunately, although these different facets of the reaction (or potential reaction) to stressful (or potentially stressful!) events are relatively intuitive, in practice they are only weakly related to each other. This is due in large part to the enormous inter-individual variation in the nature and direction of response at each of these levels given any given potential stressor. The lack of an objective measure of 'stress' makes this problem worse – although physiological responses can be objectively measured, their weak correlation with subjective measures means that one can never be certain that one is in fact measuring 'stress'.

SIGNIFICANCE TO HEALTH PSYCHOLOGY

Despite some of the limitations and complexities of studying the relationship between physiological and psychological factors, a number of studies have demonstrated this link in ways which illustrate the importance of the **biopsychosocial model** in health research generally and health psychology specifically. Positive mood has been shown to be associated with improved immune function (measured objectively using physiological measures of immune function), while psychological distress and negative subjective response to environmental stressors have been shown to be related to disease onset, poor immune function, wound healing, and a number of other measures of health and illness. Certain coping styles, which may moderate the response to environmental stressors, have also been shown to be related to physical health; for example, suppression and denial have been reported to be associated with disease onset and progression.

The PNI literature is enormous, and offers great promise for understanding the relationship between physical health and illness, social and environmental factors (in particular potential stressors), and psychological responses, coping styles, mood and so on. Kiecolt-Glaser and colleagues, for example, have published several studies demonstrating clear links between environmental factors which are typically described as stressful (such as examinations) and physical health outcomes or correlates which might be reasonably be expected to be related to physical health (such as immune function). In one very important example of such studies they investigated the incidence of minor illnesses (colds and so on) in university students, and found that these increased the closer the students were to an examination. This increase in minor illness close to examinations was accompanied by corresponding changes in immune function. Clearly a single study such as this will not provide the whole story – not all students find examinations stressful, and not all students became ill, so there are clearly other factors at play which require investigation. Nevertheless, they demonstrate the potential for exploring what has historically been described as the 'mind-body relationship'.

Further reading

Graham, J.E., Christian, L.M. and Kiecolt-Glaser, J.K. (2006) Stress, age, and immune function: toward a lifespan approach. *Journal of Behavioural Medicine*, 29, 389–400.
Discusses the importance of understanding the interactive effects of stress and age in order to determine the underlying mechanisms of the stress-health relationship and develop effective interventions in early and late life.

Vitetta, L., Anton, B., Cortizo, F. and Sali, A. (2005). Mind-body medicine: stress and its impact on overall health and longevity. *Annals of the New York Academy of Sciences*, 1057, 492–505.
Reviews evidence for the basic mechanisms of psychoneuroimmunology within the broad conceptual framework of biopsychosocial approaches to health and well being.

See also **biological and physiological models and psychophysiology**

BIOLOGICAL AND PHYSIOLOGICAL MODELS
and: PSYCHOPHYSIOLOGY

Psychophysiology, broadly defined, refers to the physiological mechanisms which underlie psychological and behavioural outcomes. For example, the amygdala is one region of the brain which has been implicated in the control of emotions, in particular fear. Although **psychoneuroimmunology** is closely related to psychophysiology, the two are treated separately here because the former can be regarded as investigating the relationship between psychological, social and

MEANING

physiological mechanisms (namely, their effects on each other), while the latter can be understood as investigating the physiological mechanisms which govern behaviour.

ORIGINS
Psychophysiological research has been incorporated within the broader science of psychology from its beginnings, and includes the study of the neural mechanisms of behaviours (for example, using surgical, electrical and chemical manipulations of the brain in controlled conditions, usually on laboratory animals for obvious reasons!), and the study of more general physiological mechanisms and behaviour. The roots of psychophysiology lie in biology, and can be traced far back into history – Descartes proposed a model of the brain (albeit incorrect in some of its specific details) which included a direct link between brain states and behaviours, while Galvani's experiments on the nature of the messages transmitted by the nerves between the central nervous system and the sensory organs remain central to our understanding of the biological basis of behaviour.

CURRENT USAGE
Historically, psychophysiological studies on human participants have relied on the measurement of cortical activity, as the electrical activity of the brain can be recorded from electrodes placed on the scalp. The resulting traces are known as an **electroencephalogram** (EEG) and represent an electrical signal from a large number of neurons. These are sometimes called brainwaves. Although EEG measures brain activity, it is capable of detecting changes in electrical activity in the brain on a millisecond-level: it does so very crudely, since it aggregates the activity across relatively large areas of the brain. EEGs are frequently used in human experimentation because the process is non-invasive. Four major types of EEG activity are typically recognized (alpha, beta, delta and theta – see Box 4.2).

Box 4.2   Major types of EEG activity

Alpha is the frequency range from 8 Hz to 12 Hz. It is characteristic of a relaxed, alert state of consciousness. Alpha attenuates with drowsiness and open eyes, and is best seen over the occipital (visual) cortex.

Beta is the frequency range above 12 Hz. Low amplitude beta with multiple and varying frequencies is often associated with active, busy or anxious thinking and active concentration. Rhythmic beta with a dominant set of frequencies is associated with various pathologies and drug effects, especially benzodiazepines.

Gamma is the frequency range approximately 26–100 Hz. Gamma rhythms may be involved in higher mental activity, including perception, problem solving, fear, and consciousness.

Delta is the frequency range up to 4 Hz and is often associated with the very young and certain encephalopathies and underlying lesions. It is also seen in deep sleep.

Theta is the frequency range from 4 Hz to 8 Hz and is associated with drowsiness, childhood, adolescence and young adulthood. Theta waves can be seen during hypnotic states, daydreaming, lucid dreaming and light sleep, and in the preconscious state just upon waking, and just before falling asleep.

Event-related potentials (ERPs) are a special case of EEG recording, and represent deflections in the EEG waveform which result from the presentation of specific stimulus (e.g. a noise) to the participant. These may be either positive (P) or negative (N) and are designated according to how many milliseconds after the presentation of the stimulus they appear on the EEG. For example, P300 refers to a positive deflection occurring 300 milliseconds after the presentation of the stimulus. ERPs can be further grouped into endogenous ERPs (occurring very soon – <100 msec – after the presentation of a stimulus, and thought to reflect early-stage processing) and exogenous ERPs (occurring later, and thought to reflect elaboration and the information processing demands of the task).

Measures of **electrodermal activity** have also been used widely, and principally reflect activity in the autonomic nervous system, such as sweat gland activity. Increased activity in the sweat glands is associated with a reduction in the electrical resistance of the skin, which may be measured using electrodes placed on the skin (usually the fingers). Emotional states such as anxiety lead to changes in autonomic nervous system activity, and a corresponding change in electrical resistance (sometimes known as the **Galvanic Skin Response** or Skin Conductance Response). It is possible to measure both the background level of skin conductance over time, and acute changes in skin conductance in response to specific stimuli or events. As an example of the latter, emotional stimuli (in particular shocking or unpleasant words and pictures) can lead to acute changes in skin conductance.

Functional magnetic resonance imaging (fMRI) measures signal changes in the brain that are due to changing neural activity. The brain is scanned at relatively low resolution (although higher than with EEG) but at a rapid rate of once every 2–3 seconds (although slower than with EEG). fMRI rests on the assumption that increased neural activity is correlated with increased demand for oxygen in those regions, and an increase in the amount of oxygenated blood relative to deoxygenated blood to compensate for this. The measure of these changes is referred to as the Blood Oxygen Level Dependent (BOLD) signal.

Positron emission tomography (PET) and **single photon emission computed tomography** (SPECT) are other neuroimaging technologies which have become increasingly widely used in neuroscience to investigate the neural correlates of behaviour. In these, a radioactive tracer substance is introduced to the participant (either by injection or inhalation), which is then taken up by metabolically active regions of the brain, on the assumption that brain regions involved in a specific behaviour will be metabolically more active during that behaviour. The amount of tracer taken up by the cells is highly correlated with the metabolic rates of those cells, and the radioactive decay of the tracer (either positron emission in the case of PET or photon emission in the case of SPECT) can be measured using an appropriate scanning device. The degree of spatial and temporal resolution which can be achieved is generally intermediate between fMRI and EEG.

SIGNIFICANCE TO HEALTH PSYCHOLOGY

The use of psychophysiological methods, and in particular neuroimaging methods (EEG, ERP, fMRI, PET and SPECT), is generally less widespread than the use of psychoneuroimmunological methods in health psychology. Nevertheless, there has been extensive study of the biological basis of various relevant behaviours using these techniques in other fields of psychology which may inform health psychology.

In particular, various personality traits, and individual responses to emotional stimuli, have been investigated in relation to the brain regions which are associated with these. Given the strong associations between personality and health, and the response to environmental stressors and health, these studies may aid in the development of comprehensive theories of the relationship between environmental and psychological factors and health, and the central nervous system mechanisms which may govern these. In an exciting example of how such studies may bring together multiple research perspectives in the future, Hariri and colleagues demonstrated that the presentation of fearful faces leads to greater activation of the amygdala than neutral control stimuli, and that the level of this activation was further dependent on which version of the serotonin transporter gene individuals possessed. Those who carried one or more copies of the 'short' allele demonstrated relatively greater amygdala activation when presented with fearful faces than those with two copies of the 'long' allele (see Box 4.3).

Box 4.3   Genetic effects on the neural substrate of fear? (*Source*: Hariri et al., 2002)

Hariri and colleages investigated the role of the serotonin gene in the processing of threat-related information. Participants completed two tasks while undergoing fMRI brain imaging. In one (A), they had to identify which of two faces matched a single target face (at the top) in terms of emotional expression, while in the other (B) they had to identify which of two faces matched

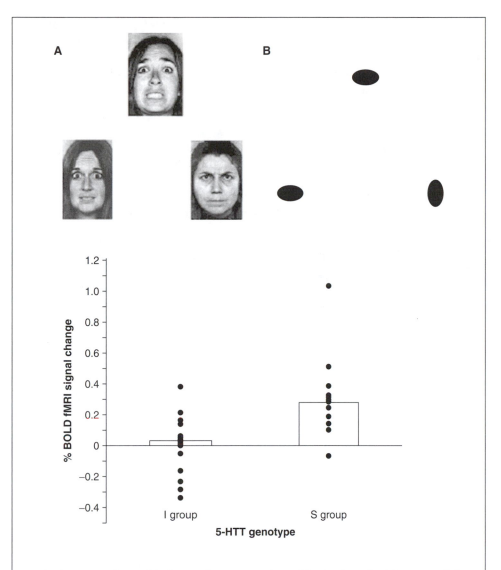

a single target shape. Task A activates a region of the brain called the amygdala, which plays a role in the processing of threat information, more than Task B. Hariri's study showed that individuals with one or more copies of the short allele of the serotonin transporter gene, which has been reported to be associated with increased risk of anxiety and depression, showed a much stronger response on Task A compared to Task B than those individuals with two copies of the long allele. This suggests that individual differences in specific brain regions may mediate the relationship between genotype and complex behaviours.

Given evidence from other studies suggesting that the serotonin transporter gene moderates the relationship between stressful life events and the risk of major depression (see Molecular Genetics), these studies when taken together point to the future integration of multiple research perspectives and a truly biopsychosocial understanding of health and illness.

Further reading

Hariri, A.R., Mattay, V.S., Tessitore, A., Kolachana, B., Fera, F., Goldman, D., Egan, M.F. and Weinberger, D.R. (2002) Serotonin transporter genetic variation and the response of the human amygdala. *Science,* 297, 400–403.

Good example of the capacity of studies which combined neuroimaging and genetic technologies to understand the neurobiological basis of complex behaviours (in this case the processing of threatening stimuli).

Pressman, S.D. and Cohen, S. (2005) Does positive affect influence health? *Psychological Bulletin*, 131, 925–971.

Unlike most studies, which focus on the ill-effects of negative mood (e.g. sadness and anxiety), this paper discusses the beneficial effects of positive mood (e.g. happiness and optimism) on health and health-related outcomes.

See also **biological and physiological models and psychoneuroim-munology; biological and physiological models and molecular genetics**

INDIVIDUAL DIFFERENCES AND HABIT

5

FIVE

INDIVIDUAL DIFFERENCES AND HABIT
and: **dispositional optimism**
unrealistic optimism
locus of control
self-efficacy
habit
personality type and health

What accounts for the observation that some people act in a healthy way and others do not? Why do people respond to perceived health threats in different ways? What factors can be used to understand why one person's interpretation of a particular set of symptoms may be distinct from another person's? Some indication of possible answers to these types of questions can be gleaned by examining a number of key psychological factors and processes that lie predominantly within each person. These key concepts include perceived control (e.g. Rotter, 1982), perceived self-efficacy (e.g. Bandura, 1997), types of optimism (dispositional and unrealistic) (e.g. Klein and Weinstein, 1997), and personality-based factors (e.g. Krantz and McCeney, 2002). In addition, recent work has started to emphasize that differences in behaviour adoption may be based on those processes concerned in the development and maintenance of habit (e.g. Stacy et al., 2000). This chapter is concerned with the relationship between these key individual differences factors and health-related experience, decision making and health behaviour. The assumption is that levels of these factors vary quantitatively between individuals to create differences in, for example, health-related decision making, symptom perception and health behaviour.

INDIVIDUAL DIFFERENCES AND HABIT
and: DISPOSITIONAL OPTIMISM

MEANING   Individual differences in generalized expectancies about positive and negative (health) outcomes have been conceptualized according to a number of factors including locus of control and self-efficacy (see the relevant concept in this chapter), as well as dispositional optimism/pessimism and explanatory style. Each of these factors has been studied by health psychologists to ascertain how they predict whether or not a person undertakes health protective behaviour, and also as to possible reasons for not behaving in a self-protective way. **Dispositional optimism** is a generalized expectancy that good things will happen in the future and bad things will not, irrespective of how these outcomes occur. Unlike locus of control and self-efficacy, dispositional optimism considers expectations of outcomes in a very general sense – locus of control and self-efficacy are more concerned with expectations about what caused these outcomes.

ORIGINS   Scheier and Carver (1985) introduced the concept of dispositional optimism as part of a behavioural self-regulatory approach for understanding goal-directed behaviour. This approach argues that goal-directed behaviour is governed by a feedback system in which the current behaviour or condition is compared against a behavioural goal. When there is an inconsistency between the goal and the conditions, the likelihood of a reduction in this inconsistency is dependent on one's expectancies about reducing such inconsistency through behavioural modification (Scheier and Carver, 1992). Optimistic individuals are likely to adopt active and directive forms of coping under such conditions, whereas pessimists may disengage in the process and use avoidance coping strategies. In other words, a generalized optimistic outlook is likely to lead to an individual having a set of expectancies about how best to achieve a goal, to believe that a desired outcome is possible and to act on these beliefs. A pessimist is more likely to 'give up' and disengage.

CURRENT USAGE   To measure dispositional optimism versus pessimism, the Life Orientation Test (LOT) was devised by Scheier and Carver (1985) and revised as the LOT-R to explicitly map onto expectancies for the future (Scheier et al., 1994). The LOT and LOT-R have good internal reliability and have been subjected to extensive validation work.

While these measures were conceptualized as measuring a single optimism-pessimism dimension, work has shown that two predominantly independent factors, optimism (based on the positive items) and pessimism (based on the negative items), are present (e.g. Robinson-Whelen et al., 1997)). In other words, being pessimistic is not just about *not* being optimistic – you can be pessimistic for some health events and optimistic for others. Optimism and pessimism have been found to predict a number of health outcomes (see Anderson (1996) for a meta-analysis of LOT studies). For instance, pessimism (and not optimism) was found to predict mortality rates in younger cancer sufferers (Schultz et al., 1996), and optimism has been shown to predict decreased distress levels in HIV positive individuals (Taylor et al., 1992) and people undergoing surgery for breast cancer (Carver et al., 1993). The question remains however – what are the mechanisms through which dispositional optimism may be adaptive for psychological and physical functioning?

One major explanation revolves around the differential use of coping strategies by optimists and pessimists. Optimists use more problem-focused, active and engaged coping styles when confronted with a health threat which guard the individual against psychological stressors (e.g. negative affect) related to physical health (Shepperd et al., 1996). In addition, optimism is associated with more health protective behaviours such as a good diet and physical exercise, emphasizing a behavioural route through which optimism might protect against certain negative health outcomes (Miles and Scaife, 2003). One recent prospective study examined the effect of pessimism and optimism on the outcome of a major life event in over 5,000 individuals and was particularly interested in studying the role of pre-existing optimism on health outcomes (Kivimäki et al., 2005). Highly optimistic people were found to return to work significantly faster and have fewer sick days than pessimistic individuals after the event, suggesting that an optimistic outlook may reduce the likelihood of experiencing health problems.

In addition to a generalized expectancy, optimism has also been thought of as a type of **explanatory style**, or the manner in which individuals attribute causes to events. Optimistic individuals are less likely to attribute internal (e.g. personal fault), stable (e.g. believing the cause of a stressful experience stems from one's own personality) and global (e.g. the stressor as being less transient, less modifiable and not generalized to other similar events) causes to stressful or negative events. Optimists attribute events to external and unstable causes, and believe these events are caused by specific situational factors. Pessimists attribute negative events to internal, stable and global causes and have a pessimistic explanatory style. Physiological evidence suggests that a pessimistic explanatory style is related to decreased immune functioning (e.g. Kamen-Siegel et al., 1991) while psychological evidence has shown a relationship with the type of self-reported illness reported and also attendance at medical clinics (e.g. Peterson and Seligman, 1987). These effects result because pessimists have maladaptive beliefs in being helpless as well as decreased self-efficacy, which create differences in the types of coping activities undertaken by this group resulting in behavioural harm.

SIGNIFICANCE TO HEALTH PSYCHOLOGY

Dispositional optimism is important because it describes an individual difference factor that is predictive both of physical health and behavioural factors. Different levels of dispositional optimism should be important for predicting the types of decisions people make when deciding which course of action to take in response to a health threat, as well as how they interpret and respond to the symptoms of illness and the onset. However, because dispositional optimism is thought of as being stable within people the feasibility of designing interventions to manipulate dispositional optimism is questionable. In addition, if optimism and pessimism are viewed as independent constructs changing optimism will not necessarily be reflected in changes in pessimism and vice versa.

Further reading

Anderson, G. (1996) The benefits of optimism: a meta-analytic review of the Life Orientation Test. *Personality and Individual Differences*, 21, 719–725.
Provides a detailed account of the utility of the key measure of dispositional optimism in psychological functioning.

Scheier, M.F., Carver, C.S. and Bridges, M.W. (1994) Distinguishing optimism from neuroticism (and trait anxiety, mastery and self-esteem): a reevaluation of the Life Orientation Test. *Journal of Personality and Social Psychology*, 67, 1063–1078.
A very useful conceptual account of the role of dispositional optimism in everyday functioning and behaviour.

See also **individual differences and habit and unrealistic optimism**

INDIVIDUAL DIFFERENCES AND HABIT
and: UNREALISTIC OPTIMISM

MEANING It is clear that central to many psychological approaches and theories in understanding why people do or do not take health protective behaviours is the concept of risk perception. An individual's appraisal of the likelihood that they will experience a particular health threat has been proposed in a number of models including protection motivation theory, the health belief model, the health action process approach and the precaution adoption process model (see Chapter 3 – Social Cognitive Models, and also Conner and Norman, 2005). In essence, these approaches have emphasized that the likelihood that a person will form an intention to behave (and thus actually behave in a specified way) is partly determined by how at risk they think they are of experiencing a negative health outcome. But how do individuals judge whether they are likely, or not, to experience either positive or negative life and health-related events in the future? One answer to this question comes from evidence that has explored the role of a comparative appraisal process in risk perception, termed **comparative optimism**, **optimistic bias** or **unrealistic optimism**.

Social comparison theory argues that individuals are motivated to seek self-understanding and self-knowledge (Festinger, 1954). People need to evaluate themselves in their social worlds, and attempt to understand whether the beliefs and opinions they hold are correct. One way they do this is by 'looking' at others and how others' behaviour or belief sets differs from their own. For example, it seems logical that one way in which people decide their own perceived likelihood of contacting a particular disease is by comparing themselves (that is, their personal perceived risks) against the risk they perceive for others. While Festinger himself did not apply the theory to health-related decision making, other social psychologists recognized the relevance of social comparison theory in providing a partial understanding of health-related decision making (see Buunk and Gibbons, 1997). For instance, Bailis et al. (2005) showed that older people, who had reduced perceptions of control in relation to their health, used positive social comparisons as a means of enhancing their own self-concept. Importantly, this mechanism was shown to predict lower mortality and hospitalization rates.

One set of evidence suggests that people show a tendency to believe that they are less likely to encounter or experience negative events in their lives compared to other people. They believe themselves to be invulnerable to negative outcomes in comparison to other people. In addition they believe themselves more likely to experience positive events in the future in comparison to other individuals. Initially coined by Weinstein (1980), this tendency is termed 'unrealistic optimism', 'optimistic bias' or 'comparative optimism'. Unrealistic optimism is a group effect. For some people responses that they are less likely to experience a health outcome may well be accurate but not everybody's risk can be lower than other individuals', as many people see themselves as 'above average risk' as 'below average risk'. Because it has been shown that the large majority of people believe their risks to be lower than a comparative other person, this optimism is unrealistic or biased (Weinstein, 1989; van der Pligt, 1998).

ORIGINS

People have been shown to be unrealistically optimistic in the face of a vast array of health and life events including precise types of cancer (e.g. Eiser et al., 1993; Fontaine and Smith, 1995), heart disease (Marteau et al., 1995) and sexually transmitted diseases (Gerrard et al., 1996). It has also been shown for behaviours that put the individual at increased risk of experiencing related negative outcomes. These include drink-driving (Albery and Guppy, 1995), other driving behaviour (Rutter et al., 1998; McKenna and Albery, 2001), smoking (McKenna et al., 1993; Rise et al., 2002), food choice (see Miles and Scaife, 2003) and even bungy jumping (Middleton et al., 1996). The bias is not culturally specific, although differences in terms of the magnitude of the bias exist across cultures according to specific cultural identity factors like construal of self (see Fontaine and Smith, 1995; Heine and Lehman, 1995). Optimistic bias has been shown in older adults (e.g. Holland,

CURRENT USAGE

1993) and younger adults (e.g. Weinstein, 1980), as well as for adolescents' perceptions (e.g. Quadrel et al., 1993; Whalen et al., 1994) and even in children as young as eight years of age (Albery and Messer, 2005).

Optimistic bias is usually measured by either an indirect method or a direct method. The indirect method involves a person making a judgment about their own risk (e.g. 'The chance of me getting lung cancer in the future is … ') and then a judgment about the average person ('The chance of the average person getting lung cancer in the future is … '). The difference between these two responses is said to represent the magnitude of the bias. The direct method requires the respondents to mark on a scale how likely they are compared to the average person of experiencing a health outcome. The midpoint of the scale is usually marked as the 'average'. Optimistic bias is determined by calculating the difference between the midpoint scale score (e.g. '0') and the mean response made by each individual. One advantage of the indirect method over the direct method is that one is able to ascertain whether different events are resulting in changes in either self or other perception. This is very important when ascertaining the effects of an intervention designed to reduce optimistic bias.

Both motivational and cognitively based explanations have been offered for the operation of unrealistic optimism (see Weinstein, 1989; Klein and Weinstein, 1997). Motivational causes focus around the idea that because people 'want' to maintain self-esteem, self-worth and avoid threat (defensive denial) so as to maintain psychological well being, they will make risk-judgments that do not destabilize but enhance self-competence (Taylor and Brown, 1988). The outcome of this process is to see oneself as 'better' than others, thus reaffirming and maximizing self-esteem and avoiding threatening information sources. Cognitive explanations emphasize how risk-relevant information is processed to lead to the observed bias. Weinstein (1980) argued that optimistic bias results from an egocentric information processing bias – when a person is unable to take another's perspective – such that when making judgments about the self based on self-protective actions, people are unlikely to understand that similar preventative actions are also undertaken by others. They focus only on themselves.

Box 5.1   The effects of personal experience on unrealistic optimism

McKenna and Albery (2001) studied the effects of previous exposure with a threat-related event on the operation of unrealistic optimism. A number of driving groups were examined who had been exposed to varying degrees of threat. One group had been involved in a severe road accident in which they had been hospitalized, a second group was involved in a severe road accident in which

---

another person had been hospitalized, a third group had been involved in a minor accident in which nobody had been injured, and the final group was a control group who had never been involved in a road accident. Measures of comparative optimism for driving skill, driving safety and future accident involvement (e.g. 'Compared to the average driver how skillful a driver do you think you are?'), as well as intended future driving speed on the motorway, were taken. Participants were marked on an 11-point scale, ranging from 'much less skillful', 'much less safe' and 'much less likely' (scored as 1), to 'much more skillful', 'much more safe' and 'much more likely' (scored as 11). The midpoint scale (6) was labeled 'average'. In addition, a number of comparative measures for other health-related events were taken to establish the generalization of any debiasing effects of driving perceptions on other aspects of a person's life.

Table 5.1 Mean responses for perceived comparative skill, safety, future accident likelihood and intended driving speed (on the motorway) for groups of accident and non-accident involved drivers (*Source*: McKenna and Albery, 2001)

Accident Group	Group			
	Skill	**Safety**	**Accident likelihood**	**Speed**
Non-accident Involved - control	*7.74* (1.59)	*8.31* (1.70)	4.39 (2.04)	*74.26* (9.62)
Minor accident	7.65 (1.57)	7.94 (1.78)	4.31 (2.12)	73.83 (8.51)
Other severe injury	7.67 (1.71)	7.98 (1.47)	4.64 (1.87)	73.07 (10.01)
Personal severe injury	*7.25* (1.65)	*7.62* (1.69)	4.57 (1.99)	*71.16* (8.41)
Group total	7.57 (1.65)	7.98 (1.67)	4.47 (1.99)	73.13 (9.27)

Note: For skill and safety responses (first two response columns), increased scores indicate increased comparative optimism. For accident involvement, increased scores indicate decreased comparative optimism.

Table 5.1 shows that only those who had experience of the most severe threat (being hospitalized after a traffic accident) showed decreased comparative risk estimates for skillfulness, safety and self-reported future speed intentions as compared to those who had experienced no threat – the control group. Comparative optimism (unrealistic optimism) is affected by personal experience of a severe health threat. In addition, no differences between the groups were found for other health events, suggesting that any effect is domain-specific.

The role of personal experience in predicting types of information processing has also been shown to be influential in understanding the operation of the bias (Weinstein, 1980; McKenna and Albery, 2001) (see Box 5.1). Personal experience makes it easier for similar events to be recalled from memory and as such this makes these events more available for recall and use. A final factor concerns the idea that people may be using a salient stereotype in their judgments such that they compare themselves with a high risk stereotypical group who may be different from themselves (Weinstein and Klein, 1995). In addition, evidence has been accumulated that optimistic bias varies as a function of how much control people think they have over future events (e.g. McKenna, 1993; Harris, 1996) but not according to how severe a health threat is deemed to be (Welkenhuysen et al., 1996).

It is assumed that being unrealistically optimistic about future health events is likely to result in a person not taking self-protective action. While this has been shown by comparing different groups of people, little evidence has shown a prospective link between the bias and actual future behaviour (e.g. Taylor et al., 1992; Rutter et al., 1998). Nevertheless, recent work has examined ways of changing, or debiasing, such optimistic perceptions and related behaviour. These have included making people accountable for their judgments (McKenna and Myers, 1997), creating a scenario in which people were to blame for the severity of an outcome (Myers and Frost, 2002), and restricting the comparison to a more similar to self target (e.g. Harris et al., 2000).

SIGNIFICANCE TO HEALTH PSYCHOLOGY If the manner in which people process health-related information is biased, resulting in the non-adoption of health protective behaviour, the study of possible cognitive biases (such as unrealistic optimism) in judging the likelihood of experiencing negative health outcomes and related decision making is fundamental. Unrealistic optimism locates this processing in a social comparative context, emphasizing that people make judgments about themselves relative to other people. The various factors found to be important in this mechanism, and which need to be overcome, can be utilized in the design and implementation of interventions created to enhance the likelihood that a person will take self-protective actions.

Further reading

Weinstein, N.D. (1980) Unrealistic optimism about future life events. *Journal of Personality and Social Psychology*, 39, 806–820.

The classic study that identified the operation of unrealistic optimism for a large number of health and non-health related life events. Provided the basis for the large body of work that has identified key operational accounts of the operation of the bias in health-related decision making and behaviour.

Klein, W.M. and Weinstein, N.D. (1997) Social comparison and unrealistic optimism about personal risk. In B.P. Buunk and F.X. Gibbons (eds), *Health, Coping and Well-being*. London: Lawrence Erlbaum. pp. 25–61.
An interesting review of the relationship between unrealistic optimism and judgments about personal risk. Explores the role of how making comparisons with others is important in predicting health and non-health related decision making.

See also **individual differences and habit and dispositional optimism; social cognitive models and health action process approach**

INDIVIDUAL DIFFERENCES AND HABIT
and: LOCUS OF CONTROL

MEANING

One of the many factors that have been implicated in the decision to undertake or not undertake health protective action is perceived control. In effect, this is about how much control a person thinks they have in determining whether or not they undertake a behaviour or attain an outcome associated with that behaviour (Wallston, 1997). This idea is central to some types of social cognition models identified in Chapter 3 (see the theory of planned behaviour) and has similarities with the concept of self-efficacy (see the self-efficacy concept in this chapter).

ORIGINS

Perceived control has its roots in **social learning theory** (e.g. Rotter, 1982; Bandura, 2000, and see social cognitive theory in Chapter 3). Rotter (1966) identified the term **locus of control** to describe the idea that over time people learn to expect that outcomes are determined by factors internal to themselves, such as their own actions or beliefs, as well as those related to external sources like chance or luck. In particular, it is argued that people can believe they have control over any reinforcement that results from doing a behaviour and that the source of this reinforcement is either internal or external to the individual.

CURRENT USAGE

Locus of control is a generalized belief. This means that people may have a predominantly internal or external locus of control across many situations, but this will have the greatest effect when the expectancies (or outcomes) of a situation are not clear or defined for the individual (see Contrada and Goyal, 2004). Rotter (1966) originally thought of locus of control as a unidimensional factor comprising a continuum with internal to external control poles. This conceptualization led to the development of the Internal-External (I-E) scale to measure individual differences along this continuum. Further work identified that internal control and external control were in fact independent constructs (not correlated with one another) and should not be thought of as ends of a continuum (e.g. Levenson, 1974). In addition this work showed that external locus of control was also multidimensional, incorporating different types of external control. This led to the redevelopment of the locus of control scale to comprise distinct constructs measuring internal control (the 'I' scale), and two external factors – powerful others controlling outcomes (the 'P' scale) and chance externality (the 'C' scale). As such, this allows for a person to be both internal and external in control at the same time. In general it has been shown that high internal locus of control is associated with beneficial health outcomes. Dalgard and Haheim (1998) in a long-term prospective study showed that an external locus of control was related to increased mortality for males. Gerits and De Brabander (1999) showed increased symptoms of depression to be associated with externality in women with breast cancer.

Wallston and colleagues developed the multidimensional **health locus of control** scale (MHLC) to capture the idea that behaviours in a particular field (e.g. health behaviours) should be predicted best by field-specific beliefs (Wallston et al., 1978) (see Box 5.2). In other words, health behaviours should be correlated best with health-related control beliefs.

Box 5.2   The condition-specific multidimensional health locus of control scale (after Wallston et al., 1994)

This version of the MHLC was developed by Wallston et al. (1994) to be condition specific. It was designed to apply to people who have an illness and this is reflected in some of the control factors included in the scale. Unlike other versions of the MHLC scale, the powerful others subscale is divided into one that taps control attributed to doctors and another which refers to control in other people. People are asked to rate each of the items (given below) in terms of how strongly they agree or disagree with them on a scale ranging from strongly disagree (scored as 1) to strongly agree (scored as 6). Wallston suggests that the word 'condition' should be replaced with the condition's name e.g. 'If I see my doctor regularly, I am less likely to have problems with my diabetes'.

1. If my condition worsens, it is my own behaviour which determines how soon I will feel better again.
2. As to my condition, what will be will be.
3. If I see my doctor regularly, I am less likely to have problems with my condition.

---

4. Most things that affect my condition happen to me by chance.
5. Whenever my condition worsens, I should consult a medically trained professional.
6. I am directly responsible for my condition getting better or worse.
7. Other people play a big role in whether my condition improves, stays the same, or gets worse.
8. Whatever goes wrong with my condition is my own fault.
9. Luck plays a big part in determining how my condition improves.
10. In order for my condition to improve, it is up to other people to see that the right things happen.
11. Whatever improvement occurs with my condition is largely a matter of good fortune.
12. The main thing which affects my condition is what I myself do.
13. I deserve the credit when my condition improves and the blame when it gets worse.
14. Following doctor's orders to the letter is the best way to keep my condition from getting any worse.
15. If my condition worsens, it's a matter of fate.
16. If I am lucky, my condition will get better.
17. If my condition takes a turn for the worse, it is because I have not been taking proper care of myself.
18. The type of help I receive from other people determines how soon my condition improves.

Scoring note: each of the items in the scale corresponds to one of the subscales – internal, chance, doctors and others (the last two scales are derived from the original powerful others dimension).
Internal questions are 1, 6, 8, 12, 13, 17
Chance questions are 2, 4, 9, 11, 15, 16
Doctors 3, 5, 14
Others 7, 10, 18

Many health behaviours have shown associations with locus of control dimensions (Mahler and Kulik, 1990). For instance, evidence has accumulated that internal health locus of control is positively related to HIV protective behaviours (Kelly et al., 1990), food choice indices (Steptoe and Wardle, 2001) and frequency of exercise (Norman et al., 1997). In addition, chance locus of control has been shown to be associated with, among other behaviours, delay in seeking medical advice (e.g. O'Carroll et al., 2001). This means that people with a more external profile are less likely to undertake health protective actions, although in one study powerful others' beliefs (external) were shown to predict an increased uptake of HIV medication (Evans et al., 2000). This may reflect a normative influence factor and one's wish to comply with what important others want us to do (see the theory of planned behaviour concept in Chapter 3). In line with social cognitive theory (see Chapter 3), it has also been argued that health locus of control is only relevant if an individual values their health – in other words, the value people ascribe to the expected outcomes of behaviour (Wallston et al., 1994). One study showed that breast self-examination was predicted most strongly among women who showed high internal locus of control and health value in undertaking the behaviour (Quadrel and Lau, 1989).

While there is evidence of the predictive utility of health locus of control in predicting health behaviours, the proportion of variance accounted for in behaviour is on average quite small, at around 10 per cent (Wallston, 1992; Norman and Bennett, 1996). A related factor, self-efficacy, has been found to be much more predictive of health and illness behaviour, and sick role behaviour (see the self-efficacy concept in this chapter).

SIGNIFICANCE TO HEALTH PSYCHOLOGY

The concept of locus of control details an individual difference type factor that predicts whether a person is more or less inclined to undertake health protective actions. In general, a high internal locus of control is more predictive of health behaviours whereas external control is associated with health compromising behaviours. This evidence indicates that such a relationship is statistically weak, accounting for a small amount of variance in behaviour. Variations of the concept have been developed and incorporated into a number of social-cognitive models including perceived behavioural control (in the theory of planned behaviour) and self-efficacy (in, among others, protection motivation theory and the health action process approach – see Chapter 3).

Further reading

Contrada, R.J. and Goyal, T.M. (2004) Individual differences, health and illness: the role of emotional traits and generalised expectancies. In S. Sutton, A. Baum and M. Johnston (eds), *The Sage Handbook of Health Psychology*. London: Sage. pp. 143–168.
A thorough review of the relationships between various individual difference-based factors, including perceptions of behavioural control, in the experience of health.

Norman, P. and Bennett, P. (1996) Health locus of control. In M. Conner and P. Norman (eds), *Predicting Health Behaviour*. Buckingham: Open University Press. pp. 62–94.
Provides a detailed overview of the role played by perceptions of control characterized by a locus of control in health-related decision making and behaviour. Includes issues related to the measurement of control, as well as a review and synthesis of relevant literature.

See also **individual differences and habit and self-efficacy; social cognitive models and theory of planned behaviour**

INDIVIDUAL DIFFERENCES AND HABIT
and: SELF-EFFICACY

In their everyday lives individuals need to feel in control of situations that affect their psychological and physical well being (see the locus of control concept in this chapter). Motivational and emotional states, and also related behaviours, are all dependent on how much control people perceive they have over situational demands. **Self-efficacy** beliefs specifically concern the perceived degree to which people have control over outcomes associated with undertaking a particular behaviour. Self-efficacy is about how confident a person is in their ability to perform a certain action and attain anticipated outcomes, whereas perceived control is more about an appraisal of environmental factors on behavioural enactment. Armitage and Conner (2002) argue that this discrimination is best thought of as the difference between internal and external sources of control – self-efficacy being an internal source (related to feelings of competence and the ability to undertake a behaviour) and perceived control as being external (an understanding of the influence of environmental factors on behaviour).

MEANING

As a concept, self-efficacy has its roots in social cognitive (learning) theory or SCT (Bandura, 1997) (see the social cognitive theory concept – Chapter 3). Self-efficacy is an individual's belief in their personal ability to arrange, plan and undertake the actions necessary to result in a particular outcome. From this conceptualization it is clear that self-efficacy beliefs are expectancy-based cognitions about control and are important determinants of behaviour. Self-efficacy expectancies determine whether certain behaviours will be used to attain certain goals, how much effort will be directed towards attaining a goal and how persistent an action will be when confronted with obstacles to behaviour. In this way self-efficacy beliefs have a profound motivational effect on the adoption of behaviour. These beliefs predict the motivation to act (Luszczynska and Schwarzer, 2005). Self-efficacy beliefs develop through vicarious experience, or the observation of another person having successfully completed a given behaviour. These beliefs also develop and change as a result of an individual experiencing situational demands and acting in an appropriate way.

ORIGINS

Bandura (1977, 1997) proposes that self-efficacy expectancies about behaving in a certain manner comprise three distinct dimensions. These are magnitude (beliefs about how well one can perform a task), strength (how much confidence a person thinks they have in their ability to perform a behaviour) and generality (how far these beliefs apply only to the current or specific behaviour or are more generally relevant to other related situations). These dimensions govern the expression of self-efficacy beliefs which are used, along with beliefs about outcome expectancy, to predict the likelihood of behavioural adoption or development. In other words, for SCT self-efficacy

CURRENT USAGE

111

forms one of two factors that determine behaviour – the other being perceived outcome expectancies. Those people who think that a behaviour will have a looked-for effect (outcome expectancy) and who believe themselves capable and competent in undertaking the behaviour (self-efficacy) will (1) be more inclined to behave in that way and (2) will exert more effort in performing the behaviour.

While the original conceptualization of self-efficacy was focused on situation-specific beliefs, the inclusion of generality as a dimension of self-efficacy expectancies has led to the development of the concept of generalized self-efficacy. This allows for the proposal that self-efficacy beliefs may be more global, more trait-like, and more stable (in much the same way as dispositional optimism – see the relevant concept in this chapter). This includes the idea that people have a general set of beliefs about their personal ability to perform a variety of behaviours across a number of situations, called 'mastery' or 'perceived competence' (Smith et al., 1995). While most work has focused on situation-specific self-efficacy, some evidence suggests that generalized self-efficacy is related to better health outcomes, health behaviours and adaptation to the onset of disease (e.g. Ormel et al., 1997; Schwarzer and Schroder, 1997).

Many of the models based on social cognitive theory (SCT) emphasize self-efficacy as an important determinant of health-related decision making and behaviour. These include extensions to the health belief model and the theories of reasoned action and planned behaviour (see the concepts in Chapter 3). Other SCT-based models specifically identify self-efficacy as a determinant in its own right of the intention to behave in a protective manner and actual behaviour directed at a health threat. These include protection motivation theory (PMT), the health action process approach (HAPA), as well as a number of stage models (e.g. the precaution adoption process model and the transtheoretical model) which think of changes in self-efficacy as being important in the transition from one stage to a subsequent decisional stage (see the relevant concepts in Chapter 3). Protection motivation theory, for example, identifies how efficacious a response is in reducing the perceived threat of a health event as one of three primary stimulus variables in fear-based appeals (the other two being the degree of severity of an event, and the likelihood of an event happening if no adaptive response is made) (Rogers, 1975). More specifically, PMT distinguishes between the types of self-efficacy used when appraising coping responses made to a health threat. These are response efficacy – beliefs that a recommended self-protective action would decrease the health threat – and self-efficacy – beliefs associated with whether this behaviour can be performed by the individual.

Schwarzer's (1992) health action process approach model proposes that types of self-efficacy are also important in determining motivational factors leading to the formation of an intention to behave in an adaptive manner, and also an individual's translation of this intention in action as part of the volition phase in the adoption of health behaviour. For example, as well as arguing that generalized self-efficacy is important at all phases in behavioural enactment, work has shown that so-called 'initiative self-efficacy' is particularly important when people are implementing intentions or planning behaviours (see the HAPA concept in Chapter 3 for further examples).

Irrespective of model type, self-efficacy has been shown to be an important predictor of motivation to behave, intention to behave and actual behavioural enactment across a number of discrete health behaviours (see Conner and Norman, 2005, for a comprehensive review). In short, increased belief that one is able to undertake a recommended course of action is associated with forming an intention to behave in that way, translating that intention into behaviour, maintaining that behaviour over time and overcoming threats or challenges to the current behaviour, such as when an ex-smoker relapses for a short-time after having given up smoking (e.g. Marlatt and Gordon's (1985) relapse prevention model).

SIGNIFICANCE TO HEALTH PSYCHOLOGY

Self-efficacy is a central individual difference factor that functions to predict a motivation to engage in health behaviour, the implementation of behavioural intention (or goal striving), and responses to illness experience (e.g. the attribution of symptoms, and so on). It has been applied in a number of models based on social cognitive theory and has also been shown to be effective in promoting changes in health beliefs and health behaviour, and maintaining change over time (see Conner and Norman, 2005; Luszczynska and Schwarzer, 2005).

Further reading

Bandura, A. (1997) *Self-efficacy: The Exercise of Control*. New York: Freeman.
The classic text that details the development and operationalization of the concept of self-efficacy in terms of behavioural self-regulation.

DeVillis, B.M. and DeVillis, R.F. (2000) Self-efficacy and health. In A. Baum, T.A. Revenson and J.E. Singer (eds), *Handbook of Health Psychology*. Mahwah, NJ: Erlbaum. pp. 235–247.
Provides a summary of the role of self-efficacy in health-related decision making and behaviour.

See also **social cognitive models and social cognitive theory**

INDIVIDUAL DIFFERENCES AND HABIT
and: HABIT

MEANING

The vast majority of behaviours that we undertake during our lifetime, including those related to health outcomes, are repeated over and over again. It is not that common an occurrence to do something for the first time but when we do so we are deliberate and conscious in the plans we have to make, and also the thinking inherent in planning the behaviour and our own evaluation of the behaviour after the event. Try and remember about first learning to ride a bicycle and the enormous amount of thinking and concentration that went into that endeavour. Doing behaviours initially is a cognitively taxing thing to undertake given the amount of processing of plans, goals, beliefs, and so on that occurs. Over time, and with the repeated enactment of a behaviour in similar environmental circumstances, we will just seem to perform the task without consciously thinking about or planning it (Ouellette and Wood, 1998). At this point the behaviour has become a **habit** or habitual in nature (Verplanken, 2005) and the best predictor of future behaviour becomes past behaviour (see Sutton, 1994). These details are nicely brought together and extended in Verplanken and Aarts' (1999) definition of habits as 'learned sequences of acts that have become automatic responses to specific cues, and are functional in obtaining certain goals and end-states' (p. 104).

ORIGINS

Habits are characterized by repetition and learning – created by doing the behaviour repeatedly. These behaviours are characterized as automatic responses to specific cues in the environment such that after repeated learning, exposure to a particular cue or stimulus will activate an automatic cognitive process which then guides behaviour (Bargh and Ferguson, 2000). **Automaticity** has a number of components. When a process or behaviour is called 'automatic' it operates outside of conscious awareness, is very difficult to control, is mentally efficient such that it can operate when cognitive resources are also being used to do other tasks, and it is also unintentional, that is, not consciously planned (Bargh, 1994). There is a plethora of research generated from experimental psychology that has sought to understand the role of automaticity in perceptual processing. Social psychologists, for instance, have been interested for many years in examining the automatic nature of social behaviour and have generated some very interesting results. For example, Bargh and his colleagues have undertaken a significant amount of work demonstrating aspects of automaticity in social perception (e.g. impression formation, and so on) and goal striving (see Bargh and Chartrand, 1999). Since health behaviours are no different from other behaviours, there is no reason why they should not be conceptualized within the boundaries of automaticity and habit as well.

CURRENT USAGE

While this holds true it is only recently that health psychologists have begun to embrace the role habits, and more importantly, automatic cognition play in the enactment of health behaviour (e.g. Stacy et al., 2000). This is an important development because social cognitive approaches (see Chapter 3) when applied to health behaviour have taken insufficient account of the role of automatic cognitive processes in the generation, development and change of health behaviour outside of the adage that 'the best predictor of future behaviour is past behaviour'. An examination of implicit or automatic cognition in health behaviour allows us to access a potential understanding of the processes that make this observation true. In a very important review of the past behaviour-future behaviour relationship for all behaviours, Ouellette and Wood (1998) make the point that the relationship holds true when well learnt behaviours occur in stable contexts and are subject to automatic processing that controls the skill. When this is the case, then the frequency of past behaviour can be seen as a habit strength and will have a direct effect on future behaviour. This in turn reflects key components of the automaticity idea seen earlier. When behaviours are subject to conscious processing (namely, deliberation with high cognitive resources) which occurs when a behaviour is not well learnt or is performed in more unstable and less predictable contexts, past behaviour only predicts the formation of an intention to act and not behaviour per se.

Previous measurement of habit has been criticized for not focusing on the key attributes of the term, relying solely on the frequency of a given behaviour as a measure. However, recent work has shown the development of a general self-report measure of habit which reflects coherently the component definition of habit detailed earlier (namely, the Self-Report Habit Index or SRHI – Verplanken and Orbell, 2003) (see Box 5.3).

Box 5.3   A measure of habitual strength: the self-report habit index (*Source*: Verplanken and Orbell, 2003)

Behaviour X is something …

1.   I do frequently.
2.   I do automatically.
3.   I do without having to consciously remember.
4.   That makes me feel weird if I do not do it.
5.   I do without thinking.
6.   Would require effort not to do.
7.   That belongs to my (daily, weekly, monthly) routine.
8.   I start doing before I realize I'm doing it.
9.   I would find hard not to do.
10.   I have no need to think about doing.
11.   That's typically me.
12.   I have been doing for a long time.

(Cont'd)

This scale was designed to reflect the core components: uncontrollability, lack of awareness, efficiency, a history of repetition and also the habit as a sense of identity. Although the sense of identity is not a classic characteristic, Verplanken and Orbell argue that habits might be deemed by the individual to be descriptive of the person.

But to measure habit and the automatic cognition that guides the enactment of habitual behaviour it may not be sufficient simply to ask participants about factors that could be important in the generation of behaviour. Take the example here of the study of addictive behaviours. McCusker (2001) points out that psychologists interested in examining the cognitive determinants of addiction as a habit are not interested in 'what people "say" about what they think, but rather make inferences about cognitive processes and structures based on behavioural responses' (pp. 49–50). In effect, researchers such as McCusker and others (e.g. see Munafò and Albery, 2006), utilize experimental paradigms that do not require the participant to consciously report their behaviour or thoughts about a behaviour, such as those based on attention and implicit memory processes (e.g. Stacy et al., 2000; Field, 2006; see also Chapter 9). This type of investigation allows the researcher to examine the automatic or implicit processing of health-related stimuli and to make suggestions of how people's thoughts and feelings are organized in the mind for guiding habitual behaviour (e.g. post-operative pain – Munafò and Stevenson, 2003; breast cancer history – Erblich et al., 2003; see also Box 5.4 and Figure 5.1).

Box 5.4   Implicit cognitive processing biases in women with or without a family history of breast cancer

Erblich et al. (2003) studied how women with (FH+) or without (FH-) a family history of breast cancer process stimuli related to cancer, another chronic illness (namely, cardiovascular disease) and negative emotional words. The idea was to examine whether stressful current concerns affect the processing of types of stimuli. Using a modified Stroop in which people responded to the colour a word is written in while ignoring the word itself, they showed that FH+ women were significantly slower to respond to the colours of cancer-related words compared to the other word types (see Figure 5.1).

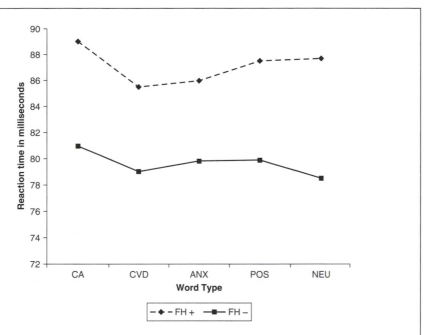

Figure 5.1   Reaction times to modified Stroop stimuli in women with (FH+) and without (FH-) a history of familial breast cancer (*Source*: Erblich et al., 2003).

Key: CA = cancer-related words; CVD = cardiovascular disease-related words; ANX = anxiety-related words; POS = positive words; NEU = neutral words

In addition, the two groups were not found to differ when asked about their perceived risks of getting breast cancer. This work showed that people with certain concerns will process related stimuli differently to other unrelated information and that this effect is not dependent on explicit risk responses. It seems that the related stimuli may automatically grab the attention of the perceiver and as such slow down the response to colour. Sharma et al. (2001) argued the case of a highly activated alcohol-specific semantic network in a similar study on problem and non-problem drinkers, and these kinds of effects have been found in addiction research generally (see Munafò and Albery, 2006). The same may have been the case in these women.

In a series of three experimental studies, Sheeran, Aarts et al. (2005) investigated how alcohol drinking behaviour may be dependent upon automatic cognitive processes. By simply categorizing people as habitual or non-habitual in their drinking behaviour, the first two experiments showed that the habitual people were fastest in responding to drinking-related words when they had been exposed previously to a condition in which the goal of socializing when drinking alcohol had been

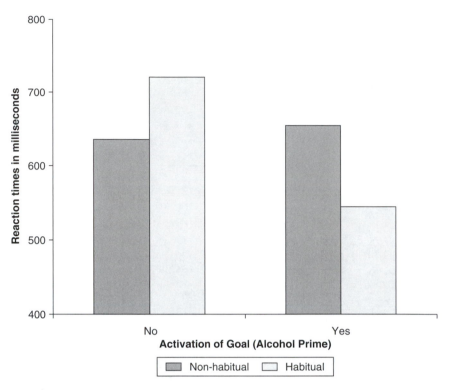

Figure 5.2   Reaction times to verify the verb 'drinking' by habit strength and goal activation type (after Sheeran, Aarts et al., 2005, Experiment 2)

Note: The above diagram shows the speed with which participants responded to whether a word presented on a computer screen was a verb or not. Half of the words presented were verbs and half were non-verbs. Of the verbs, 'drinking' was presented five times and it is the responses to these critical trials that are reported in Figure 5.2. Prior to the test, participants had been 'primed' with a concept related to drinking alcohol, namely socializing by completing a scrambled sentence task. In this task participants are presented with a number of five-letter strings and are asked to make four-word sentences. In the prime condition participants were presented with a number of scrambled sentences that included socializing-related words (e.g. associate, join, mingle, greet, and so on). Other participants in the no prime control were presented with non-socializing related words (e.g. writes, floats, and so on). In addition, participants were asked how long ago their last drinking occasion was and how much they had consumed. From these measures participants were classified into 'habitual' or 'non-habitual' in their groups.

activated, as compared to non-habitual individuals (see Figure 5. 2). This means that habit influenced the accessibility of drinking behaviour stimuli only when under conditions where a goal related to the drinking of alcohol was activated.

An important point here is that people were not aware that they had been primed with the drinking-related goal, which corresponds to the idea of unawareness as part of an automatic cognitive process. In the third experiment in this study Sheeran et al. showed that a measure of actual behaviour related to drinking

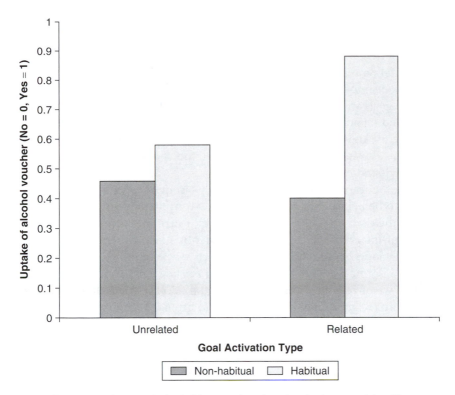

Figure 5.3   Alcohol voucher uptake by habit strength and goal activation type (after Sheeran, Aarts et al., 2005, Experiment 3)

Note: In this experiment half the participants were 'primed' with the drinking-related concept of social-izing by asking them to nominate a number of cities in the UK, Europe and the rest of the world that would be worth visiting in order to have a good social life. This was labelled the 'related goal condi-tion'. The other half were asked to nominate cities that were good for historical sites – the 'unrelated goal condition'. Participants were classified as 'habitual' or 'non-habitual' on the basis of their answers to questions about how often they had been out drinking in the past two weeks, and also about how often they had been drunk over the same time period. After priming participants were offered the choice of a £1 discount for alcohol or a £1 voucher for tea or coffee. The graph above shows the uptake of the alcohol voucher for habitual and non-habitual participants who had either been primed or not with the related goal of socializing.

(namely, the uptake of an alcoholic versus non-alcoholic drink voucher) was also dependent on habit strength and the activation of drinking goals. Briefly, those par-ticipants who had previously been primed with a drinking-related goal, in terms of good cities for socializing in (socializing being related to consumption of alcohol), and who were also scored as high in habit strength, were more likely to select the voucher which could supposedly be redeemed at a local bar/pub (see Figure 5.3). In effect, this study illustrates the dynamic influence of habit and goal activation on drinking behaviour.

This evidence provides a good example of the role of automatic thinking processes in habitual behaviour. Theoretically, the idea of this type of evidence is that the experience of a cue in the environment (e.g. in this case, socializing) activates a mental representation of behaviour – 'drinking' – in the long-term memory which contains information about beliefs associated with the behaviour, as well as behavioural goals and behavioural sequences (e.g. skills information for behaving in the associated manner). In an habitual individual this activation is fast acting; the person does not know that the representation has been activated, they cannot control it and it also increases the likelihood of that person acting in line with the stored behavioural representation.

What are the implications if we assume that some health behaviours are more than likely to be habitual in nature (subject to automatic cognitive processes) and that one of the goals of health psychology is to utilize theoretically driven ideas for the design of interventions to change maladaptive health behaviours or promote healthy behaviours? Some evidence has shown that habitual people are less attentive to new information (e.g. Verplanken and Aarts, 1999) and have an attentional bias for behaviour-related stimuli (e.g. Cox et al., 2006). As such, habitual individuals are likely to ignore new information and attend to information that is more consistent with their current behaviour. Recent work has, however, demonstrated that these attentional processes can be changed if a person is trained to attend to new information over time. In the addiction field, research suggests that the attentional bias for addiction-related cues over other cues is related to treatment outcome (Waters et al., 2003), and that by training an individual to cognitively avoid these cues by making other cues salient over time may result in a decrease in the addictive behaviour (see Franken, 2003; Wiers et al., 2006).

One alternative is to attempt to create new habits to replace existing ones. While attentional training is a mechanism that may result in the establishment of a new automatic cognitive sequence, other researchers have emphasized the use of the formation of implementation intentions to this end (see Verplanken, 2005; and the implementation intention construct in Chapter 3). Implementation intentions are likely to tap the development of habitual cognition because forcing people to plan when an action will be undertaken, what actions exactly will be undertaken and where they will be undertaking the behaviour together creates a cue-specific action plan. In other words, people are forced to plan how often they will undertake a behaviour (e.g. three times a week) and under what circumstances (e.g. last thing at night) which have the effect of transferring control for the behaviour from the person to their environmental conditions. Over time and the enactment of the implementation intention it is likely that the environmental stimulus will automatically trigger the behavioural sequence. The formation of implementation intentions has been shown to make it more likely that a person will undertake a behaviour and implement their goal intentions when presented with the relevant environmental situation, as compared to people who have not formed an implementation intention (see Sheeran, 2002; Steadman and Quine, 2004).

Some have argued that the vast majority of everyday social behaviour, of which health behaviours may be an example, is driven predominantly by automatic cognition which is fast acting, bound to stimuli in the environment, outside of people's awareness and difficult to change (Bargh, 1997). In addition, central to the concept of habit is the idea that aspects of decision-making processes and behavioural enactment processes have been transferred to these automatic processes. If this is the case, health psychologists have to embrace such reasoning in understanding how and why people undertake the behaviours they do. The role of both explicit (non-automatic factors such as self-reported beliefs, and so on) and implicit cognition (automatic processes) has to be recognized and studied in terms of the development and maintenance of health-related behaviours. In addition, the role of such processes should be considered in the design of interventions to change health behaviours, such that individuals who show increased behavioural habituation may require a completely distinct intervention compared to the behavioural novice.

SIGNIFICANCE TO HEALTH PSYCHOLOGY

Further reading

Ouellette, J.A. and Wood, W. (1998) Habit and intention in everyday life: the multiple processes by which the past predicts the future. *Psychological Bulletin*, 124, 54–74.

Provides a detailed account of the dimensions of habitual processes, how they can be conceptualised and their importance in predicting behaviour.

Sutton, S. (1994) The past predicts the future: interpreting behaviour-behaviour relationships in social psychological models of health behaviour. In D.R. Rutter and L. Quine (eds), *Social Psychology and Health: European Perspectives*. Aldershot: Avebury. pp. 71–88.

A discussion of the finding that the best predictor of future behaviour is past behaviour and how models in health psychology account for this finding.

See also **social cognitive models and implementation intentions**

INDIVIDUAL DIFFERENCES AND HABIT
and: PERSONALITY TYPE AND HEALTH

Personality is about individual differences and what makes us unique as human beings. Factors that describe ways in which people are different from one another in how they think and behave encapsulate the concept of personality. Personality refers to how psychological systems (that is, traits) are organized within an individual

MEANING

and how these cause behaviours and ways of thinking that are characteristic of that individual. Personality research in understanding health decision making, health behaviour and coping responses to the threat or onset of disease or illness has concentrated on a number of key factors including personality type (Type A, Type C, Type D, negative affectivity or neuroticism and hardiness), as well as other individual difference factors outlined in this chapter (e.g. locus of control, dispositional optimism, and so on).

ORIGINS Personality was argued in the past to be global, dispositional and trait-like (Allport, 1961). This perspective viewed personality as a personal profile that was stable over time and enduring. Personality traits were argued to group together in certain ways to form a coherent impression or typology of those individuals having these traits. For instance, an extrovert had traits that reflected sociability, impulsivity and adventurousness, whereas a psychotic type of person had traits like egocentrism and aggressiveness (Eysenck, 1982). While this view was popular in the early to mid-twentieth century, the trait approach was questioned through a growing body of evidence that suggested that traits did not always predict observed behaviour and that some consideration needed to be given to other factors that were determined more by situational factors, and referred to state-like characteristics such as situation specific mood or anxiety (e.g. Spielberger et al., 1983).

CURRENT USAGE In general, health psychologists have been interested in assessing the association between a number of personality factors and the experience of health and illness. From this work a number of propositions have been forwarded to describe the nature of this personality-illness relationship. These include the idea that personality predicts health outcome because certain personality types are more likely to undertake health compromising behaviours such as smoking and drinking. A plethora of research has also been undertaken to assess the nature of the relationship between the experience of stress, personality type and illness experience (see McCrae and Stone, 1997). The question is – does personality type mediate the effect of the experience of stress on health outcome? And if so, in what ways? Much research on the stress-personality-illness relationship has focused on **Type A behaviour** (TAB). TAB is a typology that includes competitiveness, achievement-orientated behaviour, impatience, being easily annoyed, hostile and angry, trying to achieve too much in too little time and a vigorous speech pattern (Rosenman, 1978). Early large-scale research programmes gave the impression that there was a reasonable link between TAB and coronary heart disease (CHD) (e.g. Haynes et al., 1980), although other longitudinal work has not shown such an effect (e.g. see Booth-Kewley and Friedman, 1987).

More recent work has focused on the role of **hostility** (one of the TAB characteristics) as being of particular importance (e.g. Dembrowski et al., 1989). Hostility comprises thoughts and behaviours that have as their basis the expression of anger.

People high in hostility hold particularly cynical views of their social world, and have negative expectations of others around them (Miller et al., 1996). Hostility has its affect on illness because these individuals (1) are not protected from the strain imposed by stressors through accessing support systems – the psychosocial vulnerability hypothesis (Kivimäki et al., 2003); (2) engage in health risk behaviours more often, such as drinking and smoking (Vögele, 1998); and (3) are more physiologically stress reactive (showing increased blood pressure, and so on) (Suarez et al., 1998).

Other research has also identified a personality profile associated with increased cancer risk – **Type C personality** (Temoshok, 1987). This personality type is characterized as being cooperative, appeasing, compliant, passive, stoic, unassertive, self-sacrificing and inhibiting negative affect (emotions). It has been shown that inhibiting emotional expression has a significant prospective effect on the subsequent development of cancer (Shaffer et al., 1987). Experiencing negative emotions but inhibiting expression of these and at the same time avoiding social interaction to avoid feelings of disapproval – the **Type D personality type** (Denollet, 1998) – has also been shown to be predictive of physiological indicators of coronary heart disease (Habra et al., 2003).

Other factors that have been found to be related to negative health outcomes are **negative affectivity** or NA (neuroticism) and hardiness. People low in NA have a general negative outlook on life and are more inclined to personal introspection, poorer mood and self-concept (Watson and Clark, 1984). Low NA is associated with more health complaints and lower self-rated health status, although objective health indices only show weak correlations with the profile (Evers et al., 2003). **Hardiness** is a factor that has been shown to be protective against the experience of stress (Kobasa, 1979). Commitment (a sense of purpose in life events and activities), control (the belief of personal influence over situations) and challenge (seeing adaptation and change as 'normal' and positive experiences) characterize increased hardiness. In a seminal study, Kobasa et al. (1982) showed that in situations of high stress hardiness essentially buffered the effects on illness likelihood. High hardiness people exposed to high levels of stress not only reported significantly decreased illness scores relative to low hardiness participants, they were found to be no different from people who had experienced only low levels of stress.

SIGNIFICANCE TO HEALTH PSYCHOLOGY

The role of personality factors in understanding of health decision making, health behaviour and coping responses to the threat or onset of disease or illness is important because it identifies factors for understanding why there is such diversity in people's health-related thoughts and actions. Such factors are also important because they show that objective physical markers of health or illness may be related to dispositional personality-based factors and that these factors may interact with thinking and behavioural profiles to predict health and well being.

Further reading

Contrada, R.J. and Goyal, T.M. (2004) Individual differences, health and illness: the role of emotional traits and generalised expectancies. In S. Sutton, A. Baum and M. Johnston (eds), *The Sage Handbook of Health Psychology*. London: Sage. pp. 143–168.

A general discussion of the various individual difference factors involved in predicting the likelihood of an individual experiencing health and illness. Includes a good discussion of a range of personality characteristics.

Booth-Kewley, S. and Friedman, H.S. (1987) Psychological predictors of heart disease: a quantitative review. *Psychological Bulletin*, 101, 343–362.

An excellent and detailed account of the role of a number of personality-based factors important for studying the likelihood of heart disease.

See also **individual differences and habit and dispositional optimism**

ILLNESS-RELATED AND SICK
ROLE BELIEFS

6

SIX

ILLNESS-RELATED AND SICK ROLE BELIEFS
and: **self-regulation model of illness cognition and behaviour**
   social representations of illness
   discourse and illness

In Chapter 3 we studied in some detail a number of models and approaches based on social cognitive theory including the health belief model, the theory of planned behaviour and protection motivation theory (see Conner and Norman, 2005). In general, these approaches have explored the role of various thinking processes, such as normative beliefs, outcome expectancies and the formation of action plans and goals, in the decision to undertake health-related behaviour. These approaches have also been used to identify core beliefs or processes that require intervention for a person to act in a recommended way, and have resulted in the effective design and implementation of treatments and interventions (see Rutter and Quine, 2002; Norman et al., 2000). While this work has been useful in understanding key processes that are important in why people take the health-related decisions they do and act in the manner they do, it has not fully addressed the issue of whether people think qualitatively differently when they are actually sick. What are the illness-related beliefs people have when they are experiencing it? How do people think and behave when they are sick? How and why do people behave and think in the manner they do when they are ill? This is called 'sick role behaviour'. For answers to these types of questions, we must turn to models and approaches that were developed specifically to understand illness-related and sick role thinking and behaviour.

ILLNESS-RELATED AND SICK ROLE BELIEFS
and: SELF-REGULATION MODEL OF ILLNESS COGNITION AND BEHAVIOUR

MEANING Think of the last time you woke up one morning to find that you had a headache, your throat felt a bit sore, your neck was a bit stiff and you just did not have the energy you usually have. I bet you immediately tried to work out why you were feeling this way. What was wrong with you? Could it be that you were about to get influenza, or maybe you shouldn't have had that last glass of wine the night before! In effect, in these types of situation we are trying to problem solve and this problem solving exercise appears to be based on the beliefs we have about what the causes of the symptoms may be. These beliefs will also determine what we do in response to the symptoms – take some medication, stay in bed, drink lots of fluids, or whatever – and will shape the overall personal experience of illness.

The illness beliefs we store in long-term memory are schemas or representations. As schemas (or representations) these beliefs can be thought of as mental models of an illness and are called **illness representations**. They contain information about the potential course of an illness, the symptoms associated with it, as well as what to do in the event of experiencing the illness (see Petrie and Weinman, 1997; Cameron and Leventhal, 2003; Cameron and Moss-Morris, 2004). There are large individual differences in the types of illness representations held by different people, with some, for example, believing that inoculations for common illnesses do more damage to the body than good while others fully subscribe to inoculation as a preventative measure. Regardless, it has been argued that illness representations direct how we interpret and respond to perceived symptoms. As such these representations have been used to decipher how a person makes decisions with respect to adhering to medical advice (e.g. Jessop and Rutter, 2003; Fortune et al., 2004).

ORIGINS The ways in which these representations guide responses to the perception of illness have been formally formulated in Leventhal and colleagues' **self-regulation model of illness cognition and behaviour** (SRM) (e.g. Leventhal et al., 1984, 1997, 2003). Figure 6.1 is an illustration of the self-regulation model.

Central to the model is the idea that individuals have a need to maintain an equilibrium, such that when they encounter a problem that threatens their psychological or physical being they are motivated to engage in activities (both psychological and behavioural) that work to reinstate the status quo. Illness is viewed as an unstable state that opposes the 'normal' state of being healthy and people will work towards re-establishing the norm. As such this model proposes that understanding or assigning meaning to the experience of an illness is synonymous with problem solving. More importantly, however, this problem-solving exercise serves a **self-regulatory**

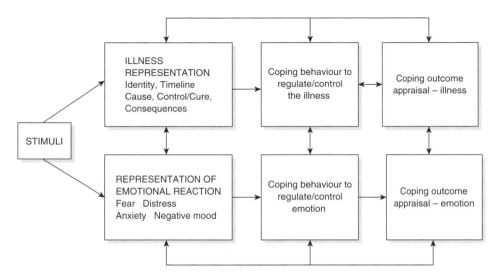

Figure 6.1   Self-regulatory model of illness behaviour (*Source*: Leventhal et al., 1984)

function such that the recognition of a problem is interpreted and responded to, and the response is then appraised with the aim of returning to the original psychological and physical condition and reinstating the goal of the status quo. An indicative metaphor could be any homeostatic system, such as a central heating system which regulates temperature by responding to thermo change. As you can see in Figure 6.1, the self-regulation model is a cognitive-affective model and emphasizes the relationship between, on the one hand, cognitively based illness representations about an illness, and on the other, a representation of the emotional impact of the illness on the individual.

Leventhal and colleagues argue that initially an individual is presented effectively with an illness message (that may be experienced as threat) either by perceiving symptoms or by being made aware of information from other sources, such as a doctor's diagnosis. Once this information has been received the individual has entered a state of disequilibrium which needs to be addressed in order to re-establish the status quo. The first stage in this task is to assign meaning to the problem by accessing, retrieving and utilizing illness representations (or cognitions). Illness representations develop from exposure and experience to the illness including personal experience, as well as other sources of information such as the media or knowing other people who have experienced a similar illness. As such you do not have to have experienced the illness in order to have formed an illness representation of it.

The SRM proposes that an illness representation is comprised of five inter-related belief components: identity, timeline, control/cure, consequences and cause (see Table 6.1). 'Identity' refers to the illness label and the symptoms that match the given label. 'Timeline' is beliefs about how long the illness will last – this can be

Table 6.1   Leventhal and colleagues' component beliefs of illness representations

Component	Belief characteristics
Identity	Illness label, diagnosis, related symptoms
Timeline	Duration of illness – acute, chronic or cyclic
Consequences	Expected outcomes of illness – effects on social, physical and psychological well being
Cause	Internal and external attributions of cause
Cure/Control	Extent to which illness can be addressed, controlled or cured

acute (transient in nature), chronic (long lasting) or cyclic (the illness will come and go over time). 'Control/cure' refers to beliefs about how far the illness or symptoms can be controlled (either internally by the individual or externally by professionals) by using medication or changing health-related behaviour. 'Consequences' are the component that reflects an individual's expectancies about the effects of the illness on their own psychological and physical functioning. Finally, 'cause' refers to an attributional process characterized by beliefs about what may have caused the illness, such as exposure to another ill person (an external attribution) or having been a smoker for 25 years (an internal attribution), depending on the illness and its associated symptoms. Once exposed to some illness-related stimulus, illness representations (characterized by the five components outlined here) are activated in long-term memory and a representation is formed based on a comparison between the current state of affairs and the existing stored beliefs. This representation in turn predicts the coping resources applied to the conditions which are then appraised by the individual to ascertain the effectiveness of the response in restoring the equilibrium. If this disequilibrium continues, the person undergoes some modification of the representation (e.g. by altering beliefs associated with controllability, perceived cause, and so on) which again feeds into a new coping response and appraisal process. This is represented by the upper branch of Figure 6.1.

Perceived symptoms or stimuli also provoke an emotional reaction, such as the worry associated with noticing the changing size and shape of a mole on the skin – an emotional representation (detailed in the lower branch of Figure 6.1). In turn this emotional representation guides coping responses aimed at alleviating the negative affect associated with symptoms which are appraised for their effectiveness in terms of self-regulatory success. The emotional representation is activated in parallel with the activation of the illness representation.

CURRENT USAGE   The majority of work in the applying and exploring the SRM has been concerned with the examination of illness representations for a number of chronic and acute illnesses (e.g. chronic fatigue syndrome – Moss-Morris et al., 1996; rheumatoid arthritis – Carlisle et al., 2005), in predicting health-related behaviour (e.g. adherence to cardiac rehabilitation programmes – Whitmarsh et al., 2003), and in response to diagnosis (e.g. Hagger and Orbell, 2006). Indeed work in this area has led to the development of the Illness Perceptions Questionnaire (IPQ) for measuring the five components of illness representations (Weinman et al., 1996), extended in the IPQ-Revised to incorporate emotional representations of illness (Moss-Morris et al., 2002; Hagger and Orbell, 2005). In one study of the illness representations about breast cancer, 249 women given either a cancer free (benign) diagnosis or a diagnosis of breast cancer completed the IPQ (Anagnostopoulos and Spanea, 2005). Results showed that the 'non-malignant' women reported exaggerated negative consequences, that environmental factors (external) were more likely perceived as a cause, and had weaker beliefs about the controllability or cure of the condition compared to 'malignant' women.

Other studies have examined the role of illness representations in health behaviours. For example, Lawson et al. (2004) reported on a cross-sectional comparative study of diabetics receiving specialist care or who had not attended a diabetic clinic for a prolonged period of time (at least 18 months). Those who had not attended a diabetic clinic reported increased negative views of control over the condition, were more pessimistic about the course of the illness (timeline) and believed the consequences of the illness to be more severe. In another investigation Whitmarsh et al. (2003) reported differences between patients who did or did not attend for rehabilitation following cardiac problems. The best predictors of increased attendance were the perception of a greater number of symptoms and more severe consequences related to the illness. In addition, attendees were shown to use more problem-focused and emotion-focused coping strategies, whereas the non-attendees used more maladaptive strategies.

Box 6.1   The relationships between illness representations, coping and psychological adjustment in people with chronic fatigue syndrome (see Weinman et al., 1996)

Basis of the research

Chronic fatigue syndrome (CFS) is a disorder that it is conceptualized as being organically based, but with psychological and behavioural responses that mediate between the physical basis and the chronicity of the syndrome. In other words, CFS has cognitive components that affect the progression of the illness. With this in mind Moss-Morris et al. (1996) applied the self-regulatory model to examine the role of illness cognitions (representations) in coping strategies applied to the management and experience of CFS among 233 sufferers.

(Cont'd)

Measures

Participants completed the Illness Perception Questionnaire (Weinman et al., 1996) to elucidate beliefs about identity, cause, timeline, cure/control and consequences and as such the CFS illness representation these people held. Coping strategies were measured using the COPE scale (Carver et al., 1989). This scale identifies and measures different types of coping. These are problem-focused or instrumental coping (characterized by planning, suppression of competing activities, and searching out social support for instrumental or problem-solving reasons), emotion-focused coping (characterized by venting emotion, identifying and using emotional social support, and the positive reinterpretation of the effects of the stressor), behavioural disengagement coping (characterized by actions to distract from the stressor), and mental disengagement coping (when a person focuses on thoughts that do not address the stressor specifically such as wishful thinking). In addition, measures of psychological adjustment and subjective well being were included.

Findings

Individual characteristics of the illness representation formed among CFS sufferers were related in the following ways:

- Illness identity, in terms of the number of symptoms reported, was related to a timeline indicative of chronicity and a belief that CFS had serious consequences for the individual.
- Beliefs about a chronic timeline was associated with beliefs about the serious consequences of the illness on a person's life and that the illness was less controllable and could not be cured easily.
- People believed that CFS was caused by psychological factors, like stress, and that these were related to a belief that the illness had serious consequences.

In addition illness representation and coping strategies were associated in the following ways.

- People who reported lots of symptoms (identity) used a vast range of different methods to address the stressor. These included emotion-focused, problem-focused, behavioural disengagement and mental disengagement coping strategies.
- Perceived consequences and a number of coping strategies were positively related. Those people who believed that there were serious consequences for them from having CFS reported using planning activities,

they had stopped themselves doing other things and had sought out emotional social support.

- Those people who thought that they could control the illness (internal) used strategies like active coping, planning, and a positive reinterpretation of the meaning of the illness.
- Responses indicative of the belief that the illness would be long lasting (that is, chronic) were related to suppressing competing activities (not doing other activities) and behavioural disengagement (e.g. using other behaviours as distracters).
- The belief that the illness had a psychological cause was shown to be related to using other activities for distraction.

Finally, those participants who reported increased symptoms, that the illness was not in their control (external), was caused by emotional factors (e.g. related to stress) and that the illness had serious consequences, displayed lower levels of psychological adjustment and greater dysfunction.

Summary

This study is useful because it identified the dynamic relationship between different components of an illness representation with the most commonly used coping strategies and outcomes in terms of well being and adjustment to illness. The research supports the basic tenets of the self-regulatory model in terms of the proposed relationship between components of the illness representation, coping strategies and the effectiveness of these strategies. However, no claims can be made about the causal relationship between the factors because the measures were all taken at the same time. To identify a causal mechanism would require illness representation components to be measured first and then the individuals would need to be followed to see which coping strategies they were using and ultimately how well they were doing (namely, their future adjustment and well being). See Petrie et al. (2002) for an intervention study which allows for more reliable causal inferences to be made.

Recent work has utilized the illness representations people hold about their illnesses to design interventions aimed at encouraging health protective behaviours. In one hospital-based randomized controlled study, Petrie et al. (2002) examined whether an individualized intervention that sought to change inaccurate and negative illness perceptions among patients who had experienced a myocardial infarction, would lead to behaviours indicative of increased health protection on discharge. Results showed that the intervention group reported more positive beliefs about their condition, were more equipped to leave the hospital setting, were likely to return to work more quickly and also showed fewer angina symptoms in the longer term. As such, providing a mechanism which addresses maladaptive illness-specific representations seems to create improved long-term adaptation to the illness experience and improved functioning.

SIGNIFICANCE TO HEALTH PSYCHOLOGY

The self-regulation model of illness cognition and behaviour has been very influential in the study of how lay people identify and respond to the threat or onset of illness. By emphasizing the dynamic interaction between cognitive representations (illness representations) and emotional representations of actually experienced or potentially experienced symptoms, the model proposes how an individual uses coping strategies to address the problems and, importantly, to appraise the response in terms of its effectiveness. Taking this self-regulatory perspective has demonstrated differences in reactivity among individuals to health threats, as well as providing one potential explanation for the adoption of maladaptive health behaviours such as non-adherence or non-compliance, and the design of effective interventions to motivate health protective behaviour.

Further reading

Cameron, L.D. and Moss-Morris, R. (2004) Illness-related cognition and behaviour. In A. Kaptein and J. Weinman (eds), *Health Psychology*. Oxford: Blackwell. pp. 84–110. An interesting and contemporary review of the key factors of the self-regulatory/ illness representations model.

Leventhal, H., Benyamini, Y., Brownlee, S., Diefenbach, M., Leventhal, E.A., Patrick-Miller, L. and Robitaille, C. (1997) Illness representations: theoretical foundations. In K. Petrie and J. Weinman (eds), *Perceptions of Health and Illness: Current Research and Applications*. Amsterdam: Harwood Academic Publishers. pp. 19–45. Provides a detailed conceptual account of the role of illness representations on the experience of illness, including key components of the self-regulatory model.

See also **social cognitive models and social cognitive theory**

ILLNESS-RELATED AND SICK ROLE BELIEFS
and: SOCIAL REPRESENTATIONS OF ILLNESS

MEANING

Social cognitive accounts propose that health-related decision making and behaviours are predicted directly by belief-based processes, and that these cognitive structures are to be found in the mind of each individual person. Other theorists, while recognizing that people are active 'thinkers' and that thinking per se determines, for the most part, the ways people behave, respond to and make sense of their social worlds, would question the idea that beliefs only operate and exist in people's heads. It is argued that such beliefs (or attitudes or any thinking-based organizational principle) appear, develop and change as a result of everyday social interaction. This approach has been formalized in social representation theory (Moscovici, 1984) and has served as the basis of one approach used in the study of illness-related beliefs.

ORIGINS

Social representation theory states that individual experience is best understood by placing the individual in their own social or cultural system (Moscovici, 1981). An individual's psychological experience of the world is the result of the ways in which they belong to groups. These groups comprise other people, within which an individual exists and shares numerous beliefs, experiences and the environment. In other words, the overarching assumption on which social representations theory is based is that a person's own identity is found in the collectivity of others' and that person's own experience.

Social representations are all the values, thoughts, knowledge and images that the collective shares. Moscovici (1988) called this collective sharing 'common consciousness'. The approach also argues that social representations influence and guide the formation and development of an individual's beliefs and attitudes about objects in the social world, and form the basis upon which groups differentiate themselves from other groups. Moscovici (1984) also argues that representations form the primary function of making unfamiliar objects or events in the social world familiar so as to create understanding and meaning of events in the world around us. In a sense, therefore, social representations guide the process of attributing meaning to unfamiliar events by searching through what is already known and familiar.

Anchoring and **objectification** are two fundamental processes identified by the theory to understand the development of social representations. Anchoring is about classifying and providing a name for unfamiliar objects by comparing that which is experienced against the collection of familiar classes of event, namely relating to a prototype. If the unfamiliar object is similar to the **prototype** it is assigned the characteristics of the prototype. If the unfamiliar is dissimilar to the prototype it is adjusted so as to fit the characteristics of the prototype. Objectification refers to the mechanism by which the unfamiliar (or abstract) is changed into concrete reality (that is, they become objectified). This process is similar to the use of metaphor in everyday language to explain and understand abstract concepts. Three processes are responsible for objectification – the translation of the abstract into the concrete (Moscovici and Hewstone, 1983); the **personification** of knowledge provides a connection between the concept and some person or group (e.g. Skinner and behaviourism) and a concrete existence for the concept; **figuration** refers to the use of metaphorical images in language to give the abstract notion a more concrete flavour (e.g. butter mountains for overproduction of foodstuffs, and so on) (Hewstone, 1986); and finally, **ontologizing** is the processes by which physical characteristics are attributed to some concept or idea, or how the immaterial becomes materialized.

CURRENT USAGE

A limited number of studies have utilized the premises outlined in social representation theory to examine beliefs about health and illness. Herzlich (1973) interviewed 80 adults to explore their social representations about the meaning of health and illness. From the detailed analysis a number of points emerged. People found it very difficult to separate the ideas of being healthy from more than not just being ill. They appeared to think of health as the outcome of balanced physical, psychological and emotional states within each person. As such when these systems are not in equilibrium a person may be said to be in a state of ill-health. In addition, it was argued that being active was the core concept taken by most people to be indicative of being healthy. The lay perception of health was that people who are active are healthy, those who are inactive (or in some way not able to be active) are unhealthy or unwell (Radley, 1994). Finally, Herzlich (1973) pointed to a further three representations that individuals have to illness and which detailed lay reactions to the experience of illness. Illness was seen as being destructive (derived from the experience of those involved in society), as a liberator (derived from those who report major social obligations) or as an occupation (derived from those who accept that illness happens and act to change the ill state to a healthy state). Not only do people appear to classify other individuals as fitting into one of the 'destructive', 'liberator' or 'occupation' categories, the work showed that all people represent ill-health in these ways and use any one of them according to the particular circumstances they find themselves in.

More recent work has extended the use of social representations to include not only how people report the experience of ill-health or well being but also how other major sources of information and communication represent these concepts (e.g. Joffe, 2003). Using the constructs of anchoring and objectification from social representation theory, Joffe (1996) was able to paint a picture of how people in the United Kingdom and South Africa were representing AIDS by studying what these people said and also by undertaking a content analysis of media reports of the illness. Joffe argued first that AIDS was anchored in the perceived peculiar behaviour of other people because, on the whole, individuals were able to distance themselves from the threat of disease, namely, 'I don't inject drugs (or have unprotected anal intercourse) and cannot be at risk of contracting HIV/AIDS'. However, Joffe (1996) also noted that these types of beliefs have been objectified (when an abstract notion is transformed into a concrete image), with the emergence of AIDS as affecting all groups and being reflected in media images of tombstones. In other words, people's fears associated with the threat of AIDS were made more concrete and represented as such. A similar representational picture emerged among young people in Zambia, who attempted to distance themselves from the threat of HIV/AIDS by representing it as being associated with deviant sexual acts and also by viewing it as a Western disease (Joffe and Bettega, 2004).

While social representations theory is not new, research in the domain of health psychology has been more limited than that undertaken utilizing social cognitive theory. Social representations are important in the study of how people think about illnesses because they take account, in effect, of shared thinking or shared beliefs and are important for determining and establishing identity within a group. Understanding that people use these shared beliefs, and use them in a predictable manner, adds another dimension by taking the interpretation of thinking processes outside of people's heads and into the consensual social world. While work has been carried out in establishing how individuals represent different illnesses, little has emerged to examine the role of these representations in formulating actual health-related behaviour.

SIGNIFICANCE TO HEALTH PSYCHOLOGY

Further reading

Joffe, H. (2003) Social representations and health psychology. *Social Science Information*, 41, 559–580.

Outlines the role of social representations in understanding how and why people adopt (or do not adopt) healthy behaviours. Provides an interesting synthesis of the everyday thinking processes involved in the experience of health and illness.

See also **illness-related and sick role beliefs and discourse and illness**

ILLNESS-RELATED AND SICK ROLE BELIEFS
and: DISCOURSE AND ILLNESS

Like social representation theory (see the concept in this chapter), psychologists who emphasize discursive mechanisms for understanding experience and behaviour reject the social cognitive approach on the grounds that it assumes perceptions (including illness- or health-related ones) as being static and existing only in people's minds. **Discursive psychologists** would argue that experience is predominantly social in nature and is concerned not with inferred, unobservable and static beliefs (as in social cognitive approaches), but with how language and discourse are used to describe experience. This approach also emphasizes explicitly that what people say should be interpreted in terms of both current and historical context.

MEANING

Discursive psychology has its roots in **social constructionism** (Gergen, 1973). Social constructionists suggest that social experiences are forever changing and as

ORIGINS

135

such we can only examine how the world appears at the time at which we are looking at it. In addition, theorists argue that knowledge and experience of the social world are created (or constructed) by language, culture and history (McGhee, 2001). Ultimately, reality is argued to be socially constructed through interactions in the social world. Given these ideas, for social constructionists the best way to understand why people behave in the ways they do is to study what they say and how they say it while taking account of current context in the individual's personal history (Gough and McFadden, 2001). For social constrctionists, language is fundamental in understanding the constructions people hold about their social worlds. As well as being a communication device for transmitting feelings and thoughts, language is also an action because it plays a major role in constructing the social world (Potter and Wetherell, 1987).

One predominant method for studying language is through the use of **discourse analysis** in which the researcher seeks to undertake a 'reading' or 'interpretative account' of the text or conversation by isolating a number of strategies used by participants in their language. For example, so called **interpretative repertoires** of discourse are isolated. These are the types of metaphors and images used in everyday talk to 'construct' an object (Wetherell, 1997). These repertoires are used in contradictory ways by the same person in differing contexts such as the goals that people bring to their interactions. Take as an example the types of repertoires that people may use about drug addicts. When discussing drug addicts, one interpretative repertoire may be that drug addicts are dangerous people, thieves, irresponsible, untrustworthy and a drain on society. Another may be that drug addicts are the victims of social conditions, helpless, controlled by an evil drug, and so on. These repertoires are contradictory and may be used by the same person when talking about 'drug addicts'. A related area of study is the use of narratives (or the stories people tell – written or verbal) to analyse and interpret the experience of illness. According to Murray (1997) people construct stories about their illness experiences as a means of providing meaning for themselves and in order to generate control or ownership over the illness.

CURRENT USAGE

Over recent years there has been a move towards providing more social constructionist accounts of health beliefs and behaviours (see Murray, 2004) and the use of discursive methods of enquiry (Willig, 1998, 2004). For example, one study examined discourse in mothers with asthma about their illness experience (Radtke and van Mens-Verhulst, 2001). When discussing the causes of the illness these women invariably produced the standard medical conception and at the same time distanced their illness far away from their role as a mother. In another study Gillies and Willig (1997) examined discourse in cigarette smokers. They were particularly interested in how women constructed their smoking behaviour and how these constructions were embedded in that smoking behaviour. Results showed that, in general, these women appeared to construct their accounts of smoking in terms of a discourse that was related primarily to addiction. In particular, the participants viewed their smoking behaviour as a result of physiological addiction (to the chemical nicotine) and psychological dependence. They also perceived themselves as victims of these dependency processes. In effect, it seems that these types of discourse point towards the idea that for these participants smoking was about some external agency. In other words, smokers are helpless and not in control – the dependency has passed the behaviour in effect onto the environment, and as such the smoker is not at fault or to blame for their behaviour. For Gillies and Willig (1997) the discourse of addiction used in the construction of smoking behaviour acts in a way that is disempowering for the smoker. If a person constructs their smoking in terms of physiological and psychological addiction and that addiction manifests itself in helplessness or challenged control (that is, a self-regulatory process), the chances are that these participants are unlikely to give up. This work complements other perspectives on the nature of addiction (e.g. see Orford, 2001) and provides an interesting language-based account of the meaning (or construction) of personal behaviour.

A recent method for using discourse to examine the illness representations of individuals and the experience of health and ill-health takes a phenomenological approach and is called **interpretative phenomenological analysis** (IPA) (Smith, 1996). IPA 'explores personal experience and is concerned with an individual's personal perception or account of an object or event, as opposed to an attempt to produce an objective statement of the object or event itself' (Smith and Osborn, 2003: 51). IPA also emphasizes the significance of the researcher in the dynamic process of understanding what the participant is 'saying'. It assumes that there is an association between what people say and how they think and feel about an object in their social worlds. As such, IPA results in the staged identification of a number of key themes in the transcripts of detailed participant interviews (see Smith and Osborn, 2003, for a detailed examination of IPA procedures).

IPA has been used to examine a number of health-related issues including obesity surgery (Ogden et al., 2006), risk perception in genetic testing (Smith et al., 2002) and vulnerability to heart disease (Senior et al., 2002) among others (see Brocki and Wearden, 2006, for a full review). For example, in a study of chronic benign lower back pain Osborn and Smith (1998) identified four key themes that represented the meaning of experience of the ailment for patients. These were the need to search for an explanation of the illness; seeking to understand the predicament by comparing oneself to others; not being believed or judged appropriately by other people; ultimately withdrawing from others.

SIGNIFICANCE TO HEALTH PSYCHOLOGY

Discursive approaches to the study of illness beliefs and behaviours are useful to health psychology by incorporating an emphasis on how people's beliefs and behaviours may be constructed in the social world as opposed to being strictly determined by internal cognitive mechanisms. In addition, using discursive approaches considers the role of context and history in a participant's reports about some experience, such as ill-health. However, how the constructions utilized by people in their language about a health issue are translated into the decisions made by them in particular contexts, and the behaviours adopted subsequently have not been the main focus of enquiry.

Further reading

Murray, M. (ed.) (2004) *Critical Health Psychology*. London: Palgrave.
An interesting account of health psychology emphasizing what can be learnt from exploring people's experience of health and illness through, among other factors, discourse about their experience.

Smith, J.A. and Osborn, M. (2003) Interpretative phenomenological analysis. In J.A. Smith (ed.), *Qualitative Psychology: A Practical Guide to Research Methods*. Thousand Oaks, CA: Sage. pp. 51–80.
Details a contemporary qualitative and interpretation method for exploring how people experience health and illness. Used quite extensively in current research.

See also **illness-related and sick role beliefs and social representations of illness**

ACUTE AND CHRONIC ILLNESS

7

SEVEN

ACUTE AND CHRONIC ILLNESS
and: **coronary heart disease**
   HIV/AIDS
   cancer
   sexually transmitted disease
   hospitalization and surgery
   disability

One of the ultimate goals of health psychology is to understand the causes and consequences of illness, and develop interventions to reduce the burden of disease. In this chapter we discuss some of the predominant acute and chronic illnesses which affect large numbers of individuals across the lifespan. These include coronary heart disease and cancer, two of the leading causes of early death in the developed world, and disability which, while not necessarily life-threatening, presents a substantial burden on both the individual and society. We also discuss the impact of hospitalization and surgery, events which can present a psychological threat in addition to the physical impact of the surgery. In particular, we focus on the role that health psychology can play, both in understanding the causes of these illnesses, and in intervening to reduce the risk of them occurring.

ACUTE AND CHRONIC ILLNESS
and: CORONARY HEART DISEASE

MEANING **Coronary heart disease** (CHD) is caused by hardening of the arteries (known as atherosclerosis), following the accumulation of fatty deposits (known as plaques) on the arterial walls, in particular affecting those arteries which directly supply the heart. While the symptoms and signs of CHD can be seen in the advanced stages of the disease, it is common for most individuals with CHD to show no evidence of disease for several years. Disease progression can continue for some time in the absence of symptoms or signs, with the first onset of symptoms often being a heart attack (**myocardial infarction**), caused by an interruption of the blood supply to the heart due to blockage.

ORIGINS CHD is one of the leading causes of death in the developed world, accounting for approximately one third of all deaths (in particular, among men aged below 65 years). There is a marked variation in the incidence of CHD across socio-economic groups, with those in manual employment at higher risk of suffering death from CHD. In middle age, the risk of death from CHD is far higher in men than in women, although after 65 years of age the risk is approximately equal for males and females.

Cross-cultural research has indicated that there are marked differences in the incidence of CHD across countries, and in particular death rates from CHD. For example, individuals in Russia have very high death rates from CHD, while those in France and Japan have very low rates. Within Europe, the northern countries typically demonstrate a higher incidence of CHD, while the southern countries show lower incidence. These findings suggest an important role for lifestyle factors, and in particular diet, in CHD.

CURRENT USAGE It has been recognized for some time that lifestyle factors strongly influence the risk of CHD (see above). These include a family history of CHD, cigarette smoking, elevated blood pressure, high levels of low density lipoprotein (LDL) and low levels of high density lipoprotein (HDL) cholesterol, physical inactivity, diabetes, obesity and stress. Risk factors for CHD can be broadly classified as modifiable and non-modifiable. Examples of modifiable risk factors include lifestyle factors such as physical inactivity, obesity, stress, smoking and so on, while examples of non-modifiable risk factors include socio-economic status, sex, family history and educational status.

Prevention of CHD targets modifiable risk factors, which include decreasing cholesterol levels, reducing obesity and hypertension, increasing levels of physical activity, adopting a healthy diet, stopping smoking, and consuming a moderate quantity of alcohol. In the case of diabetes, there is little evidence that good blood sugar control actually reduces the risk of CHD. There has been considerable interest in the consumption of omega-3 fatty acids in the diet to reduce the risk of CHD, although the evidence that these are effective is mixed.

In addition to focusing on modifiable risk factors, there is considerable current scientific interest in other physiological mechanisms, which may account for the substantial inherited risk of CHD (since family history remains one of the strongest risk factors). For example, one such marker is low density lipoprotein, so that individuals with CHD are advised to avoid fats that are readily oxidized (e.g. saturated fats) and to limit carbohydrate consumption to reduce production of LDL cholesterol while increasing HDL cholesterol. In other words, identification of biological markers for CHD may serve to validate the effectiveness of behavioural interventions designed to address modifiable risk factors such as diet, as well as identify individuals at higher risk of CHD who might benefit most from these behavioural interventions.

Given the importance of CHD as a leading cause of death in the developed world, and given the large number of modifiable risk factors which are known to contribute to the incidence of CHD, health psychology has a considerable amount to offer in terms of understanding and modifying the behaviours which increase CHD risk. For example, up to a quarter of deaths caused by CHD are related to cigarette smoking, while diet (and in particular cholesterol levels) is another major modifiable risk factor. Both of these are amenable to behavioural interventions delivered by health psychologists.

SIGNIFICANCE TO HEALTH PSYCHOLOGY

There is also interest in risk factors related to personality, and the most extensively investigated of these is **Type A personality**, first described by Friedman and Rosenman in 1959. A Type A personality is characterized by high levels of time urgency and impatience, competitiveness, hostility and activity, and has repeatedly been shown to be a risk factor for CHD. Nevertheless, there remains debate regarding whether the association between Type A personality and CHD operates directly due to intrinsic factors (e.g. an inherited disposition to both Type A behaviour and CHD), or indirectly via the effects of the behaviours associated with the Type A personality (such as poor diet, increased tobacco and alcohol consumption, lack of sleep, and so on). It should be noted that the relationship between Type A behaviours and CHD remains controversial, with its strength, nature and even direction frequently debated.

Stress is another risk factor for CHD which is relevant to health psychology, in particular given the central role of **psychoneuroimmunology** in the understanding of the subjective experience of stress and its impact on health. While exposure to environmental stressors has robustly been demonstrated via the increase in the risk of CHD, this is heavily influenced by the *subjective perception* of these stressors. In particular, perceived lack of control over environmental stressors (for example the demands of one's job) appears to be an important risk factor for CHD.

Health psychology, therefore, plays a role both in the understanding of the aetiology of CHD, and in its prevention. Behaviour modification of a range of lifestyle factors, including smoking, diet, exercise and alcohol consumption, has been shown to result in important reductions in the risk of CHD. Such programmes typically offer health education on the benefits of behaviour change (such as the promotion of smoking cessation or the consumption of five portions of fruit and vegetables daily). These interventions are sometimes allied with motivational counseling, group support and telephone follow-up in more intensive programmes. While time-intensive in the short term, these programmes are extremely cost-effective in the long term because of the prolonged benefits of sustained behavioural change to the health of the individual and, on a larger scale, the public health of the population targeted.

Similar interventions have also been developed to target Type A behaviours, which typically focus on health education, relaxation, and a reduction in work demands, to counter the high levels of hostility and stress typical of the Type A personality. Stress management more generally, comprising relaxation techniques and general life management (e.g. time management), has been shown to reduce many of the risk factors associated with CHD, including elevated blood pressure and cholesterol and Type A behaviours.

Further reading

Fekete, E.M., Antoni, M.H. and Schneiderman, N. (2007) Psychosocial and behavioral interventions for chronic medical conditions. *Current Opinion in Psychiatry*, 20, 152–157.
Reviews the evidence for a range of psychosocial and behavioural interventions for chronic diseases including cardiovascular disease, HIV/AIDS and cancer.

Matthews, K.A. (2005) Psychological perspectives on the development of coronary heart disease. *American Psychologist*, 60, 783–796.
Provides an overview of advances in understanding the aetiology of heart disease, and accumulating evidence for the importance of psychosocial predictors of clinical and subclinical coronary disease.

Sebregts, E.H., Falger, P.R. and Bar, F.W. (2000) Risk factor modification through nonpharmacological interventions in patients with coronary heart disease. *Journal of Psychosomatic Research*, 48, 425–441.
Reviews the evidence for the effectiveness of behaviour modification interventions designed to target modifiable risk factors to reduce the risk of coronary heart disease.

See also **addictive behaviours and alcohol; addictive behaviours and tobacco**

ACUTE AND CHRONIC ILLNESS
and: HIV/AIDS

MEANING The **human immunodeficiency virus** (HIV) is a retrovirus that causes **acquired immunodeficiency syndrome** (AIDS), a condition in humans in which the immune system begins to fail over a prolonged period, eventually leading to life-threatening infections. Infection with HIV occurs by the transfer of bodily fluids; the three major routes of transmission are unprotected sexual intercourse, contaminated needles, and mother-to-child transmission (at birth, or via breast milk). Screening of blood products for HIV infection in the developed world has largely eliminated transmission through blood transfusions or infected blood products in these countries.

AIDS was first identified as a new syndrome in 1981, and because the first cases were restricted to the homosexual population it was considered to be specific to this group. However, following the occurrence of AIDS in haemophiliacs shortly after its initial identification, and the observation that at least half of the reported cases did not occur in homosexual men, it became increasingly clear that the syndrome was the result of a viral infection. This could account for the infection of haemophiliacs, through their treatment with blood products, unlike early explanations which focused on supposed lifestyle factors among homosexual groups. Subsequently, HIV was identified in 1983. It is a retrovirus (namely, a virus which contains RNA – ribonucleic acid), and specifically a lentivirus (which means that it has effects which develop slowly over a long period of time).

ORIGINS

AIDS is now considered pandemic in humans, with over 30 million individuals worldwide living with HIV/AIDS, including approximately 1 million children. When HIV infection occurs there may be a period of several years before any impact on immune function is detectable. When this occurs it is typically reflected in a reduction in the number of T-helper cells (also known as CD4 cells) available, accompanied by the onset of symptoms. AIDS is diagnosed once symptoms reach a specific threshold, reflected in the individual contracting one of several opportunistic diseases associated with impaired immune function. It is now possible, however, to assess the concentration of viral particles in the blood to give an index of the degree of infection by HIV prior to the onset of symptoms.

CURRENT USAGE

Medical treatments for HIV/AIDS include both treatments for the opportunistic disease which characterizes the onset of AIDS, and anti-retroviral treatment to inhibit HIV reproduction and delay the onset of AIDS. The latter requires adherence to a strict medication regimen (indeed, a large number of individuals fail to adhere to the regimen because of the complexity), is not successful for all individuals, and can result in serious side effects (also leading to poor adherence). Most importantly, while antiretroviral treatments may inhibit HIV reproduction they are not a cure for the disease. AIDS is fatal and most individuals with the syndrome die within a few years of diagnosis. It remains unclear what factors influence survival following the onset of AIDS, but there is considerable variation between individuals. Some of this variability may be due to genetic factors, but there is also evidence that psychobiological factors, such as high levels of stress reactivity, may be associated with a poorer prognosis.

In large part due to the uncertainty regarding the aetiology of HIV/AIDS in the early 1980s, the condition has aroused strong feelings of fear and uncertainty, frequently leading to discrimination. Initially it was not uncommon for stories in the media to appear reporting that those diagnosed with AIDS suffered various forms of discrimination, from losing their jobs to being refused treatment by health workers. This situation has improved considerably over the last two decades, but a diagnosis of AIDS still results in fear and discrimination from others. Those diagnosed with AIDS frequently report that one of the consequences which is most difficult to cope with about their condition is the lack of physical contact with others resulting from this fear. An unfortunate consequence of the stigma associated with HIV/AIDS is that some delay being tested for HIV because of fears about the implications of the diagnosis.

SIGNIFICANCE TO HEALTH PSYCHOLOGY

Given the still limited understanding of the aetiology and progression of HIV/AIDS, in particular with respect to lifestyle factors which may promote survival, it might not be clear at first glance what health psychology has to offer. However, the chronic nature of the illness, and in particular the very strong emotional and social consequences of diagnosis, suggest that psychosocial interventions may be valuable in managing these consequences, for example by reducing distress. Behavioural interventions have been shown to be effective in reducing distress, improving sleep and managing pain (in the later stages of the disease).

There are also a number of other ways in which health psychology may inform our understanding and treatment of HIV/AIDS, although many of these require further research. For example, since exposure to HIV is usually a consequence of specific behaviours (e.g. needle sharing among intravenous drug users, unprotected sexual intercourse, and so on), health education and motivational counseling interventions may serve to modify key health behaviours which increase the risk of infection.

There is also considerable research interest in behavioural factors which influence susceptibility to the HIV virus, the progression of the disease and the onset of AIDS, and survival following the onset of AIDS. This research draws heavily on **psychoneuroimmunology**, given the central importance of immune function in the disease. There is evidence, for example, that peripheral lifestyle factors such as drug use and other unhealthy behaviours may not only increase risk of *exposure* to HIV, but may also increase the risk of *infection* following exposure, possibly by impairing immune function prior to the exposure. These factors may also influence the progression from HIV infection to the onset of AIDS, via the same mechanisms. The psychoneuroimmunological study of HIV/AIDS is enhanced by the ability to accurately index disease progression via the measurement of T-helper (CD4) cell activity.

Some studies have also suggested that psychological factors, such as **locus of control** and **self-efficacy** beliefs, have an impact on disease progression and survival, via effects on immunosuppression (see Psychoneuroimmunology for a more detailed discussion of these processes). These effects may not be unique to HIV/AIDS (effects of mood and stress on immune function occur in all individuals), but may be of particular importance because of the nature of the disease. In particular, active coping styles (as opposed to passive, fatalistic coping) have been associated with relatively improved immune function. Interventions to promote such coping styles may therefore be valuable in treating HIV/AIDS.

Further reading

Chippindale, S. and French, L. (2001) HIV counselling and the psychosocial manage-ment of patients with HIV or AIDS. *British Medical Journal*, 322, 1533–1535.
Brief overview of the role of counseling and psychosocial interventions in the man-agement of patients with HIV or AIDS, in the context of an holistic (that is, biopsy-chosocial) model of healthcare.

Fekete, E.M., Antoni, M.H. and Schneiderman, N. (2007) Psychosocial and behav-ioral interventions for chronic medical conditions. *Current Opinion in Psychiatry*, 20, 152–157.
Reviews the evidence for a range of psychosocial and behavioural interventions for chronic diseases, including cardiovascular disease, HIV/AIDS and cancer.

See also **acute and chronic illness and sexually transmitted disease; biological and physiological models and psychoneuroimmunology**

ACUTE AND CHRONIC ILLNESS
and: CANCER

Cancer is one of the leading causes of death in the developed world. It is a broad class of diseases or disorders, the principal characteristic of which is the uncon-trolled division of cells, and the spread of these to other regions and systems, lead-ing to **tumours** (also called **neoplasms**). This spread may occur through direct growth into adjacent tissue, or by transfer and implantation into more remote sites. The latter process is called metastasis, and involves the transportation of cancer cells through the bloodstream of lymphatic systems. Cancer may affect people at all ages, but risk tends to increase with age for the majority of cancers.

MEANING

Tumours can be classified into two kinds: **benign** (which do not spread), and **malig-nant** (which do spread, for example by metastasis). In antiquity, benign tumours were described by Hippocrates as *oncos* (from the Greek for swelling, and from which we derive the modern word oncology, to describe the branch of medicine that deals with tumours). Malignant tumours were described as *carcinos* (from the Greek

ORIGINS

for crab, probably because of the physical appearance of solid malignant tumours, and from which we derive modern words such as carcinogenic, to mean anything capable of promoting cancer). Understanding of the nature of cancer advanced considerably in the eighteenth century with the widespread use of the microscope, while the discovery of radiation in the nineteenth century led to the first effective non-surgical treatment for cancer. The discovery in the twentieth century of marked differences in the incidence of various cancers across countries indicated a possible role for environmental and lifestyle factors in the aetiology of cancer.

CURRENT USAGE

Cancer is one of the leading causes of death in the developed world (and the second leading cause of death in the UK and most developed countries, accounting for approximately one quarter of all deaths). Among men, the main cancers associated with mortality (in rank order) include lung cancer, colorectal cancer and prostrate cancer, while among women they are breast cancer, lung cancer, colorectal cancer, ovarian cancer and cervical cancer. It is notable that the majority of the increase in cancer death rates in the second half of the twentieth century was due to deaths from lung cancer.

There are four main subdivisions or types of cancer. Carcinomas are malignant neoplasms of cells of the skin and organ lining or certain organs including the digestive, respiratory and reproductive tracts, and account for the majority (approximately 80 per cent) of human cancers. Lymphomas are cancers of the lymphatic system (which is the network of vessels carrying lymph, circulating through various organs involved in the production and storage infection-fighting cells). Sarcomas are malignant neoplasms of muscle, bone and other connective tissue such as cartilage. Leukemias are the cancer of organs involved in blood production, such as bone marrow.

The two main factors influencing prognosis for cancer are the site of the cancer and how early it is detected. Diagnosis involves blood or urine tests (to reveal hormonal abnormalities which may reflect cancer), imaging techniques such as X-ray (to detect tumours in internal organs), and the tissue sampling or biopsy of a potentially cancerous site (for analysis for the presence of cancerous cells). Treatments include surgery (to remove large clusters of cancerous cells), radiological treatments (to destroy or inactivate cancerous cells using intense radiation) and chemotherapy (to kill rapidly dividing cells, such as cancerous cells, using powerful drugs), all of which may be used individually or in combination. Again, a decision regarding the best treatment will depend on the site of the cancer and how early it is detected. Radiation therapy and chemotherapy both carry the risk of severe and potentially problematic side-effects, such as fatigue, nausea, vomiting, hair loss and sterility.

SIGNIFICANCE TO HEALTH PSYCHOLOGY

Health psychology can inform our understanding and treatment of cancer in two broad ways: one is the extent to which psychosocial factors are involved in the aetiology of cancer and a subsequent prognosis (for example, by increasing or decreasing risk), while another is the extent to which the consequences of cancer (such as distress) can be understood and managed within a psychosocial framework.

Behavioural factors clearly play an important role in increasing or decreasing the risk of cancer. The most striking example of this is the relationship between cigarette smoking and lung cancer, with approximately 90 per cent of lung cancer cases being diagnosed in smokers. In general, tobacco use is associated with almost a third of cancers, while diet also plays a role in a similar proportion. Alcohol use and sexual activity also are important, although much less so than tobacco consumption and diet. Environmental factors, such as stressful life events, have also been reported to increase the risk of cancer, although the evidence for this is not clear-cut. This may be due to the variation in how life events are *perceived* across individuals, and subjective stress may be more strongly associated with cancer, for which there is evidence from animal studies.

Psychological and cognitive factors, such as personality and coping style, also play a role, both in the risk of cancer and in the progression of the disease. The **Type C personality** (see also Coronary Heart Disease), characterized by passivity and a perceived helplessness, has been reported to be related to the risk of cancer, as has a perceived lack of control over stressors. Coping strategies may also be related to behaviours which increase the risk of cancer or influence prognosis – for example, coping strategies which involve smoking or drinking alcohol in response to stress.

As with all chronic illnesses, cancer involves a number of specific threats and difficulties. In addition, the frequently progressive nature of cancer means that these change over time, potentially becoming worse and more complex. To add to this, many of the treatments which exist for cancer lead to further difficulties – for example, the side-effects of chemotherapy, in particular fatigue, nausea and vomiting (all of which can be extremely severe), are highly distressing for the patient. Other side-effects, such as hair loss, can lead to social embarrassment and potential stigmatization, given societal fears of cancer. Even though cancer is not transmissible, patients frequently report a reduction in close and physical contact, which can be distressing (see also HIV/AIDS).

A substantial proportion of cancer patients demonstrate symptoms of depression, anxiety, anger and grief, although the strength of these symptoms varies over time, and some individuals do not demonstrate a severe emotional response. Active coping styles and feelings of control have been reported to be associated with lower levels of emotional distress, while passivity, helplessness and rumination are associated with higher levels of distress. There is also some evidence that active coping styles are associated with improved prognosis and greater longevity, with personality and environmental stress also playing a role. These relationships are complex, however, and considerable debate remains regarding whether psychosocial factors do indeed play a role in cancer survival.

One unique and highly specific role for psychology in cancer relates to the nausea and vomiting associated with chemotherapy, and in particular the *anticipatory* nausea and vomiting which sometimes precedes this. Anticipatory nausea and vomiting arises through a process of **classical conditioning**, whereby the chemotherapy becomes associated with other cues such as the treatment room, or the clinical staff administering the treatment. In some cases, the foods consumed in the last meal prior to the chemotherapy come to trigger nausea and vomiting, as a learned taste aversion. One promising approach to counter this has been to eat a novel and strongly flavoured food in between the last meal and the chemotherapy treatment, so that it is *this* which becomes disliked, rather than foods in the normal diet. Other psychosocial treatments used in cancer patients include pain management techniques (involving **relaxation** and **biofeedback**), body image counseling (in particular following surgical interventions, for example for breast cancer), and training in active and adaptive coping strategies.

Further reading

Fekete, E.M., Antoni, M.H. and Schneiderman, N. (2007) Psychosocial and behavioral interventions for chronic medical conditions. *Current Opinion in Psychiatry*, 20, 152–157.
Reviews the evidence for a range of psychosocial and behavioural interventions for chronic diseases, including cardiovascular disease, HIV/AIDS and cancer.

Uitterhoeve, R.J., Vernooy, M., Litjens, M., Potting, K., Bensing, J., De Mulder, P. and van Achterberg, T. (2004) Psychosocial interventions for patients with advanced cancer – a systematic review of the literature. *British Journal of Cancer*, 91, 1050–1062.
Systematic review of psychosocial intervention studies designed to improve Quality of Life in cancer patients, in particular in the domain of emotional distress and emotional functioning.

See also **acute and chronic illness and coronary heart disease; acute and chronic illness and HIV/Aids**

ACUTE AND CHRONIC ILLNESS
and: SEXUALLY TRANSMITTED DISEASE

MEANING **Sexually transmitted diseases** (STDs) are diseases caused by sexually transmitted infections that have a substantial probability of transmission between humans by means of sexual contact. Some of the these can be also transmitted by other means such as mother-to-child transmission (e.g. at birth or via breast milk), or through needle sharing among intravenous drug users. Clinicians are increasingly using the term **sexually transmitted infection** as distinct from the **sexually transmitted disease**, since infection does not necessarily mean that symptoms are present (see HIV/AIDS).

Until relatively recently in the history of medicine, STDs were generally incurable, and treatment was limited to symptom management. The discovery of antibiotics, however, meant that many STDs became curable. In addition, public health campaigns in the 1960s and 1970s resulted in increased public awareness of STDs. These two factors have resulted in a marked decline in the prevalence of STDs in the developed world.

ORIGINS

In the 1980s, genital herpes and in particular HIV/AIDS emerged into the public consciousness as STDs that remained incurable. In particular, HIV/AIDS has a long asymptomatic period, during which time HIV can be transmitted to others. Vigorous public health campaigns were initiated to improve public awareness of HIV/AIDS, and to dispel initial misconceptions that the disease was limited to certain groups only. Nevertheless, HIV/AIDS is now pandemic, in particular in developing countries (see HIV/AIDS).

Sexually transmitted diseases can be classified into four broad groups of infection: viral (e.g. Chlamydia and gonorrhea), bacterial (e.g. hepatitis B, herpes simplex, HIV), parasitic (e.g. pubic lice), and protozoal (e.g. trichomoniasis, a form of vaginitis). The most effective method for the prevention of sexual transmission of sexually transmitted infections (STIs) and subsequent STDs is to avoid sexual contact with an infected individual. The asymptomatic and covert nature of STDs, however, means that this is difficult to achieve in practice without testing for infection status. While this is possible among partners in a romantic relationship, it is impractical in other settings such as casual sexual intercourse. If a person chooses to have sexual intercourse with a partner whose infection status is unknown, condom use markedly reduces the likelihood of infection, although it will not completely protect against the risk of infection due to the possibility of breakage and the risk that the pathogen may be present outside the protected skin.

CURRENT USAGE

As well as the widespread availability of condoms, it is increasingly possible to purchase home testing kits for common STDs such as Chlamydia (which is highly prevalent in countries such as the UK, affecting up to 10 per cent of young adults aged under 25). These have the advantage of avoiding the stigma associated with attending a genitor-urinary or sexual health clinic, although questions have been raised regarding the appropriateness of tests which, if positive, require medical treatment and advice (for example, informing other partners who may also be infected).

Modern society increasingly emphasizes sexual intercourse as an activity, as opposed to a means to reproduction, although the acceptability of this varies enormously across countries. Sexual activity is common and there has been considerable research interest into sexual behaviour, and in particular contraception use and the practice of 'safe sex' (namely, barrier contraception), among young people. Health psychology can play a prominent role in understanding sexual health behaviours and decision-making processes regarding contraception use.

SIGNIFICANCE TO HEALTH PSYCHOLOGY

A number of factors appear to influence decision making regarding contraceptive use, including the age of the individual (young people are less likely to use contraception), sex (women are more likely), socio-economic status (although this remains controversial) and educational level (with higher education attainment associated with greater likelihood of use). It is unclear, however, what mechanisms mediate these relationships, and to what extent they are amenable to intervention.

Of more relevance to health psychologists are a number of intrapersonal factors which have been shown to influence contraceptive use, as these are more likely to be amenable to intervention. For example, knowledge about contraceptive use, STDs and the risks and consequences of infection is relatively weakly related to sexual health behaviour, but this is against a background of relatively poor overall knowledge. Actual attitudes to contraception use appear to be linked more strongly to behaviour, and recent public health campaigns have attempted to address attitudes, for example by emphasizing personal responsibility and maturity as being associated with contraceptive use.

Given the strong influence of interpersonal (such as peer influence, parental attitudes) and situational (e.g. accessibility of contraception, spontaneity) factors, it is perhaps unsurprising that intrapersonal factors such as attitudes are only modestly related to actual behaviour. Health behaviour models such as the **Health Belief Model**, the **Theory of Reasoned Action** and the **Theory of Planned Behaviour** have all attempted to model the relationship between attitudes and sexual health behaviour.

In general, the Health Belief Model has been unsuccessful in predicting condom use, for a number of possible reasons, such as the emotional nature of sexual activity, the interactive nature of the exchange (namely, two people are required to make the decision!) and, in particular, a failure by young people to acknowledge their personal susceptibility. The Theory of Reasoned Action and the Theory of Planned Behaviour have had more success at predicting condom use, although this success is still modest in absolute terms, with the most important predictors (in the context of these models) being those which relate to normative beliefs regarding condom use among peers, friends, previous sexual partners and so on.

In general, the variety of populations between which normative beliefs regarding sexual behaviour may differ (e.g. adult versus adolescent, religious versus non-religious, heterosexual versus homosexual) suggests that it may always be difficult to establish a single model which strongly predicts condom use and other sexual behaviour. The social, interactive and transactional nature of sexual activity also presents another challenge to **social cognition models**, which typically focus on individual cognitions. Finally, there is widespread evidence of **optimistic bias**, the tendency to believe that one is less at risk than the average member of society, among young people in general, and with respect to perceptions of susceptibility to STDs in particular.

Further reading

Donovan, B. (2004) Sexually transmissible infections other than HIV. *Lancet*, 363, 545–556.

Outlines the prevalence of a range of STIs other than HIV, discusses their role in the transmission of HIV, and looks at the necessary public health, social and political measures required to tackle their spread.

van Empelen, P., Kok, G., van Kesteren, N.M., van den Borne, B., Bos, A.E. and Schaalma, H.P. (2003) Effective methods to change sex-risk among drug users: a review of psychosocial interventions. *Social Science and Medicine*, 57, 1593–1608.

Reviews behavioural and psychosocial interventions designed to target modifiable risk behaviours (specifically, sexual risk behaviours) among drug users, who are a particularly high risk group.

See also **acute and chronic illness and HIV/Aids**

ACUTE AND CHRONIC ILLNESS
and: HOSPITALIZATION AND SURGERY

MEANING

Hospitalization refers to the admission to hospital as an inpatient for a period which may be brief or extended but which typically entails at least one overnight stay. Some patients undergo diagnosis and/or therapy and then leave without an overnight stay (**outpatients**), while others are admitted and stay overnight or for several weeks or months (**inpatients**). Hospitals are usually distinguished from other types of medical facilities by their ability to admit and care for inpatients. Hospitalization is a potentially stressful experience in its own right, but this may be exacerbated by the nature of the condition, for which the patient may be undergoing diagnostic tests or medical procedures undertaken during the hospitalization period. In particular, surgical procedures are widely regarded as stressful and threatening, due to unpredictable and uncontrollable features of the procedure such as loss of consciousness during anaesthesia.

ORIGINS

Hospitals in various forms have existed for several centuries, and can be traced back to antiquity. During this time, the function served by hospitals and their equivalent has varied substantially – in the Middle Ages, for example, they served a wider range of functions, including as almshouses for the poor. The word is derived from the Latin word *hospes*, meaning host. Hospitals in the developed world, in a role similar to that which we would recognize today, began to become common in the eighteenth century.

As medical science advanced and the number of effective treatments increased rapidly, networks of hospitals funded by the public and private sector became established across Europe and North America.

CURRENT USAGE

The trend in recent years has been for inpatient stays to be reduced, with many minor procedures now being carried out on an outpatient basis to further reduce the length of time spent in hospital by patients. While this is partly for cost-saving purposes, it is also driven by evidence that shorter hospital stays do not seem to be associated with poorer health outcomes. Given the fact that hospitalization is a potentially stressful experience, as well as being one that carries risks in itself (for example as a result of exposure to the MRSA virus, an antiobiotic-resistant bacterium that increases the risk of potentially life-threatening illnesses such as pneumonia, in particular among vulnerable groups such as hospitalized patients), this trend is likely to continue. Indeed, a recent White Paper in the UK identified the reduction in length of stay as a component of efficiency – one of the key performance indicators against which hospitals would be appraised.

Nevertheless, there is an inherent tension between reducing the length of stay in order to increase throughput (thus allowing more patients to be treated and potentially reducing costs per patient), and maintaining an appropriate standard of care. Furthermore, it is not in fact clear that such initiatives will serve to reduce costs. One consequence may be an increase in high intensity days of hospital care during early hospitalization, at the expense of lower intensity days of care at the end of a hospital stay. Another consequence may be a shift in cost onto other community healthcare providers, as well as relatives and so on.

Against this background, hospitalization and surgery continue to be central features of medical care in developed countries. While there is debate regarding the optimal length of duration of hospitalization, certain procedures necessarily can only be carried out in a hospital environment, principally because of the attendant risks they may carry (such as anaesthesia during surgery), and the recovery time during which high levels of care are required.

SIGNIFICANCE TO HEALTH PSYCHOLOGY

There are two broad elements of hospitalization which are of relevance to health psychology. One is the extent to which hospitalization in itself constitutes a stressor, thereby potentially influencing the response to treatment, while another is the extent to which psychological interventions can serve to prepare patients for the stressful features of hospitalization and thereby improve the response to treatment and subsequent recovery. While this is true for hospitalization in general, surgery is widely regarded as one of the more stressful and anxiety-provoking reasons for hospitalization. This has therefore been the focus of much of the research into the effects of hospitalization on patients.

There are clear features of hospitalization which are potentially threatening, including the procedures themselves, anaesthesia and loss of consciousness, pain, and the time spent in an unfamiliar environment. In addition, sleep patterns and eating habits may be disrupted while in hospital. As with other potential stressors (see Psychoneuroimmunology), unpredictability and a lack of perceived control contribute to the extent to which a period of hospitalization is perceived as stressful. It may also be valuable to distinguish between threats related to the procedure itself and other immediate aspects of hospitalization and surgery, versus threats related to outcomes such as the result of treatment.

Emotional responses to surgical procedures are dominated by anxiety, with some evidence that anxiety peaks post-surgery, possibly due to anticipatory anxiety regarding the outcome of the surgery. There is also evidence that emotional response may vary across different surgical procedures. High levels of worry and rumination are also common, which may show concern about the surgical procedure but which may also show concern regarding other unrelated matters such as work and home, possibly due to a loss of control during the period of hospitalization. Physiological responses tend to be those associated with exposure to a stressor (see Psychoneuroimmunology). There is some evidence that high levels of emotional distress (and its physiological correlates) prior to surgery predict poor outcome. This relationship may not be straightforward however – it has been proposed that a moderate level of anxiety is optimal, with very low and very high levels of anxiety being maladaptive. This was described by Janis in 1958 as 'the work of worry' and is proposed to allow the patient to prepare for surgery. However, the majority of research to date suggests a simple linear relationship, with high levels of preoperative anxiety associated with poor outcome, including time to discharge and pain. The most compelling evidence suggests effects of anxiety and pain on immune function, which may in turn affect wound healing and recovery.

The evidence for an association between preoperative and postoperative distress, and subsequent wound healing and recovery, has led to attempts to develop preoperative interventions to promote recovery from surgery. Egbert and colleagues in 1964 reported that preoperative advice and relaxation resulted in marked improvements in postoperative recovery. A large number of studies have subsequently investigated the effects of similar intervention on recovery, and there is growing evidence that they are effective, possibly resulting in improvements of approximately 20 per cent on a variety of recovery measures such as self-reported pain, medication consumption and time to discharge. These interventions may operate via effects on the immune function, or by promoting 'well' behaviours (or reducing 'unwell' or maladaptive behaviours), although these two possibilities are by no means mutually exclusive.

Further reading

Kiecolt-Glaser, J.K., Page, G.G., Marucha, P.T., MacCallum, R.C. and Glaser, R. (1998) Psychological influences on surgical recovery: perspectives from psychoneuroimmunology. *American Psychology*, 53, 1209–1218.
Outlines a biopsychosocial model of surgical recovery, based on evidence that stress and anxiety are related to poorer surgical recovery, and that these factors also influence wound healing (see Psychoneuroimmunology).

Larson, M.R., Duberstein, P.R., Talbot, N.L., Caldwell, C. and Moynihan, J.A. (2000) A presurgical psychosocial intervention for breast cancer patients: psychological distress and the immune response. *Journal of Psychosomatic Research*, 48, 187–194.
Randomized controlled trial of a preoperative psychosocial intervention among breast cancer patients, indicating evidence for improvements in both immune response and psychological measures in the treatment group.

Munafò, M.R. and Stevenson, J. (2001) Anxiety and surgical recovery: reinterpreting the literature. *Journal of Psychosomatic Research*, 51, 589–596.
Systematic review of the literature on the relationship between preoperative psychological variables (e.g., mood) and postoperative recovery measures (e.g., mood and immune response).

Rosenberger, P.H., Jokl, P. and Ickovics, J. (2006) Psychosocial factors and surgical outcomes: an evidence-based literature review. *Journal of the American Academy of Orthopaedic Surgeons*, 14, 397–405.
Reviews several studies on the role of psychosocial variables (e.g. depression, social support) as predictors of outcome following surgery.

See also **biological and physiological models and psychoneuro-immunology; pain and acute pain**

ACUTE AND CHRONIC ILLNESS
and: DISABILITY

MEANING **Disability** is a significant impairment of function relative to some usual standard, defined as the norm within a population. This can include physical, sensory, cognitive, or intellectual impairment, and in some cases may be considered a mental health issue (e.g. learning disabilities). These impairments of function may occur due to disease or accident during the lifespan, or may be present from birth. This usage is associated with a **bio-medical model** of disability, while a more comprehensive definition focuses on function as an interaction between a person and the environment, with a particular emphasis on the role of societal norms and attitudes in ascribing labels to conditions described as disabilities, and the resulting stigma and social exclusion which may arise from such labelling.

ORIGINS Historically, a number of models have evolved to explain the presence of altered or impaired function in certain sections of society. For example, in the past disability was associated with moral degeneration, or occult practices such as witchcraft. This has frequently included a religious component. With the development of modern bio-medicine, disability has increasingly come to be understood in the context of impaired function in specific bodily systems which leads to consequent behavioural impairment, with further personal and social consequences. Lay conceptions of disability continue to adhere, at least in part, to a charity model whereby individuals with disabilities are regarded as victims of circumstances and deserving of pity.

The two most common models of disability in current use are the **bio-medical model** and the **social model**. The bio-medical model frames disability as a loss or impairment of function resulting from disease, injury or another bio-medical condition. Treatment is viewed in the context of medical care provided by appropriate healthcare professionals, with a focus on curing or, if this is not possible, symptom management and behaviour modification to minimize impairment and maximize adjustment. Any social issues related to disability are viewed primarily in terms of an appropriate healthcare policy to enable optimal bio-medical care. The social model, by contrast, views the principal issue as social and societal, related to the integration of certain individuals within society. Disability is not regarded as a feature of an individual, but instead as a complex aggregate of conditions and behaviours, many of which arise as a result of the response of society and the environment to the individual (e.g. perceptions of the inability of individuals with disabilities to perform tasks which they are in fact capable of performing). As a result, social action and change are necessary to manage disability, to enable individuals with disabilities to participate fully in society. The social model of disability places an emphasis on the human rights of the individual.

CURRENT USAGE

The social model has increasingly impacted on the bio-medical model, in particular with respect to how disabilities are described. For example, it is now common practice to emphasize the individual first, with the disability being described in a way which does not imply a modification of the person. Examples include 'a person with schizophrenia', or 'a person with Down's syndrome'. Similarly, equipment employed in the management of the consequences of disability is described as something which provides assistance. An example might be 'a person who uses a walking stick', as opposed to 'a person dependent on a walking stick'.

As the populations of developed countries age, an increasing proportion of those populations come to live with various disabilities. As a consequence, there is increasing focus on morbidity (as opposed to mortality) as an important indicator of the health of a society, and consequently on the study of the impact of disability. While epidemiological studies typically focus on crude measures of morbidity, such as days of sick leave taken within a specific population, health psychologists focus more closely on the level of functioning within an individual.

SIGNIFICANCE TO HEALTH PSYCHOLOGY

Function can be defined in a variety of ways, from simple physical definitions which emphasize the ability of the individual to complete specific tasks (e.g. walk a certain distance), through to definitions and measures which emphasize the personal and social context within which such behaviours take place (e.g. the ability to complete tasks associated with daily living, such as washing onself). These were originally developed to assess the level of functioning in the elderly, in order for appropriate measures to be taken to maximize functioning and independence. More recently, these measures of physical function have been supplemented by more subjective measures of health status, which place greater emphasis on the extent to which an individual rates him or herself as healthy.

These various objective and subjective measures are together taken to reflect **quality of life**, which is ideally considered in conjunction with *quantity* of life when considering the benefits of an intervention. In other words, an intervention which extends life by several years, but which offers markedly reduced quality of life over that time period, may be considered less desirable than one which offers less quantity of life but greater quality of life.

However, a definition of quality of life may be problematic, not least because this definition may differ markedly between individuals. The World Health Organization has defined quality of life as 'a broad ranging concept affected in a complex way by the person's physical health, psychological state, level of independence, social relationships and their relationship to the salient features in their environment'. Even if this definition is accepted (and there is by no means a shared consensus that this is the best definition), it does not necessarily help us in operationalizing or measuring quality of life. As a result, several measures intended to measure quality of life have proliferated, some generic and others specific to certain diseases and disabilities, some objective and others subjective, some unidimensional and others multidimensional, and so on.

Despite the difficulties in assessing the subjective impact of disability using measures of quality of life, the emphasis on subjective health measures (as opposed to traditional measures of mortality and morbidity which assume that health can be indexed objectively) has the potential to include the subject of the measurement much more closely in the decision-making process regarding treatment. Furthermore, quality of life measures are increasingly being used as outcome measures in intervention studies, indicating a shift away from traditional measures of morbidity and, in particular, mortality as outcome measures. Indeed, there is some evidence that these constructs are themselves inter-related, with quality of life having been shown to predict longevity, albeit indirectly in a number of studies (e.g. stressful life events and mortality). This illustrates the growing importance of the **biopsychosocial model** in modern medicine. Health psychology has an important role to play in understanding and operationalizing quality of life.

Further reading

Ebrahim, S. (1995) Clinical and public health perspectives and applications of health-related quality of life measurement. *Social Science and Medicine*, 41, 1383–1394.

Discusses issues related to the design and construct of various measures of health-related quality of life, with respect to the psychometric properties of these tests and their validity as measures of quality of life.

Hayes, J.A., Black, N.A., Jenkinson, C., Young, J.D., Rowan, K.M., Daly, K. and Ridley, S. (2000) Outcome measures for adult critical care: a systematic review. *Health Technology Assessment,* 4, 1–111.

An extremely detailed and comprehensive review of a range of outcome measures for patients following adult critical care, including health-related quality of life instruments.

See also **pain and chronic pain**

8
EIGHT

PAIN

PAIN
and: **pain theories**
     neurological models
     behavioural models
     endogenous opioids
     acute pain
     chronic pain

A central feature of many illnesses is pain, and this is often one of the most distressing and debilitating features of an illness. In this chapter we describe historical and current pain theories, including neurological models which assume a biological basis for pain, and behavioural models which focus on the relationship between pain behaviours and the social context within which they occur. Modern theories of pain place great importance on the role of psychological factors in modifying the subjective response to injury, and we outline the potential role of endogenous opioids in this. The distinction between acute and chronic pain is highlighted and discussed in separate chapters, with an emphasis on the similarities and differences in the mechanisms which explain these phenomena. We discuss the ways in which acute pain can, if it remains unresolved, over time give rise to chronic pain, and the complex social and behavioural factors which sustain chronic pain behaviours.

PAIN
and: **PAIN THEORIES**

Pain is defined as 'an unpleasant sensory and emotional experience associated with actual or potential tissue damage, or described in terms of such damage', derived from the Latin for punishment. Pain is a subjectively unpleasant sensation which is distinct from **nociception**, which is a measurable physiological event *usually* associated with subjective pain. A sensation of pain can exist in the absence of nociception (e.g. phantom limb pain). The pathways which carry information about inflammation and damage, including the spinal cord and the brain, are characterized in terms of nociception. These mechanisms are an integral part of the body's defences, providing early warning of impending damage and triggering physiological (via nociception) and behavioural (via subjective pain) responses to avoid or minimize that damage.

MEANING

For most of history, pain has been regarded largely in mechanical terms. For example, Sextus reports the Epicurean claim that 'it is impossible for what is productive … of pain not to be painful', which implies linear causality. Descartes, in particular, argued that pain is evidenced by the withdrawal of the relevant body part from the noxious stimulus, as a result of nerve action. These models regard the pain mechanism and the subsequent behavioural response as distinct from the individual's subjective experience of pain. This mechanistic behaviourism continues to have a pervasive influence on scientific thinking, and the distinction between the mechanistic response to stimulation and the subjective experience distinction still lingers in the current distinction between nociception and pain.

ORIGINS

Pain can be classified as either **acute** or **chronic**. While both may differ in terms of duration, a more helpful distinction is to regard acute pain as that which serves to protect after injury and promote healing, and chronic pain as a disease of pain which does not serve this function. Generally, healthcare professionals regard acute pain as an appropriate symptom of various disease states and procedures, which can be treated by removing the cause of the pain, and managed in the interim with appropriate treatments such as analgesic medications. In some cases, however, 'acute pain' fails to resolve after the expected period, so that the pain itself becomes a disease state (that is, chronic). This may occur even when the original injury that gave rise to the first episode of acute pain has resolved, or when the injury fails to resolve fully (for example, as in some cases of low-back injury).

CURRENT USAGE

While chronic pain was originally defined as pain that has lasted six months or longer, it is now generally defined as a 'disease of pain', recognizing that simple duration of experience cannot clearly distinguish between long lasting acute pain versus chronic pain. It has no specific time limit (unlike acute pain, which is generally expected to resolve within a specific time limit). It may have no apparent cause (namely, no obvious underlying physical pathology), and will serve no clear biological purpose (unlike acute pain, which promotes behaviours consistent with healing). Partly due to the unpredictable characteristics of chronic pain, including uncertainty regarding its duration, it can lead to psychological distress and a feeling of helplessness. The most common causes of chronic pain include low-back pain, headache, recurrent facial pain, cancer pain, and arthritic pain. The one consistent fact of chronic pain is that, as a disease, it cannot be understood in the same terms as acute pain. The failure to adequately make this distinction (both by healthcare professionals and, more commonly, by those who suffer from chronic pain) is a major cause of distress, social isolation, and helplessness.

Various sub-types of pain exist, classified according to the site of injury and the relevant components of the nociceptive pathway (pain-signalling neurons) which are involved. Cutaneous pain (e.g. due to minor cuts and burns) is caused by injury to the skin or superficial tissues. Somatic pain (e.g. due to bone fractures) originates from ligaments, tendons, bones, blood vessels, and nerves, and is characterized by a dull, throbbing pain of longer duration that cutaneous pain. Visceral pain originates from the body's internal organs (viscera), and is typically felt as an aching pain of longer duration than somatic pain. Both somatic and visceral pain may be either local (that is, felt at the site of injury) or referred (namely, where the sensation is localized to an area unrelated to the site of injury). Referred pain can be explained by current neurological models of pain which describe the convergence of multiple pain receptors (including those from both visceral and somatic receptors) on the same spinal cord neurons which transmit nociceptive information to the brain. An example of referred pain is **phantom limb pain**, which is the sensation of pain from a limb that has been lost or injured so that the nociceptive pathways in that limb are no longer active. **Neuropathic pain** can occur as a result of injury or disease to the nerve tissue itself, giving rise to activity in nociceptive pathways which is interpreted by the brain as the result of injury (giving rise to the subjective experience of pain), even though there is no obvious physical injury at the site where the pain is felt.

SIGNIFICANCE TO HEALTH PSYCHOLOGY

Several important features of pain mean that psychological concepts and theories are required for a full understanding of pain. For example, while the bio-medical treatment of acute pain is generally good (e.g. using analgesic medications), these same treatments are frequently ineffective in the treatment of chronic pain. Also, there is wide variation between individuals, and within individuals across different situations, in the subjective pain reported in response to comparable levels of tissue injury. In a seminal (1946) paper, Beecher reported that soldiers and civilians suffering comparable levels of injury differed substantially in their pain reports and requests for medication to relieve their pain. He argued that this may be due, in part, to the 'meaning' of the pain: for soldiers it reflected an end to combat and their transfer to a safe environment (e.g. a field hospital), whereas for civilians it represented a threat, associated with uncertainty and a possible loss of income. Phantom limb pain also represents a challenge for traditional, mechanistic models of nociception and pain, due to the lack of an apparent physical basis for the pain.

While modern **neurological models** can go some way to explain these apparent anomalies, **behavioural models** have become increasingly important in the understanding of pain, and in particular chronic pain.

An increasing acceptance of the role of psychological factors in pain has led to a number of psychological and behavioural pain management interventions. These are particularly popular when bio-medical interventions such as analgesic medication have met with limited success (e.g. in the case of some examples of chronic pain). Relaxation techniques aim to reduce stress and anxiety, and consequently reduce pain, while biofeedback techniques adopt a similar approach but use various feedback methods to increase the ability of the individual to exert control over bodily functions (e.g. heart rate). Operant conditioning methods aim to promote, via positive reinforcement, non-pain behaviour (e.g. increased levels of activity), while at the same time attempting to extinguish pain behaviours (e.g. a reliance on medication). Cognitive methods focus on the diversion of attention away from the pain, and positive imagery. Hypnosis has also been used, but may operate via similar mechanisms to cognitive methods (namely, distraction and positive imagery).

Further reading

Keefe, F.J., Abernethy, A.P. and Campbell, L.C. (2005) Psychological approaches to understanding and treating disease-related pain. *Annual Review of Psychology*, 56, 601–630.
Review which discusses the limitations of the bio-medical model of pain and outlines the development of psychosocial models of pain, and psychosocial interventions for pain management.

See also **pain and neurological models; pain and behavioural models**

PAIN
and: NEUROLOGICAL MODELS

Neurological models of pain attempt to understand the experience of subjective pain in terms of activity along specific nociceptive pathways. These pathways include specific pain receptors and transmitters, which project to an isolated pain centre in the brain via a spinal pathway. Various models which include these basic elements exist, ranging from simpler models such as Specificity Theory, through to more complex models such as Pattern Theory and **Gate Control Theory**, which incorporate distinct roles for subtypes of pain receptors and transmitters.

MEANING

Descartes described the relationship between injury and pain as analogous to the relationship between pulling a rope in order to ring a bell. This conception of the

ORIGINS

mechanisms of pain resulted in Specificity Theory, proposed by Muller and developed by von Frey in the mid- to late-1800s. According to this model, pain information could only be transmitted along sensory nerves, with activity initiated by peripheral pain receptors. Extensions to von Frey's theory included the ascription of unique types of pain, associated with specific pain fibre types. For example, A-delta fibres were identified as those principally involved in the transmission of information about cutaneous pain, while C fibres were identified as those involved in somatic and visceral pain. The **spinothalamic tract** was also identified as crucial in the transmission of pain information. A critical limitation of Specificity Theory, however, is the assumption that there exists a direct and invariant relationship between a physical stimulus and a sensation felt by an individual. There are numerous commonplace examples of physical injury existing in the absence of pain, for example when the individual is distracted (e.g. by sporting competition).

A reaction against Specificity Theory in fact began before its inadequacies and limitations had been fully described. In particular, referred pain, where the sensation of pain occurs at a site other than where the injury has occurred, is difficult to accommodate within Specificity Theory. Goldschneider proposed Pattern Theory (sometimes called Patterning Theory) to account for phenomena such as referred pain, and visceral hypersensitivity (when severe pain is reported in response to very mild stimulation). The central feature of Pattern Theory is a role for the central summation of peripheral sensory and nociceptive information. This summation was proposed to occur at the dorsal horn, at the base of the spine, with further transmission up the spine and on to the brain only occurring if the level of activity exceeded a specific threshold. The most simple variant of Pattern Theory suggests that the sensation of pain is the result of spatial and temporal patterns of neural transmission, as opposed to individual transmission pathways unique to pain information. While the notion of central summation has been retained in modern theories, Pattern Theory fails in the assumption that transmission pathways are not unique to nociceptive or pain information, whereas in fact there is a great deal of receptor and transmitter specificity.

CURRENT USAGE Modern neurological theories of pain include elements of both Specificity and Pattern Theories, but extend these to account for several important physiological and behavioural phenomena. These include the high degree of physiological specialization of receptor units and pathways in the central nervous system, the role of temporal and spatial patterning in the transmission of information in the nervous systems, and the clinical phenomena of spatial and temporal summation, the spread of pain and the persistence of pain after healing. Melzack and Wall described the Gate Control Theory of pain in the mid-1960s, which also introduced psychology into the understanding of pain. This model is illustrated in Figure 8.1.

The central feature of Gate Control Theory is the 'gate' itself, which is hypothesized to be located at the base of the spinal cord. This receives ascending input from peripheral nerve fibres, including large (C) and small (A-delta) fibres, so that nociceptive information from the site of injury is summated and transmitted to the

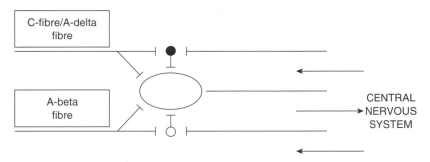

Figure 8.1 The Gate Control Theory of pain (*Source*: Melzack and Wall, 1965)

Note: The Gate Control Theory proposed that C-fibre and A-delta fibre transmission activated excitatory systems that excited output cells in the 'gate'. This activity was also controlled by inhibition resulting from A-beta transmission. A mechanism is also included whereby psychological and cognitive factors (descending factors) can modify the balance of activity in these output cells.

brain. It also receives descending inputs from the brain, which account for the role of, for example, distraction and mood in modulating pain response. The gate integrates information from both ascending and descending inputs and produces a net output. If this output is above a certain level it is transmitted to an action system in the brain, giving rise to the subjective experience of pain. Therefore, it is the net output of the gate, and not activity in the peripheral nerve fibres, which is the closest neurological correlate of the subjective experience of pain.

Gate Control Theory represents an important advance in the bio-medical understanding of pain as it integrates the complexity of inputs arising from central and peripheral sites which modulate the subjective experience of pain. Importantly, it also introduces a role, at least conceptually, for psychological factors, offering the possibility of explaining the impact of psychological interventions such as relaxation on pain perception.

The extent to which the gate is 'open' or 'closed' depends on a number of physical, emotional and behavioural factors. Physical factors which serve to open the gate include injury and the activation of relevant nerve fibres, while those which serve to close the gate include medication and the stimulation of small A-beta fibres which transmit the sensation of light touch (which is why rubbing an injured area reduces the sensation of pain). Emotional factors include anxiety and depression (which open the gate) or happiness and relaxation (which close the gate), while behavioural factors include distraction (which also serves to close the gate). The incorporation of these factors into what essentially remains a neurological model of pain has resulted in the development and increasing acceptance of psychological and behavioural interventions for pain relief, including relaxation and biofeedback techniques (which attempt to reduce pain by reducing anxiety and tension), and cognitive techniques (which attempt to achieve pain relief via distraction and positive imagery).

Nevertheless, the model has limitations, not least that it continues to assume a largely or entirely organic basis for pain, and is designed principally to explain

SIGNIFICANCE TO HEALTH PSYCHOLOGY

acute pain. It is less successful in explaining chronic and pathological pain, in particular that which lacks an obvious organic pathology related to it. Alternative models, and in particular **behavioural models** of pain, are therefore required to fully understand all aspects of pain, and in particular **chronic pain**.

Further reading

Dickenson, A.H. (2002) Gate control theory of pain stands the test of time. *British Journal of Anaesthesia*, 88, 755–757.

A review of almost 40 years of research into the Gate Control Theory of pain, which argues that the theory has stood up well to empirical investigation and remains an effective model of pain.

Melzack, R. and Wall, P.D. (1965) Pain mechanisms: a new theory. *Science*, 150, 971–979.

The original research article which describes basic elements of the Gate Control Theory of pain.

See also **pain and behavioural models; pain and acute pain; pain and chronic pain**

PAIN
and: BEHAVIOURAL MODELS

MEANING   The way in which an individual responds to the subjective experience of pain may play a role both in the nature of that experience, and in the likelihood of it continuing. Pain behaviours in response to acute pain are typically regarded as promoting healing and recovery, or seeking assistance from others. For example, facial expressions may signal to others that the individual is in pain, while protecting behaviour and limping may reduce the strain on the injured area. Avoidance of activity will also serve to promote healing and recovery. These behaviours should serve to reduce pain until the injury which has caused it has resolved. However, in cases where the pain does not resolve, these behaviours may be positively reinforced, through attention and acknowledgement from others, and via secondary gains such as time off work and financial compensation. **Behavioural models** suggest that these reinforcement processes may, in certain circumstances, serve to maintain pain behaviours and the subjective experience of pain.

ORIGINS   While modern neurological models of pain, such as the Gate Control Theory, go a long way to addressing the limitations of simpler, mechanistic models of the past, they are still largely designed to explain acute pain. This resulting gap in our understanding of chronic pain, and in particular chronic pain in the absence of any detectable underlying pathology, gave rise to behavioural models of pain. Fordyce, in the late 1960s, proposed that the persistence of chronic pain over time presents greater scope for psychological, social and behavioural factors to come into play and begin to influence an individual's subjective experience of pain. Specifically, Fordyce argued that the nature of the chronic pain syndrome (see Chronic Pain) presents opportunities for unconscious learning, in the context of an operant conditioning model. Requests for pain medication, for example, are reinforced by attention from others and the prescription of medication. Attention and medication, in this case, act as reinforcers to the behaviour of medication request. This behavioural model therefore suggests ways in which pain behaviours can be modified in order to treat the chronic pain syndrome.

CURRENT USAGE

Fordyce's (1976) insights into the role of operant conditioning processes in maintaining pain behaviour and the chronic pain syndrome remain current. Fordyce's model turns on the premise that the behaviours typical of the chronic pain patient (inactivity, medication request, medication consumption, and so on) are reinforceable by the environment and other individuals. Behaviours have consequences, and if those consequences can be characterized as favourable, the behaviours eliciting them will tend to be reinforced. These favourable consequences have been termed **gain**, and subdivided into primary, secondary and tertiary gain.

Primary gain refers to an interpersonal, psychological or behavioural mechanism for the reduction of pain or distress (e.g. short-term pain relief), **secondary gain** to the interpersonal or environmental advantage supplied by the behaviour (e.g. attention, sympathy, and so on), and **tertiary gain** to the advantage that someone other than the patient may gain from the behaviour (e.g. the gratitude of the patient to the care giver). There is substantial evidence for the effects of interpersonal and environmental reinforcers. For example, if a supportive spouse is present during a clinical interview a patient may rate the subjective pain higher, whereas with an unsupportive spouse present the reverse is true. The operant reinforcement of these behaviours is not conscious, and any 'advantage' supplied by these behaviours should be understood in the context of a patient who believes that the pain is likely never to resolve.

SIGNIFICANCE TO HEALTH PSYCHOLOGY

Behavioural models of pain have had a substantial impact on psychological and behavioural interventions for the management of chronic pain. The treatment of chronic pain behaviours, according to behavioural models, relies on the extinction of associations between specific pain behaviours and subsequent reinforcers. This would mean in practice that patients would not be given pain medication on request, for example, but on a fixed schedule. In parallel, an attempt is made to *establish* new associations between well behaviours and reinforcers, such as giving strong encouragement to patients who attempt to be self-mobile. In this way, an attempt is made to reverse the development of the behavioural state of the patient and to achieve a higher level of function.

The results of studies assessing the efficacy of behavioural treatment programmes are striking; some report marked reductions in medication consumption and increases in activity and independent living. Psychological adjustment is also generally improved and distress reduced following such programmes, which typically require the involvement of family members to ensure that behavioural modifications are extended beyond the treatment setting to the home. These improvements are generally in the context of a population previously seriously disabled by their condition and unable to function independently, and where traditional medical interventions have consistently failed to provide relief. Such programmes are not without their critics, however: claims have variously been made that patients are simply being taught to be stoical, or that the selective nature of admission to such programmes means that the results are not generalizable. Fordyce's response to such criticism is that the goal of behavioural treatment programmes is not to modify nociception, but to render the patient functionally independent by modifying behaviour. Nevertheless, whether this was intended or not, patients treated using an operant model tend to report reduced levels of pain and require less medication.

As well as being a clinically valuable consequence, the reduction in self-reported pain and medication consumption following behavioural treatment raises important questions regarding the relationship between injury, nociception and the subjective experience of pain. Patients also demonstrate improvements in self-efficacy and locus of control beliefs, and there has been recent interest in the role of cognitions in the subjective experience of pain. Psychological treatment programmes now include a cognitive component designed to enhance cognitive strategies for improving the patient's sense of efficacy and control over the condition. Modern multidisciplinary pain clinics rely on both neurological and cognitive-behavioural conceptions of pain, and focus on improving function (in particular independent living), reducing reliance on medication and medical services, and increasing social support and social interaction.

Further reading

Keefe, F.J., Abernethy, A.P. and Campbell, L.C. (2005) Psychological approaches to understanding and treating disease-related pain. *Annual Review of Psychology*, 56, 601–630.

Review which discusses the limitations of the bio-medical model of pain and outlines the development of psychosocial models of pain, and psychosocial interventions for pain management.

Sharp, T.J. (2001) Chronic pain: a reformulation of the cognitive-behavioural model. *Behavioral Research and Therapy*, 39, 787–800.

Discusses current interpretations of Fordyce's behavioural model of chronic pain behaviours, and argues for an extension of this model to incorporate a cognitive-behavioural perspective.

See also **pain and chronic pain**

PAIN
and: ENDOGENOUS OPIOIDS

An **opioid** is a chemical substance that has a primarily pain-relieving function in the body. These agents work by binding to opioid receptors, which are mainly located in the central nervous system and the gastrointestinal tract. The receptors in these two organ systems mediate both the beneficial effects (e.g. pain relief), and the undesirable side-effects (e.g. respiratory depression). Endogenous opioids are those which are produced naturally in the body, while other opioids (morphine, heroin, pethidine) are either extracted from opium, or are semi- or fully synthetic. The term 'opiate' properly refers to natural opium alkaloids (e.g. morphine) and semi-synthetic opioids derived from them (e.g. heroin).

MEANING

Opioids extracted from plants, and synthesized from these products, have been used widely in human society throughout history, for both their psychoactive and pain-relieving properties, although in developed countries the use of opioids for non-medical purposes is now illegal. The active ingredient in opium, morphine, was isolated by Serutner in the 1800s and named after Morpheus, the Greek god of dreams. However, the endogenous opioid system, which mediates the effects of opium, heroin and other opioids, remained unclear until the late 1960s. Endogenous opioids were first isolated in the 1970s by Hughes and Kosterlitz in animal studies, and then subsequently isolated in humans.

ORIGINS

Opioids bind to specific opioid receptors in the central nervous system and in other tissues. There are at least 17 major classes of opioid receptors, although only four are common: mu (μ), kappa (κ), sigma (σ) and delta (δ). Different properties of opioids (e.g. analgesia, respiratory depression, physical dependence, and so on) are mediated by different receptors. Endogenous opioids are opioid peptides that are produced naturally in the body, and are classified into three broad types: **endorphins**, dynorphins, and enkephalins. Dynorphins act through kappa-opioid receptors, and are widely distributed in the central nervous system. Enkephalins include met-enkephalin and leu-enkephalin, the former acting through the mu- and delta-opioid receptors and widely distributed in the central nervous system, and the latter through the delta-opioid receptor. Endorphins act through the mu-opioid receptors and are more potent than other endogenous opioids at these sites. Beta-endorphin, in particular, has wide ranging effects on behaviour, including sexual behaviour and appetite.

CURRENT USAGE

The role of endogenous opioids in regulating behaviour is an important biological component of any biopsychosocial model, in particular with respect to their role in mediating pain response. Endogenous opioids have been suggested to explain several important pain phenomena, such as the impact of psychological factors on

SIGNIFICANCE TO HEALTH PSYCHOLOGY

pain perception (as in Beecher's (1946) study of wounded soldiers – see Box 8.1), and may contribute to the 'descending signals' which form a part of Melzack and Wall's (1965) Gate Control Theory. This offers a possible mechanism by which psychological factors such as anxiety, for example, may modulate pain perception, via relationships between anxiety and endogenous opioid activity (although this remains speculative).

Box 8.1 Beecher's study of american soldiers

In 'Pain in men wounded in battle' (1946), Henry Beecher wrote that 'Three-quarters of badly wounded men, although they have received no morphine for hours ... have so little pain that they do not want pain relief medication, even though the questions raised remind them that such is available for the asking. This is a puzzling thing and perhaps justifies a little speculation'.

In this seminal study of wounded American soldiers, Beecher illustrated that the subjective experience of pain is not simply the result of the degree of tissue damage involved. Comparisons with severely injured civilians (even though their injuries tended to be, if anything, less severe than those of the soldiers) indicated that civilians reported far higher levels of subjective pain.

Of course, one possibility is that soldiers are simply trained to be more stoical than the average civilian (although the fact that their pain behaviours differ so markedly is still relevant to the question of what influences subjective pain response). An alternative explanation, favoured by Beecher, is that one reason for the difference between soldiers and civilians was due to the *meaning* of the pain, and the environment in which they found themselves. For a civilian, hospitalization is a threatening, frightening event, whereas for soldiers (certainly in contrast to battle), hospital represents a place of relative safety which means that the immediate danger has passed.

Evidence such as that provided by Beecher illustrated the deficiencies of early neurological models of pain, and highlighted the necessity of some form of influence of signals from the brain ('descending signals' in the Gate Control Theory) to account for how psychological factors are able to so strongly modify the subjective experience of pain.

A number of non-pharmacological interventions for pain relief may also act in part via their effects on the endogenous opioid system. Acupuncture, for example, is increasingly acknowledged to be an effective method of pain relief, and pre-treatment with naloxone (an opioid antagonist which blocks the effects of opioids) appears to block acupuncture analgesia (suggesting that the effects of acupuncture are mediated partly by the endogenous opioid system). Acupuncture analgesia may also operate via stimulation of A-delta (sharp pain) and A-beta fibres (light touch), which serve to maximally inhibit the transmission of C-fibre (dull, throbbing pain) information. Therefore, pain therapies and interventions previously considered to be on the fringes of modern medicine are now being understood in the context of Gate Control Theory and endogenous opioid activity. Another non-pharmacological method of pain relief, which may operate via similar pathways as acupuncture, is Transcutaneous Electrical Nerve Stimulation (TENS). In this, mild electrical stimulation is applied to peripheral nerves to achieve pain relief, and TENS appears to be particularly effective in the treatment of **chronic pain**.

Endogenous opioids therefore play an important role in the understanding of pain mechanisms and pain behaviours, and may offer a biological pathway via which psychological and behavioural factors related to pain perception can operate. In particular, their role complements the basic features of Gate Control Theory and may explain a mechanism via which 'descending signals' exert their influence.

Further reading

Kaptchuk, T.J. (2002) Acupuncture: theory, efficacy, and practice. *Annals of Internal Medicine*, 136, 374–383.
Discusses the evidence for the effectiveness of acupuncture as a pain management intervention, and also the evidence that acupuncture activates endogenous opioid mechanisms.

Sluka, K.A. and Walsh, D. (2003) Transcutaneous electrical nerve stimulation: basic science mechanisms and clinical effectiveness. *Journal of Pain*, 4, 109–121.
Describes theories that support the use of transcutaneous electrical nerve stimulation as a pain management intervention, such as the Gate Control Theory and the release of endogenous opioids.

See also **pain and neurological models; pain and acute pain; pain and chronic pain**

PAIN
and: ACUTE PAIN

Acute pain may be simply defined as pain that arises quickly, usually in response to a readily identifiable injury or pathology, and that lasts a relatively short period of time. A more complex definition would also incorporate the fact that acute pain

MEANING

is generally an adaptive and appropriate response to injury or impending injury, which serves to promote physiological and behavioural changes that result in optimal healing and recovery. It has been reported as the primary symptom in around 80 per cent of medical presentations, emphasizing its salience for patients at least.

ORIGINS

While generally being regarded as the 'normal' manifestation of some physical pathology, the range of syndromes and diseases where there is pain that resolves (namely, is acute) is vast, in contrast to the relatively narrow range of conditions where pain does not resolve (namely, is chronic). In the past it was usual to distinguish between acute pain and chronic pain solely on the basis of duration – for example, pain lasting six months or longer was typically considered chronic pain, on the assumption that this was sufficient time for any physical pathology to resolve. However, this definition does not accommodate specific cases of repeated acute pain (e.g. burns treatment, where there are episodes of acute pain during treatment, which are repeated over a long period of time). Therefore, more recent conceptualizations of acute pain place an emphasis on its central role in the healing process (as distinct from chronic pain, which may be regarded as pathological and not part of the normal healing process).

CURRENT USAGE

Clearly there is no linear relationship between the degree of injury or pathology and the subjective experience of pain (see neurological models and endogenous opioids). Similar levels of injury can result in very different levels of pain across individuals, and this remains the case whether one is considering post-operative pain, headache, or any other form of acute pain. While factors that influence pain threshold (the point at which stimulation becomes painful) and pain tolerance (the point at which pain becomes unbearable) have been studied in a laboratory setting, the models of pain used (e.g. the cold pressor task, which requires participants to keep their hand in a container of ice water) are of questionable ecological validity.

SIGNIFICANCE TO HEALTH PSYCHOLOGY

The centrality of acute pain as a symptom of most physical illness makes it an important treatment target. Moreover, the role of psychological factors in pain, as described in current models such as Gate Control Theory (see neurological models), suggest that health psychology has a role to play both in explaining individual differences in pain response, and in developing interventions to reduce or manage pain. While the majority of psychological interventions have been developed for use in chronic pain (see behavioural models), there are applications in the acute pain setting.

These include **relaxation** and **positive imagery**, in particular when the acute pain is in response to a particular treatment (such as debridement, where dead skin is removed periodically from burn sites). The importance of self-efficacy and control beliefs has also been suggested to play a role in explaining pain response, in particular in post-operative patients. This may explain the success of **Patient Controlled Analgesia** (PCA) which has become increasingly widely adopted in post-operative environments. PCA allows patients to administer their own doses of pain-relieving medication (albeit with safe-guards to prevent overdose). Evidence suggests that patients given PCA demonstrate substantially lower self-reported pain and medication consumption than those who are administered analgesic medication either by hospital staff or by continuous intravenous infusion. It has been suggested that the element of control over one's environment and post-operative recovery central to PCA is part of the reason for this improvement, as well as the clear advantages of having relatively immediate and predictable pain relief.

Further reading

Hudcova, J., McNicol, E., Quah, C., Lau, J. and Carr, D.B. (2006) Patient controlled opioid analgesia versus conventional opioid analgesia for postoperative pain. *Cochrane Database Syst Rev, CD003348.*
Systematic review and meta-analysis of studies comparing the effectiveness of patient controlled analgesia with conventional (that is, clinician or nurse administered) analgesia for post-operative pain.

Keefe, F.J., Abernethy, A.P. and Campbell, L.C. (2005) Psychological approaches to understanding and treating disease-related pain. *Annual Review of Psychology*, 56, 601–630.
Review which discusses the limitations of the bio-medical model of pain and out-lines the development of psychosocial models of pain, and psychosocial interven-tions for pain management.

See also **pain and neurological models; pain and endogenous opioids**

PAIN
and: CHRONIC PAIN

MEANING

Chronic pain refers to persistent pain which endures over a period longer than that which healing normally takes place within. This is typically taken to be longer than three months in duration, although some have argued that this period should be longer and only pain lasting longer than six months should be considered chronic. It is a persistent state of subjective pain where the cause of the pain either cannot be removed or cannot be identified. Chronic pain is often associated with long-term incurable or intractable medical conditions or disease, but may also occur in the absence of any identifiable pathology. Increasingly, chronic pain has begun to be understood as a pathological state in its own right, which may develop over time but where the duration of pain is not necessarily a defining characteristic.

ORIGINS   In the past the treatment of pain has relied on a narrow conception of the aetiology of chronic pain, implementing pharmacological and surgical techniques in an attempt to achieve pain relief. **Behavioural models** of pain suggest that these interventions, as well as allied consequences such as bed rest and reliance on others, may in fact serve to maintain and exacerbate pain behaviours, resulting in quite negative effects on the patient in the long term. A broader conception of pain and its aetiology, however, has resulted in a more **biopsychosocial** conception of chronic pain, and has led to the development of behavioural interventions which have proved very successful in some patients. The danger, however, is that the identification of psychological, behavioural and social factors which contribute to the development and maintenance of chronic pain leads to the view that chronic pain is a distinctly different entity from acute pain. Instead it might be more helpful to regard chronic pain as a pathological condition arising from behaviours and other factors which serve an adaptive purpose in the short term but which become increasingly maladaptive as pain persists.

CURRENT USAGE   Chronic pain can exist as an unresolved symptom where there is an obvious underlying physical pathology (sometimes, but not always, associated with a degenerative condition). Examples include low back pain (although there are cases of this where a physical cause cannot be identified), cancer pain, rheumatoid arthritis and multiple sclerosis. In the case of chronic pain in the absence of degenerative disease, it is assumed that if healing takes place at the site of the original injury, persistent pain is the consequence of behavioural and central nervous system changes that have taken place over time (see behavioural models).

One possible mechanism via which persistent nociception may give rise to pathological chronic pain is **central neural plasticity**. This refers to the modification of central nervous system function over time in the presence of persistent signaling along specific pathways. There is evidence, for example, of sustained changes in central nervous system excitability following noxious stimulation which can be maintained even in the presence of local anaesthesia at the site of injury. These changes may take the form of spontaneous activity in pain pathways, lowered thresholds for activation, and increased sensitivity to stimulation. Pathological chronic pain states seem, at least in part, to be the result of long-term structural and organic changes in pain pathways resulting from persistent activation.

Chronic Pain Syndrome (CPS) is a common problem that presents a major challenge to healthcare professionals because of its complex and unclear aetiology, and typically poor response to medical intervention. It has been suggested that CPS might be a learned behavioural syndrome that begins with a noxious stimulus that causes acute pain (frequently, but not exclusively, low back pain) that persists over time. Gradually, pain behaviours are reinforced externally or internally (gain), so that these behaviours persist in the absence of nociception. Patients with several psychological syndromes (e.g. major depression, hypochondriasis) are more prone to developing CPS. Core features of CPS have been described by Sternbach (1987) as the Six Ds: Dramatization of complaints, Drug misuse, Dysfunction, Dependency, Depression, and Disability. Behavioural models of pain, and interventions based on these models, typically target the CPS itself, rather than the pain per se, in order to increase function (see behavioural models).

Individuals with chronic pain, in particular where there is no clear pathology associated with the pain, have historically met with minimal success when treated with traditional bio-medical interventions. Analgesic medication, for example, is typically ineffective in patients with Chronic Pain Syndrome, who frequently require escalating doses to achieve modest pain relief, resulting in problems of dependence, in particular in the case of opiate medication. It is notable that patients whose chronic pain results from clearly identifiable pathology (e.g. cancer) do not typically experience problems of dependence, despite often taking similarly high doses of analgesic opiate medication.

The development of more sophisticated neurological and, in particular, behavioural models of pain and the Chronic Pain Syndrome has resulted in the development of novel interventions, such as behavioural treatments based on operant conditioning models, which target features of chronic pain more successfully. Clearly there is considerable variation in the types of chronic pain which may present, and the aetiologies of these differ widely. At the very least, persistent pain is highly aversive and distressing, so that psychology has a role to play in managing and ameliorating this distress, and promoting coping strategies to enhance self-efficacy and control beliefs. In more specific cases, the persistence of the pain may have given rise to behavioural changes which themselves have become problematic and limiting for the individual, in which case psychological (and in particular behavioural) interventions may prove successful.

SIGNIFICANCE TO HEALTH PSYCHOLOGY

Further reading

Campbell, L.C., Clauw, D.J. and Keefe, F.J. (2003) Persistent pain and depression: a biopsychosocial perspective. *Biological Psychiatry*, 54, 399–409.
Highlights recent research findings on the relationship between persistent pain and depression and discusses advances in theories of pain that incorporate a role for emotional factors in the aetiology of pain.

Pearce, J.M. (2002) Psychosocial factors in chronic disability. *Medical Science Monitor*, 8, RA275–281.
Review of psychosocial factors, including interactions with carers, family and so on, that give rise to **secondary gain** and **tertiary gain**, and contribute to the development and maintenance of **sick role** behaviours.

See also **pain and behavioural models; acute and chronic illness and disability**

9
NINE

ADDICTIVE BEHAVIOURS

ADDICTIVE BEHAVIOURS
and: **disease models**
neurobiological models
social and behavioural models
alcohol
tobacco
behavioural addictions

Addictive behaviours are particularly interesting to health psychologists because they highlight the close relationship between social, psychological and physical factors in health and illness. While the majority of addictive behaviours include some form of substance, such as alcohol and tobacco, there is also some evidence that addictive behaviours can occur in the absence of substance use. This chapter outlines historical and current models of addictive behaviours, including disease models (which place an emphasis on the impact of prolonged substance use), neurobiological models (which regard addictive behaviours as a consequence of specific learning processes), and social and behavioural models (which extend the conception of addictive behaviours as reflecting learning processes to take into account contextual factors and the role of habit). Alcohol and tobacco use are given as examples of substances with addictive potential which, in part because of their widespread use, have a major impact on public health and society in general. Finally, behavioural addictions such as problem gambling are described, with an emphasis on the challenge of accommodating these behaviours within traditional conceptions of addictive behaviours.

ADDICTIVE BEHAVIOURS
and: DISEASE MODELS

The **disease model** or **bio-medical model** of **addiction** describes addiction as a life-long disease involving biological and environmental aetiological factors. The traditional bio-medical model of disease requires only that an abnormal condition be present that causes discomfort, dysfunction, or distress to the individual with the disease, and takes into account that this may be the result of biological, psychological or social causes, even if these remain poorly understood. The bio-medical disease model assumes that some factor (e.g. the substance used, the intrinsic characteristics of the individual, or a combination of both) ultimately gives rise to the disease state.

MEANING

In previous centuries addiction was widely regarded to be a consequence of free choice and personal responsibility, with the excessive consumption associated with addiction considered to result from an intrinsic weakness in the individual and deserving of scorn and punishment. This model has been described as the **moral model** of addictive behaviours, since individuals such as alcoholics were thought to have 'chosen' to behave in that way. Punishment was regarded as the appropriate treatment within this model, as this enforced an acknowledgment of personal responsibility by the individual, who was ultimately responsible for his or her behaviour. It is notable that the pervasive social and cultural attitudes of the time strongly influenced the medical conception of addictive behaviours (or, possibly, vice versa), and this relationship continues in current models of addictive behaviours.

ORIGINS

In the nineteenth century, addictive behaviour increasingly came to be understood as a bio-medical problem which could be conceptualized as a **disease** state. Early bio-medical models placed the emphasis on the **substance**, so that exposure to alcohol, for example, was a prerequisite for developing dependence on that substance. Treatments based on this model emphasized removal of the substance and subsequent abstinence as appropriate. This represented an important shift from earlier moral models and placed a far higher priority on treatment as opposed to punishment. Some elements of this model are retained in current bio-medical models, since it is clearly necessary for an individual to be exposed to a substance in order to become dependent upon it. There is considerable current debate, however, regarding whether total lifelong abstinence is a necessary treatment goal.

CURRENT USAGE

Disease models in the twentieth century extended the original conception of addictive behaviours as disease by placing more emphasis on the intrinsic characteristics of the individual. One limitation of the simple bio-medical model which emphasizes the role of exposure to a substance as causative in the development of dependence is that by no means all individuals exposed to a substance become dependent upon it. The vast majority of alcohol consumers, for example, are what might broadly be described as social drinkers, despite regularly exposing themselves to large quantities of a potentially highly dependency-forming substance. Various intrapersonal and biological (e.g. genetic) factors may predispose an individual to addiction when exposed to a particular substance. Again, elements of this conception are retained in modern models and integrated with earlier disease concepts which place an emphasis on exposure to the substance.

SIGNIFICANCE TO HEALTH PSYCHOLOGY

Psychological concepts of addiction have augmented modern bio-medical models. In particular, **social learning theory** has been used to explain behavioural features of addiction, and the extent to which they occur and develop within a social context. This has resulted in a gradual shift from the use of the term 'addiction' to 'addictive behaviour', to encompass the spectrum of behaviours associated with substance use and dependence.

Social learning theory regards addictive behaviours as learned behaviours which may be triggered by social and environmental contingencies (e.g. the desire that smokers may have to smoke a cigarette when they enter a bar that has been associated with cigarette smoking in the past). In this respect, addictive behaviours are no different from other learned and habitual behaviours, although the contribution of a specific substance may result in very strong learning processes. This role for learning processes has now been incorporated within bio-medical models, which emphasize roles for the substance, the characteristics of the individual, and the context within which these behaviours occur, and give rise to learned associations and habits.

Early bio-medical disease models regarded addiction as a discrete, irreversible state, which was 'located' within the individual, and emphasized lifetime abstinence as the optimal treatment model. More current biopsychosocial models retain a role for the substance in triggering addictive behaviours (although see behavioural addictions), and for the individual in explaining the different susceptibilities observed between different people when exposed to the same substance. However, these models also integrate a role for learning processes (which may have important biological correlates) and the importance of habit and learned environmental contingencies (in particular triggers for substance use, such as the sights, smells and sounds associated with the use of a substance in the past). According to this model, addictive behaviours can be treated by 'unlearning' the habits and contingencies which have become established, so that 'normal' behaviour patterns become re-established. Lifetime abstinence may be desirable if achievable, but is generally not regarded as a *necessary* condition for treatment.

There are substantial medical and social costs associated with tobacco and alcohol use in the United Kingdom. Many individuals have difficulty in reducing their consumption (even social drinkers frequently find it difficult to cut down because of the social pressure to drink alcohol in the majority of social contexts), so that understanding addictive behaviours is important both to allow for the refinement of treatment models and in order to improve public health. In addition, the recent liberalization of gambling laws in several developed countries (in particular Australia and the United Kingdom) has led to a concern that the prevalence of **problem gambling**, which is sometimes described as a **behavioural addiction** (namely, one lacking a psychoactive substance), may soon increase.

Further reading

Drummond, D.C. (2001) Theories of drug craving, ancient and modern. *Addiction*, 96, 33–46.
Reviews the principal theoretical models of drug craving, provides some directions for future research, and challenges the widely held assumption that craving is the underlying basis for addictive behaviours.

Robinson, T.E. and Berridge, K.C. (2003) Addiction. *Annual Review of Psychology*, 54, 25–53.
Comprehensive review of current neurobiological models of addiction, with a particular emphasis on problem drug use, and covering major theoretical explanations of the transition from drug use to addiction.

Lyvers, M. (1998) Drug addiction as a physical disease: the role of physical dependence and other chronic drug-induced neurophysiological changes in compulsive drug self-administration. *Experimental and Clinical Psychopharmacology*, 6, 107–125.
Reviews evidence which suggests that persistent drug-induced changes in the physical brain may underlie addictive behaviour, consistent with the general notion of addiction as a physical disease.

See also **addictive behaviours and neurobiological models; addictive behaviours and social and behavioural models**

ADDICTIVE BEHAVIOURS
and: NEUROBIOLOGICAL MODELS

Neurobiological models of addiction place an emphasis on the role of the central nervous system, and activity in specific neurotransmitter pathways, in explaining addictive behaviours. In particular, changes in the activity of these pathways resulting from chronic drug use is thought to be the underlying pathology associated with addictive behaviours, with the emphasis here on the role of the **dopamine** pathway. Neurobiological models rely heavily on a bio-medical view of addictive behaviours as representing a disease. Variation in the susceptibility of different individuals **MEANING**

to drug addiction is thought to reflect primarily individual differences in the activity and sensitivity of these relevant neurotransmitter pathways.

ORIGINS

In the past, addiction was primarily a pharmacological term that specifically referred to the use of a tolerance-inducing drug in sufficient quantity as to eventually cause **tolerance** (namely, the requirement that greater dosages of a given drug be used to produce a comparable effect over time). This was considered to be the underlying biological basis of addiction within bio-medical conceptions of addictive behaviours. This remains a feature of most addictive behaviours, as well as the capacity for substances which are potentially addictive to cause a **physical dependence** (namely, to elicit marked withdrawal symptoms if drug use is abruptly terminated) and a **psychological dependence** (namely, to elicit cravings and psychological distress if the drug use is terminated). More recently, however, neurobiological models have emphasized the role of learning in addictive behaviours, with the disease state of addiction (as understood within these models) reflecting the consequence of dysfunction learning processes over time.

CURRENT USAGE

Modern neurobiological models of addiction emphasize the capacity of drugs of abuse (e.g. heroin, cocaine, alcohol, nicotine, and so on) to powerfully activate pathways in the central nervous system related to motivation and reward. Although different drugs of abuse exert their psychoactive effects via a range of neurotransmitters, it has been increasingly agreed within neurobiological models of addictive behaviours that all share the capacity to elicit the release of dopamine in specific brain regions, such as the Ventral Tegmental Area and the Nucleus Accumbens. It is dopamine, operating within these specific brain regions, which is thought to govern the regulation of motivational and appetitive behaviours, and in particular to play a role in the learning processes whereby we 'learn' that specific substances are palatable or desirable. Generally this is healthy; for example, sweet tastes activate these pathways because they usually indicate high-calorie foods which, in an evolutionary context, it is appropriate and desirable to seek out.

Potentially addictive substances, however, appear to *strongly* elicit a release of dopamine in these regions. A large number of animal studies have demonstrated that the acute administration of drugs of abuse causes dopamine release, especially in these brain regions, while recent advances in neuroimaging techniques (see psychophysiology) have provided similar evidence of dopamine release following drug administration in humans. Eventually, through associative learning processes (e.g. **classical conditioning**) cues associated with the drug (such as the taste and smell of a cigarette which delivers nicotine) come to elicit dopamine release and trigger behaviours involved in seeking out the drug. The repeated use of substances which lead to dopamine release in these pathways is thought to result in permanent or semi-permanent changes to the brain (**neuroadaptations**), the upshot of which is that the drug, and the cues associated with it, begin to 'grab' the attention of the individual disproportionately and then exert a strong influence over behaviour. For example, alcohol-dependent individuals frequently report strong cravings for alcohol and the urge to drink when they experience smells associated with alcohol, such as of particular drinks or bars. Those that favour the bio-medical disease models of addiction see these neurobiological changes in the brain as evidence that addiction is a disease.

For these reasons, neurobiological models of addictive behaviours characterize addiction as a disease of learning, although a very specific one related to the capacity of the brain to 'learn' the effects of specific drugs via their effects on dopamine release, and to subsequently assign a high 'priority' to the drugs themselves, and the cues associated with them. While these models are able to account for the wide variation in susceptibility to addiction across individuals, for example by incorporating a role for genetic variation in influencing the sensitivity of relevant neurotransmitter pathways (in particular dopamine pathways), they place little if any emphasis on the role of social and interpersonal factors in addictive behaviours.

SIGNIFICANCE TO HEALTH PSYCHOLOGY

At first glance, neurobiological models of addiction and addictive behaviours appear to be far better suited to bio-medical and disease conceptions of addiction rather than psychological ones. However, the central role of learning in these models suggests that behavioural interventions designed to 'reverse' these learning processes may be appropriate, in which case psychologists may have a great deal to offer in the formulation of novel interventions to treat addictive behaviours.

As described above, one important theoretical consequence of neurobiological models is that cues associated with a drug should eventually, over time and following repeated pairings with the drug itself, acquire the capacity to elicit drug seeking behaviours themselves. Indeed, many individuals attempting to abstain from drug use report that they find it most difficult to maintain abstinence when in those environments which have previously been associated with using the drug (e.g. ex-smokers when going into a bar where they had previously smoked). Various experimental techniques exist for exploring whether cues do indeed acquire this capacity to capture attention in drug users, and most attempt to measure the degree of selective bias (sometimes called **attentional bias**) towards specific cues in drug users compared to non-users (see Box 9.1).

Box 9.1   Attentional bias for drug-related cues

The tendency for cues associated with drug use to capture attention in drug users has been demonstrated using various experimental methods, and in various drug-using groups.

In the modified Stroop task, participants engage in a colour-naming task, while words are simultaneously presented. These words are coloured, and the task

(Cont'd)

---

is to name the colour of the word. The words may belong to a neutral or drug-related category, and evidence for attentional bias consists of a relative slowing of colour-naming reaction times when the drug-related word is present relative to when a neutral word is present. The assumption is that these stimuli 'capture' the attention and thereby limit the information processing resources available to the primary task (naming the colour).

The attentional probe task is a reaction time task, with either a word or picture presented prior to the appearance of a visual probe (e.g. a dot) to which participants have to respond as fast as possible. The stimuli may belong to a neutral or drug-related category, and appear as pairs of relevant and neutral stimuli, after which these stimuli are removed and replaced with a visual probe in *either* the previous location of the drug-related or the neutral stimulus. Evidence for attentional bias consists of relatively faster reaction times when the probe appears in the previous location of a drug-related stimulus, compared to when it appears in the previous location of a neutral stimulus.

Field and Eastwood (2005) found that heavy social drinkers who completed a modified version of the visual probe task, where the probe always appeared either in the location of an alcohol-related cue or a neutral cue, showed modified attentional bias after the procedure compared to before. In addition, those who were trained to attend towards the alcohol-related cues drank more alcohol in a taste test after the experiment, compared to those who were trained to attend towards the neutral cue. This suggests that attentional biases may play a causal role in drinking behaviour, and may also be a target for clinical intervention.

These biases towards drug-related cues, and the capacity of these cues to trigger drug-seeking behaviours as well as physiological (e.g. increased heart rate) and psychological (e.g. subjective craving) responses, have important treatment implications. For example, encouraging individuals to monitor situations which appear to trigger drug cravings (such as specific locations or even other people), for example by keeping a diary, can enable those individuals to develop strategies to avoid potentially 'high-risk' situations.

More recently, a number of studies have suggested that it might be possible to re-train' these biases, using similar experimental techniques to those developed to show that these biases existed in the first place (see Box 9.1). In these studies, individuals are trained to attend away from drug-related cues. The evidence is very preliminary, but there are some encouraging early findings which suggest that, following this period of training, individuals are less responsive to drug-related cues than those who have not been trained in this way. It remains to be seen, however, whether these novel interventions will prove to be effective in highly dependent individuals, and whether any positive effects will generalize beyond the laboratory environment and influence responses to drug-related cues in the everyday environment.

Further reading

Drummond, D.C. (2001) Theories of drug craving, ancient and modern. *Addiction*, 96, 33–46.
Reviews the principal theoretical models of drug craving, provides some directions for future research, and challenges the widely held assumption that craving is the underlying basis for addictive behaviours.

Robinson, T.E. and Berridge, K.C. (2003) Addiction. *Annual Review of Psychology*, 54, 25–53.
Comprehensive review of current neurobiological models of addiction, with a particular emphasis on problem drug use, covering major theoretical explanations of the transition from drug use to addiction.

Robinson, T.E. and Berridge, K.C. (2000) The psychology and neurobiology of addiction: an incentive-sensitization view. *Addiction*, 95, S91–117.
Discusses evidence that mesolimbic dopamine systems play a role, including evidence that neural sensitization happens in humans, and the implications of incentive-sensitization for the development of therapies in the treatment of addiction.

See also **addictive behaviours and social and behavioural models; biological and physiological models and psychophysiology**

ADDICTIVE BEHAVIOURS
and: SOCIAL AND BEHAVIOURAL MODELS

MEANING

Social models and **behavioural models** of addiction emphasize the role of **habit** in addictive behaviours, which it is argued are learned according to the principles of **social learning theory**. These models do not necessarily deny the importance of **neurobiological models** in explaining some of these processes, but place far greater emphasis on the role of interpersonal and social factors (such as peer influences and observational learning), as well as intrapersonal factors (such as self-esteem, coping behaviours and attributional style), in the development of addictive behaviours.

ORIGINS

While disease models of addiction place an emphasis on the role of exposure to the substance as the primary causal agent in the development of addictive behaviours, social theories have historically placed an emphasis on the role of environmental factors. Such theories hypothesize that addictive behaviours develop and are sustained as a result of environmental pressures (generally negative) such as unemployment, poverty, violence, family dysfunction, and so on. These influences act as social stressors and substance use is considered to be a **coping strategy** in response to the psychological distress resulting from these pressures. Addictive behaviours result from the maintenance of this coping strategy, which leads to an eventual reliance on substance use as a means of adapting to these environmental stressors. While this is clearly a valuable extension to simple disease conceptions of addictive behaviours, purely social models of addictive behaviours have increasingly been replaced by social learning models which emphasize both the role of environmental stressors and behavioural learning phenomena in these behaviours. It is worth noting that these theories are not necessarily incompatible with **neurobiological models** of addictive behaviours, and may be better understood as explaining these phenomena at different levels of explanation.

CURRENT USAGE

Social learning theory argues that substance use and addictive behaviours arise through a process of behavioural acquisition and reinforcement, driven by **classical conditioning** and **operant conditioning** mechanisms. These theories have evolved from simple classical and operant conditioning theories through to more complicated social learning theories that point to the interactions between personal dispositions and environmental situations. There is general agreement that a complex behaviour like substance misuse cannot be acquired through a single learning mechanism. Several contingencies appear to reinforce or maintain substance misuse including the psychopharmacological properties of specific drugs, the social aspects of substance use, the individual's ability to tolerate aversive environments and/or aversive physical states related to substance use, and the individual's need to alter unpleasant psychological states.

The role of **classical conditioning** processes in social learning theories of addictive behaviours lies in their capacity to generate associations between substance use and outcomes initially unconnected with the use of the substance. For example, a social environment (an **unconditioned stimulus**, or US), may be relaxing (an **unconditioned response**, or UR). If alcohol is consumed in this environment (a **conditioned stimulus**, or CS), this will come to be associated with the UR (feeling relaxed), so that eventually the CS alone (namely, alcohol consumption) will elicit the feeling of relaxation (a **conditioned response**, or CR). Both internal and external cues can be associated with drug cues. Internal cues typically include subjective feelings of pleasure and relaxation, while external cues can include other people or specific contexts or situations. Note that **neurobiological theories** of addictive behaviours attempt to describe the brain pathways involved in these learning processes.

In addition, classical conditioning processes can occur in conjunction with **operant conditioning** processes. Operant conditioning refers to the process whereby behaviours which result in favourable outcomes tend to increase in frequency. This may be via a process of **positive reinforcement** (whereby positive consequences are *achieved* as a result of the behaviour) or **negative reinforcement** (whereby negative consequences are *avoided* as a result of the behaviour). In the context of addictive behaviours, positively reinforcing consequences of drug use may be elevated mood or increased social acceptance (which may be one process via which peer pressure exerts an influence on substance use), while negatively reinforcing consequences may be the reduction of subjective stress or (in acutely abstinent individuals) the removal of **withdrawal symptoms**.

Social learning theories imply that treatment should focus on creating and maintaining behavioural change, usually through a structured system of behaviour modification. In other words, the behavioural changes associated with addictive behaviours are reversible in broadly the same way as any other behaviour. Note, however, that neurobiological theories, which also argue that learning processes underlie the development of addictive behaviours, suggest that the **neuroadaptations** which give rise to these learned behaviours may be permanent or semi-permanent, and are therefore potentially less amenable to change than social learning theories would suggest. It is possible that the classical and operant conditioning processes which occur in addictive behaviours, because they relate to the effects of substances such as alcohol, nicotine, heroin, cocaine and so on, may be more powerful than those which occur in other behaviours related to **natural reinforcers** (such as food and water).

SIGNIFICANCE TO HEALTH PSYCHOLOGY

Although the use of illegal drugs, and in particular those with high physical and psychological dependency potential such as heroin and cocaine, remains relatively rare in developed countries (with the possible exception of marijuana, where use is widespread within certain age groups), other substances with high dependency potential such as alcohol and nicotine are widely used socially. The use of these substances also increases the risk of a number of negative health consequences, such as the increased risk of a variety of cancers and coronary heart disease. Psychologists, therefore, have a role to play in understanding the causes of addictive behaviours and in developing treatments for those seeking to reduce their use or to abstain entirely.

While disease models of addiction typically prescribe some form of **replacement therapy** in order to promote abstinence (for example, nicotine replacement therapy in smokers or methadone maintenance in heroin users), social learning theory emphasizes behaviour modification through appropriate rewards and punishments for specific behaviours. **Aversion therapy**, for example, seeks to pair punishments with behaviours associated with drug use (e.g. electric shocks whenever a cigarette is smoked). However, these therapies have generally been found to be ineffective, largely because the punishment contingencies are established in a controlled environment and do not appear to generalize to everyday life. Other approaches also grounded in social learning theory include financial incentives for abstinence (namely, financial rewards for avoiding smoking), which can be successful, although this success is modest once the period of financial reward ends, and **cue exposure** procedures, which involve exposing the drug users to cues which have become associated with the drug in order to gradually extinguish these associations. Cue exposure procedures can also include cognitive elements to encourage the development of coping strategies to deal with cravings arising from the presence of drug-related cues. Note that cue exposure techniques are distinct from cue avoidance techniques, which teach the individual to simply avoid these cues (for example, by avoiding environments which trigger urges to use a drug). **Group therapy** has also been demonstrated to be a successful treatment for addictive behaviours, and includes ongoing support between pairs of treatment-seeking individuals who establish a 'contract' between themselves to remain abstinent, and maintain contact to ensure each is adhering to this.

Psychologists can also inform **public health** interventions which are designed to modify behaviour at a population level, rather than at an individual level. For example, brief advice to stop smoking by general practitioners has been shown to increase smoking cessation rates by 5 per cent. Although small in absolute terms, this effect if applied across the entire smoking population of the United Kingdom has the potential to result in a very large number of individuals stopping smoking. More recently, governmental interventions such as restricting access to cigarettes (for example by increasing duty on cigarettes, so that prices increase) and banning smoking in workplaces and public places have increased, and a number of developed countries now have or are introducing restrictions on smoking in public places and workplaces. The advertising of potentially addictive substances is also increasingly restricted and, in some cases, banned altogether. Note that social learning theory would argue that banning smoking advertising and smoking in public places would eventually extinguish the association between these cues and the drug use itself, so that the benefits of these interventions would extend beyond simply restricting access or exposure.

Further reading

Drummond, D.C. (2001) Theories of drug craving, ancient and modern. *Addiction*, 96, 33–46.
Reviews the principal theoretical models of drug craving, provides some directions for future research, and challenges the widely held assumption that craving is the underlying basis for addictive behaviours.

Orford, J. (2001) Addiction as excessive appetite. *Addiction*, 96, 15–31.
Outlines the excessive appetite model of addiction, arguing that a broader conception of what constitutes addiction is required that places more emphasis on the socio-cultural processes within which addictive behaviours take place.

McCusker, C.G. (2001) Cognitive biases and addiction: an evolution in theory and method. *Addiction*, 96, 47–56.
Discusses anomalies in conceptions of addiction which depend on self-reported subjective experiences, and outlines advances on understanding grounded in cognitive neuroscience which may complement these traditional approaches.

See also **addictive behaviours and neurobiological models; addictive behaviours and tobacco**

ADDICTIVE BEHAVIOURS
and: ALCOHOL

MEANING

Alcohol, when used alone, generally refers to ethanol, which is a very strong and unique smelling, colourless, volatile liquid formed by the fermentation of sugars. It also often refers to any beverage that contains ethanol. Alcohol is a psychoactive substance, with depressant effects. The sale and consumption of alcohol are generally restricted, and in particular there are typically restrictions placed on the sale of alcohol to young people. The manufacture and consumption of alcohol are found in the majority of cultures and societies, and the consumption of alcohol frequently takes place in a social context and plays a role in social events.

ORIGINS

Alcohol has been widely consumed since prehistoric times, as a component of the standard diet, for hygienic or medical reasons, for its relaxant and euphoric effects, for recreational and social purposes, and so on. In the past, alcoholic drinks (in particular beer) were used to supplement normal diets because of their high calorific content, and were used as a substitute for water when its long-term storage (for example, on naval vessels) was unhygienic.

The negative consequences of alcohol use, in particular with respect to alcohol abuse and dependence, have been for as long as alcohol has been used in human societies. The framework within which alcohol abuse and dependence has been understood has changed, however, as conceptions of addiction have changed, for example from **moral models** to **disease models**. Moral models gave rise to the Temperance Movement in the eighteenth and nineteenth century, which encouraged total abstinence from alcohol. This, in turn, led to **prohibition** in the USA in the early twentieth century, which made the sale of alcohol illegal, although this period was short-lived. Now alcohol is generally widely available in developed countries (except in those which prohibit it for religious reasons, such as Islamic countries), but its sale is restricted.

CURRENT USAGE Most people in developed countries try alcohol at some time in their lives, although a large proportion report lifetime abstinence, frequently for religious reasons. Social alcohol consumption is widespread, therefore, although the prevalence of alcohol consumption and the amount consumed varies considerably between males and females, and across age groups. There are also cultural differences in the pattern of alcohol consumption: although individuals in southern European countries consume large quantities of alcohol, this tends to be consumed with food in modest amounts on separate occasions, while individuals in North American and northern European countries are more likely to '**binge**' drink (namely, consume four to five or more drinks on a single occasion, typically without food and leading to intoxication).

Alcohol consumption is a risk factor for a number of conditions, including liver disease, brain damage, and certain cancers (possibly by enhancing the carcinogenic effects of other chemicals), although there is also evidence that moderate consumption is protective against coronary heart disease and strokes. There therefore seems to be a curvilinear relationship (that is, U-shaped) between alcohol consumption and overall mortality, with modest alcohol consumption (roughly equivalent to one small drink daily and minimal binge drinking) associated with the lowest overall mortality. Contrary to popular belief, there is no strong evidence that alcohol consumption is strongly related to obesity, possibly because the calorific content of alcohol is not efficiently used. Alcohol also appears to increase metabolic rate significantly, thus causing more calories to be burned rather than stored in the body as fat. In the United Kingdom, the recommended maximum weekly alcohol consumption for men is 21 Units and for women 14 Units. A Unit is equivalent to a single 125 ml glass of 8 per cent strength wine, or half a pint (roughly 250 ml) of beer at 3 per cent strength, although there has been a trend in recent years for larger volumes of higher strength to be sold (e.g. a typical glass of wine is now between 175–250 ml and 12–14 per cent strength, equivalent to up to 3 Units).

In the first half of the twentieth century per capita alcohol consumption in the United Kingdom fell rapidly, but from the late 1950s to the end of that century alcohol consumption began to increase steadily. In the last ten years, evidence from the General Household Survey has shown that the proportion of men consuming more than the recommended weekly intake has remained stable, but has increased markedly (by around 50 per cent) in females. In young women (aged 16–24 years) this increase has been even more pronounced, with the proportion drinking more than 14 Units per week doubling over this period. Unfortunately the General Household Survey does not include data on binge drinking specifically, but given known patterns of drinking, especially in young adults, it is likely that much of this increase represents binge drinking.

Binge drinking was previously referred to as alcohol consumption over an extended period of time (e.g. two days or more). However, a widely used and current definition of a binge is five or more drinks on a single occasion for males, and four or more for females. There is some debate as to whether this constitutes an appropriate definition, but it continues to be widely applied. While binge drinking is rare in most of Europe, it is widespread in North America, the United Kingdom, Australia and other English-speaking nations. This perceived culture of binge drinking is increasingly becoming viewed by politicians and the media as a serious social problem, partly due to health reasons, but mostly due to its association with violence and anti-social behaviour.

Partly due to high levels of binge drinking, a large number of individuals in the United Kingdom drink heavily on a regular basis. This can lead to psychological dependence, in particular if drinking alcohol is used as a coping strategy for work-related or interpersonal stress. This can lead to social and occupational impairments, and is described as **problem drinking** (as distinct from **alcohol dependence** or **alcoholism**), and sometimes is described as **alcohol abuse**. Characteristic features of problem drinking include drinking alcohol to intoxication on a regular basis, and regularly drinking alcohol during the day, or alone. Problem drinking is more common among males than females, and most likely to develop between the ages of 18 and 30.

Those who are problem drinkers or regularly abuse alcohol are at increased risk of alcohol dependence, defined as a physical dependence on alcohol resulting in marked withdrawal following the cessation of use. Individuals with alcohol dependence (namely, alcoholics – although this term is used with decreasing frequency) have a high tolerance for alcohol, and frequently experience periods of memory loss, that on occasion can result in chronic memory loss. In severe cases alcohol dependence can result in **Korsakoff's Syndrome**, the primary symptoms of which include marked anterograde and retrograde amnesia. Problem drinking and alcohol dependence can both lead to serious social problems such as job loss and marital breakdown, so that alcohol abuse represents an important social issue in many societies around the world.

SIGNIFICANCE TO HEALTH PSYCHOLOGY

Psychology has a role to play in understanding the development of alcohol abuse, both for why people become problem drinkers, and in the treatment of alcohol dependency problems. The primary reasons for drinking alcohol are social and cultural, at least with respect to why people start drinking. The general acceptability of alcohol consumption in social contexts provides a strong model for adolescents through social learning processes, who perceive alcohol consumption to be a sociable and adult behaviour. Once alcohol consumption has begun, the pharmacological factors associated with this begin to play a role. Alcohol is a reinforcing substance which activates the reward pathways described in the **neurobiological models** of addiction, and also has other pharmacological effects (such as providing relaxation and improving mood, at least in appropriate contexts), so that various positive and negative reinforcement processes will sustain the behaviour. The role the reduction of tension and anxiety plays in the maintenance of alcohol consumption and development of problem drinking has been referred to as the **tension-reduction hypothesis**.

There is growing evidence that levels of alcohol consumption, and in particular alcohol dependence, are under a degree of genetic influence (see twin, family and adoption studies and molecular genetics). Twin studies have generally found a higher level of concordance for problem drinking between monozygotic (identical) twins compared to dizygotic (non-identical) twins. There is also some evidence that the subjective response to first drinking alcohol predicts subsequent problem drinking, with those who appear to be less sensitive to the effects more likely to become problem drinkers. The evidence for this remains controversial, although there is general acceptance that genetic factors do contribute to the likelihood of problem drinking. Other familial factors, such as modeling parents' drinking behaviour, also contribute to the observation that drinking patterns tend to be transmitted across generations within families.

A variety of treatment models for alcohol dependence exist, some of which encourage lifetime or permanent abstinence and others of which aim to allow the individual to return to controlled drinking following treatment. Due to the physical dependence which accompanies alcohol dependence, a period of detoxification is usually necessary, which results in severe withdrawal symptoms. For this reason, detoxification is often conducted in a controlled medical environment, using medication to control the symptoms.

Psychological and behavioural treatments for alcohol dependence include **aversion therapy** techniques, which pair the consumption of alcohol with a drug which induces nausea when alcohol is consumed (which is typically done over a series of controlled drinking sessions following injection of the drug). Theoretically, this should lead to a conditioned aversion for alcohol through a process of classical conditioning. These therapies are sometimes moderately successful, although potentially distressing for the patient and may have limited efficacy if the effects do not generalize to the world outside of the clinical setting in which the therapy took place. **Self-monitoring** and **stress management** techniques have also been show to be effective, by enabling the individual to identify internal and external triggers for alcohol consumption (and thereby avoiding these) and to develop alternative coping strategies to deal with the feelings of anxiety and stress.

Although medical and psychological treatments for alcohol dependence are effective, their long-term benefits are reduced because of the problem of relapse. The level of drop-out from treatment programmes is generally high, and only a minority of those who successfully complete their treatment programme maintain their abstinence or controlled drinking for a year or more following treatment. Common reasons for relapse include a lack of alternative coping strategies – so that when faced with stressors in the environment the individual reverts to alcohol consumption as a coping strategy – and the social pressure to drink. Cues in the environment can also continue to trigger cravings and urges to drink for a long period following treatment (see neurobiological models).

Further reading

Enoch, M.A. (2006) Genetic and environmental influences on the development of alcoholism: resilience vs. risk. *Annals of the New York Academy of Sciences*, 1094, 193–201.
Discusses the key time frame for the development, and prevention, of alcoholism, which lies in adolescence and young adulthood, and the role of severe childhood stressors in vulnerability to addiction.

Field, M. and Eastwood, B. (2005) Experimental manipulation of attentional bias increases the motivation to drink alcohol. *Psychopharmacology (Berl)*, 183, 350–357.
Reports evidence that attentional biases for alcohol-related cues in social drinkers can be modified, and that these modified biases can influence subsequent drinking behaviour.

Kadden, R.M. (2001) Behavioral and cognitive-behavioral treatments for alcoholism: research opportunities. *Addictive Behaviors*, 26, 489–507.
Reviews evidence for the effectiveness of behavioural and cognitive-behavioural treatments for alcohol dependence, and suggests research directions to improve these treatment models.

See also **addictive behaviours and neurobiological models; addictive behaviours and social and behavioural models; addictive behaviours and tobacco; biological and physiological models and twin, family and adoption studies; biological and physiological models and molecular genetics**

ADDICTIVE BEHAVIOURS
and: TOBACCO

Tobacco consumption in developed countries exists predominantly in the form of **MEANING** manufactured **cigarettes**, although other delivery mechanisms are available, including cigars, pipes, and '**smokeless tobacco**' products such as chewing tobacco and snuff. People become physically dependent on tobacco principally because of the nicotine contained in it, which is now acknowledged to be the primary addictive constituent, although other chemicals present in tobacco, as well as additives introduced in the manufacturing process, may also contribute to the addiction potential of such products. While it is nicotine that is the primary addictive constituent, it is the **carbon monoxide** produced by burning tobacco (in non-smokeless products) and other chemical constituents (which form a residue called **tar**) which contribute principally to the harmful health effects of tobacco consumption.

ORIGINS
Tobacco was introduced to the Western world following the exploration of the North American continent by European expeditions. Initially, tobacco was used for 'medicinal purposes', but by the beginning of the sixteenth century, consumption for pleasure was becoming widespread, initially in the form of pipe smoking and snuff taking. The manufactured cigarette was developed at the beginning of the twentieth century which, allied to production methods that produced a mellower tobacco for easier inhaling, resulted in a rapid increase in the popularity of cigarette smoking, with up to 60 per cent of the male and 40 per cent of the female population of developed countries smoking at the peak of smoking prevalence in the 1950s and 1960s. Following the publication of seminal research by Richard Doll and Austin Bradford Hill in 1950, indicating a strong relationship between cigarette smoking and **lung cancer**, however, smoking prevalence began to decline.

CURRENT USAGE
While the use of other tobacco products (e.g. cigars and various smokeless products) continues, the majority of tobacco consumed is in the form of manufactured or self-rolled cigarettes. Cigarette smoking will therefore be focused on in this section. Despite a reduction in the prevalence of smoking in developed countries since the 1950s, it remains widespread, with prevalence ranging from roughly 20 per cent to 40 per cent across countries. Prevalence continues to be substantial in developing countries, however, and the rate of decline in developed countries has slowed considerably in recent years. In addition, smoking prevalence within a country tends to vary considerably with **socio-economic status**, with higher rates of smoking in poorer socio-economic groups. One consequence of this is that existing disparities in health between wealthier and poorer groups in society tend to be exacerbated. Cigarette smoking also tends to be more prevalent among males than females, although in many countries such as the United Kingdom this difference has reduced since the 1950s.

Tobacco consumption, and in particular cigarette smoking, is linked with a number of adverse health effects. In particular, smoking is linked to an increased risk of a number of cancers, including a highly increased risk of **lung cancer**, as well as **coronary heart disease** and **chronic obstructive pulmonary disease** (including emphysema and chronic bronchitis). Cigarette smoking has also been shown to be linked with **infertility** and **subfertility** (in both males and females) and a number of mental health conditions, including **depression** and **schizophrenia**. However, it remains unclear whether smoking increases the risk of mental health problems, or individuals with mental health problems are more likely to smoke (possibly in an effort to 'self-medicate' their symptoms). There has also been recent interest in the health effects of **environmental tobacco smoke** (also described as **passive smoking**), which is now generally acknowledged to be linked with the same broad health effects as direct smoking, although the degree of risk is substantially lower in absolute terms. Cigarette smoking is also linked to an increased likelihood of the use of other substances, including alcohol as well as illegal drugs such as cannabis, although it is not clear whether this is due to any direct causal effects.

While smoking has acknowledged and well-understood negative health effects, a few marginal health benefits have been observed in smokers, reducing their risk of several diseases, such as **Alzheimer's disease** and **Parkinson's disease**. It should be noted that the increased risk of terminal illness from smoking is still widely believed to outweigh the benefits and these examples should not be taken as evidence that smoking is healthy or beneficial overall.

The increasingly well-known negative health effects of smoking, allied to public health campaigns and policy directives motivated by these effects, such as reducing or prohibiting tobacco advertising, increasing the rates of duty and taxation on tobacco products, and restricting access by raising the age at which individuals are able to purchase tobacco products, have together been successful in reducing the prevalence of smoking in developed countries. A number of countries are also now introducing bans on smoking in public places and workplaces, in large part because of growing evidence and concerns regarding the negative health effects of **environmental tobacco smoke** (usually described as **passive smoking**). Despite this general reduction in prevalence, however, certain groups (in particular low income groups) continue to smoke at levels only slightly lower than levels in the 1950s. In addition, the rate at which adolescents are starting to smoke remains high, and there is even some recent evidence that this rate is increasing, in particular among females. Possible reasons for this continued uptake of smoking by young people include smoking continuing to be perceived as an adult behaviour, peer pressure, a desire to demonstrate independence from their parents and other adult authority figures, and the use of smoking as a means to control weight (in particular among females).

While a large proportion of individuals will experiment with trying one cigarette, only the minority progress to becoming regular smokers. Factors such as parental smoking, sibling and peer smoking, and positive attitudes to smoking (e.g. regarding smoking as glamorous or adult) are related to an increased likelihood of progression to regular smoking. Once regular smoking is established, exposure to nicotine over time results in eventual **physical dependence** and **psychological dependence** in most smokers, although a substantial proportion remain so-called **chippers** – social smokers who do not appear to be nicotine dependent and find it relatively easy to stop smoking. Among those who are nicotine dependent, however, stopping smoking is extremely difficult, with **relapse** rates comparable to those found in alcohol and heroin dependence.

One reason for this variation in who is likely to become tobacco dependent is genetic variation (see twin, family and adoption studies, and molecular genetic studies). As with other substances (see alcohol), the similarity in smoking behaviour is greater between identical (monozygotic) twins compared with non-identical (dizygotic twins), suggesting a genetic influence. Recent molecular genetic studies have identified a number of candidate genes which may influence the likelihood of smoking initiation (possibly via effects on personality measures such as novelty seeking), the risk and degree of nicotine dependence, smoking cessation success, and so on. Some studies have also identified genetic variants which appear to modify the response to pharmaceutical smoking cessation aids such as nicotine replacement therapy, raising the possibility than in the future it may be possible to prescribe a kind (or dose) of treatment on the basis of an individual's genotype, to maximize the chances of success.

SIGNIFICANCE TO HEALTH PSYCHOLOGY

There are a number of psychological reasons why an individual may progress from experimentation with cigarettes to regular smoking. These include smoking to increase **positive affect** (mood), to decrease **negative affect** (e.g. stress reduction), the development of habitual smoking (which may operate outside of conscious awareness), and the development of psychological dependence (e.g. via positive and negative reinforcement processes, perhaps related to mood regulation). Social learning models of cigarette smoking are informative, not least because of the strong **social context** within which cigarette smoking takes place (see alcohol). A biopsychosocial model would include the physical dependence potential of nicotine, and the withdrawal symptoms which accompany acute abstinence from smoking (which include irritability, cravings for cigarettes, weight gain and mouth ulceration, for a period lasting four or more weeks).

Interventions to assist individuals attempting to stop smoking may include pharmacological or behavioural treatments, or a combination of these. Until recently, the only pharmacological aid with proven efficacy was **nicotine replacement therapy** (NRT), on the basis that reduction of the **withdrawal symptoms** associated with abstinence by replacing nicotine levels would mean that cessation could be maintained. Various NRT products exist, such as gums, patches and nasal sprays, and all have been shown to roughly double the chances of success. Recently, other medications which don't include nicotine, such as bupropion and varenicline, have been developed. Although these act in very different ways (for example, bupropion is an atypical anti-depressant), their effectiveness is roughly similar to NRT products, although using multiple medications in conjunction may be particularly effective, in particular if they are allied with **behavioural support**.

Smoking cessation services, which offer group or individual therapy, can help people who want to quit. Most smoking cessation programmes offer a combination of behavioural support, motivational interviewing, cognitive-behavioural therapy, group therapy, and advice on appropriate pharmacological treatments. Programmes in the United Kingdom are available through the National Health Service. The **Stages of Change Model** of Prochaska and DiClemente (1983) has been used to understand the process of smoking cessation (see Figure 9.1), highlighting the processes involved in the transition from being a smoker to being a non smoker, across four basic stages of Precontemplation, Contemplation, Action and Maintenance.

There is also research on the **Health Belief Model**, the **Theory of Reasoned Action** and the **Theory of Planned Behaviour** in relation to predictors of smoking

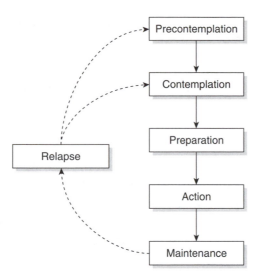

Figure 9.1   The Stages of Change in Smoking Cessation (*Source*: Prochaska and DiClemente, 1983)

Note: Prochaska and DiClemente described the Stages of Change Model of behaviour change, which has been widely applied to addictive behaviours such as smoking cessation. The model describes the stages through which an individual moves, from not considering change (precontemplation), to a desire to change (contemplation), followed by actual behaviour change (preparation and action) and the continuation of this change (maintenance). Since behaviour change, particularly in the context of addictive behaviour, is hard to maintain, there is also a role for relapse, after which the individual may revert to one of the earlier stages (precontemplation or contemplation). The model is helpful in roughly characterizing whether or not someone is ready and willing to, for example, stop smoking (since without this willingness any attempt is unlikely to be successful), but has been criticized for assuming that relapse should be followed by regression to the earlier stages of precontemplation or contemplation. For this reason, a distinction is sometimes made between a lapse (a minor slip, such as smoking a single cigarette) and a relapse (reverting to regular, daily smoking).

and, in particular, smoking cessation. Individual perceptions of perceived susceptibility, perceived behavioural control, and past cessation attempts have been shown to predict the likelihood of smoking cessation. Health education campaigns have therefore focused on these factors in an attempt to modify them and thereby increase rates of cessation, for example by increasing perceptions of perceived susceptibility to tobacco-related disease.

Further reading

Munafò, M., Clark, T., Johnstone, E., Murphy, M. and Walton, R. (2004) The genetic basis for smoking behavior: a systematic review and meta-analysis. *Nicotine and Tobacco Research*, 6, 583–597.

Reviews the evidence for a genetic contribution to smoking behaviour, and in particular the influence of various candidate genes on smoking behaviours such as smoking initiation, smoking persistence, and nicotine dependence.

Tiffany, S.T., Conklin, C.A., Shiffman, S. and Clayton, R.R. (2004) What can dependence theories tell us about assessing the emergence of tobacco dependence? *Addiction*, 99, 78–86.
Summarizes three reviews in the same article, which cover theories from the perspectives of negative reinforcement, positive reinforcement, and cognitive and social learning theory.

See also **addictive behaviours and neurobiological models; addictive behaviours and social and behavioural models; addictive behaviours and alcohol; biological and physiological models and twin, family and adoption studies; biological and physiological models and molecular genetic studies**

ADDICTIVE BEHAVIOURS
and: **BEHAVIOURAL ADDICTIONS**

MEANING   **Behavioural addictions** refer to those behaviours which share the characteristics of addictive behaviours but which do not involve the use of a **substance** or pharmacological agent (sometimes described as chemical addictions, to distinguish these from behavioural addictions). A number of examples of possible behavioural addiction have been suggested recently, such as sex, internet and video game addictions, although the most widely investigated is **gambling addiction**. This is sometimes referred to as **problem gambling**, since there remains considerable controversy regarding whether this constitutes a genuine addictive behaviour.

ORIGINS   Gambling has had many different meanings, depending on the cultural and historical context, but it is currently defined in economic terms, referring to 'wagering money or something of material value on an event with an uncertain outcome with the primary intent of winning additional money and/or material goods'. Typically, the outcome of the wager is evident within a short period of time. It is generally controlled to some degree by legal restrictions, due in large part to the acknowledged potential social consequences of excessive gambling, while in some countries it is illegal, in most cases because of religious prohibitions on gambling in those countries (e.g. Islamic countries).

Table 9.1   Criteria for a diagnosis of pathological gambling
(*Source*: American Psychiatric Association, 2000)

Pathological gambling is defined as persistent and recurrent maladaptive gambling behaviour meeting at least five of the following criteria:

Preoccupation	Frequent thoughts about gambling experiences
Tolerance	Larger/more frequent wagers to achieve a 'high'
Withdrawal	Restlessness or irritability when gambling ceases
Escape	Gambling to improve mood or escape stressors
Chasing	Attempting to win back losses with more gambling
Lying	Hiding the extent of gambling to others
Loss of control	Failure to reduce gambling
Illegal acts	Breaking the law in order to obtain gambling money
Risked significant relationship	Gambling despite risking or losing a relationship
Reliance on others	Requesting financial assistance from family/friends

Pathological gambling is diagnosed in the presence of five or more of these symptoms IF this behaviour is not better accounted for by a possible manic episode.

The psychological effects of gambling, and the potential for this to result in problem gambling, have been acknowledged for some time. Dostoevsky describes these effects in the novel *The Gambler*. Gambling Research Australia have defined problem gambling as ' … characterised by difficulties in limiting money and/or time spent on gambling which leads to adverse consequences for the gambler, others, or for the community'.

Problem gambling is an urge to gamble despite harmful negative consequences or the desire to stop. The term is preferred to 'compulsive gambling' among many professionals, as few people described by the term experience true compulsion in the clinical sense. For similar reasons, the term is also preferred to 'gambling addiction'. Problem gambling often is defined by whether harm is experienced by the gambler or others, rather than by the gambler's behaviour. Severe problem gambling may be diagnosed as clinical **pathological gambling** if the gambler meets certain criteria (see Table 9.1).

CURRENT USAGE

There is some evidence that the likelihood of problem gambling is related to the degree of success experienced after initial experiences. This may be regarded as analogous to evidence that the risk of dependence on chemical substances is related to the effects experienced when a drug is first used. There is also some evidence that the brain processes involved in problem gambling are similar to those involved in chemical addictive behaviours, although this evidence is mixed and controversial.

The prevalence of problem gambling is approximately 5 per cent in developed countries, with pathological gambling occurring at a lower rate of approximately 1 per cent. However, this varies substantially between countries, and appears to be higher in countries where gambling is less regulated (e.g. Australia and the United Kingdom) compared to those where it is more strictly controlled (e.g. the United States).

In the United Kingdom, legislation regulating gambling has recently been updated to provide appropriate protections for children and vulnerable adults, as well as extending the coverage of the regulatory framework to internet gambling services, which are growing rapidly in popularity. There are concerns, however, that this legislation will ultimately result in wider access to gambling, with an attendant increased risk of problem gambling and pathological gambling.

SIGNIFICANCE TO HEALTH PSYCHOLOGY
Few behavioural treatments for problem gambling currently exist, but the possible existence of addictive behaviours which can develop in the absence of a chemical substance raises important questions regarding the mechanisms of addictive behaviours. In particular, problem gambling can be readily understood in the context of **social learning theory**, and in particular positive and negative reinforcement processes allied with social processes, but less readily in the context of **neurobiological models** (although these would still argue for a biological basis to the relevant learning processes). For example, there are current concerns (with some evidence to support these concerns) that increasing the availability of gambling results in an eventual increase in the prevalence of problem gambling (as an increase in the availability of drugs increase the risk of problems of addictive behaviours related to these drugs).

Given the potential for **psychological dependence** to develop as a result of positive and negative reinforcement processes, it is relatively uncontroversial that behavioural addictions such as problem gambling can be characterized in these terms, since these behaviours can give rise to subjective feelings of elation, a distraction from stressful live events, and so on. Other behaviours which give rise to powerful positive and negative reinforcement processes include sex, internet and computer use, eating, self-harm and work, and these have all variously been described as 'behavioural addictions'. Given the potentially important role of these reinforcement processes, behavioural treatments which do exist follow broadly the same model as those for chemical addictive behaviours, although clearly replacement therapies (e.g. nicotine replacement therapy for tobacco addiction) are not possible in the case of behavioural addictions.

Further reading

Pallesen, S., Mitsem, M., Kvale, G., Johnsen, B.H. and Molde, H. (2005) Outcome of psychological treatments of pathological gambling: a review and meta-analysis. *Addiction*, 100, 1412–1422.
Investigates the short- and long-term effect of psychological treatments of pathological gambling and factors relating to treatment outcome and concludes that they yield very favourable short- and long-term outcomes.

Potenza, M.N. (2006) Should addictive disorders include non-substance-related conditions? *Addiction*, 101, 142–151.

Argues that there are substantial similarities between pathological gambling and substance use disorders, and that addictive disorders should include non-substance use disorders (namely, behavioural addictions).

See also **addictive behaviours and social and behavioural models; addictive behaviours and neurobiological models**

10

TEN

HEALTH PROMOTION AND INTERVENTION

HEALTH PROMOTION AND INTERVENTION
and: **health promotion**
  persuasion processes
  fear appeals
  doctor-patient communication
  adherence

In Chapter 3 (Social Cognitive Models) we saw how a number of models and approaches have been developed or applied to change individuals' health-related decision making (intention formation) and subsequent health-related behaviour. These approaches are important because they detail specific psychological factors that require intervention in order for change to occur. These include models such as the precaution adoption processes model, the transtheoretcial model of behaviour change, protection motivation theory and the health action process approach. These approaches have identified change processes within the individual. In this chapter we build on these ideas, but also focus on identifying some of the key concepts that have been developed and applied by health psychologists in the field of health promotion. We are more interested here to study what we know about how to encourage individual change through population-based intervention. One example here is the large-scale advertising campaigns to encourage healthier eating habits or less risky driving behaviours. The key question we are asking here is: what are the key psychological processes that can be effective in understanding the promotion of a healthy (unhealthy) lifestyle? It is not so much *what* we need to change but *how* we maximize the likelihood of change.

HEALTH PROMOTION AND INTERVENTION
and: **HEALTH PROMOTION**

MEANING

Health psychology is concerned with how psychological processes are important for understanding how we maximize longevity and facilitate quality of life. **Health promotion** builds on this assumption and concerns 'any event, process or activity that facilitates the protection or improvement of the health status of individuals, groups, communities or population' (Marks et al., 2005: 393). With such an overarching definition, health promotion is about all interventions, environmentally based or behaviourally based, that seek to address and allow for changes in individual and population health status. Some of these interventions will be based on matching the intervention to the individual or group (see for example intervention-based stages/phases of change in Chapter 3) while others will be focused on intervening with the masses, such as large-scale health education programmes.

ORIGINS

At some point in our lives we have all been the recipient of some form of health promotion activity whether it be through being exposed to health promotion leaflets in general practitioner's surgeries or viewing the large-scale messages developed for television, radio or billboards. We have been exposed to health education or promotion at all points in our lives. Figure 10.1 gives a few examples of health promotion activity.

Health promotion is as old as the discipline of health psychology. Indeed the idea that there is some mileage in designing interventions to facilitate cognitive and behavioural change in individuals and groups of individuals so as not to experience negative (health) outcomes is probably as old as psychology itself. Nevertheless, the development of various models for understanding how and why people take the health-related decisions they do (e.g. the health belief model – Chapter 3), and whether by knowing this we can design interventions to encourage people and groups to form decisions and behave in a less health-compromising manner, have been central for the operation and development of health psychology as a discipline.

CURRENT USAGE

Health promotion concerns environmentally based interventions as well as those focused on the behaviour of individuals, groups or even populations. Environmentally based interventions encompass public policies developed by significant health-related organizations (e.g. the World Health Organization) and are applied within individual countries (Bennett and Murphy, 1997) such as the focus on creating a healthy environment (in schools, workplaces and neighbourhoods) adopted by the UK government's Our Healthier Nation programme

Figure 10.1   Examples of health promotion leaflets

Book a flu jab today

Anyone can get flu but it can be more serious for people aged 65 years or over and people of any age (including children over 6 months of age) with a serious medical condition, particularly those with serious heart or respiratory disease. You may also be at an increased risk if you have diabetes that requires medication, have serious kidney or liver disease or if you have lowered immunity due to disease or treatment.

If you fall into one of these groups, you are more vulnerable to the effects of flu (even if you feel fit and healthy) and

could develop more serious illnesses such as bronchitis and pneumonia, potentially putting you in hospital. It could also make any existing condition worse.

That's why it pays to get your flu jab in the autumn before flu starts to circulate. Because the virus constantly mutates, it's necessary to get the jab every year, to protect you against the latest strains of the virus.

So make an appointment with your GP today. The flu jab is free and available between September and early November.

© Crown copyright 2005
Produced by COI for the Department of Health
269742 1p 1.7m Jul05 (CHO)

If you require further copies of this title quote 269742/*If you knew about flu* and contact:

NHS Immunisation Information
DH Publications Orderline
PO Box 777
London
SE1 6XH
Phone: 08701 555 455
Fax: 01623 724 524

E-mail: dh@prolog.uk.com
Textphone (for minicom users): 08700 102 870
for the hard of hearing (8am to 6pm, Monday to Friday)

For more information on
immunisation, visit our website
at www.immunisation.nhs.uk

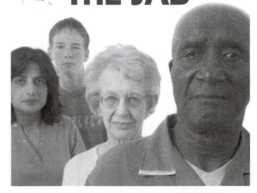

Flu jab →

NHS

IF YOU KNEW ABOUT FLU YOU'D GET THE JAB

NHS
Immunisation Information

Flu jab →

Fight flu this winter

How do I know when I've got flu?

Flu symptoms hit you suddenly and severely. They usually include fever, chills, headaches and aching muscles, and you can often get a cough and sore throat at the same time.

Don't wait until there's an epidemic: contact your GP or practice nurse and get your flu jab this autumn before the virus appears in the winter.

Who needs a flu jab?

Ask your GP about having a flu (influenza) vaccination if:

- you're 65 or over

or if you have any of these problems (however old you are):

- a serious heart or chest complaint, including asthma
- serious kidney disease
- diabetes
- lowered immunity due to disease or treatment such as steroid medication or cancer treatment

Your GP may also advise you to have the flu jab if you have serious liver disease.

If you live in a residential care home, talk to your nurse or the manager.

If you are the main carer for older or disabled people then you should ensure that they are vaccinated (if recommended) and also seek advice from your GP as to whether you should be vaccinated so that you can continue to look after them.

Isn't flu just a heavy cold?

No. Colds are much less serious and usually start gradually with a sore throat and stuffy or runny nose.

How serious is flu?

Catching flu is a nasty experience for most people. But it can also lead to really serious illnesses like bronchitis and pneumonia, which may mean you need hospital treatment. A lot of people, mainly older people, die from flu every winter.

How do I catch flu?

Flu is a highly infectious illness, which spreads very rapidly by coughs and sneezes from people who are already carrying the virus.

When am I most at risk from flu?

Flu reappears every winter, usually over a short period of a few weeks, so a lot of people get ill around the same time. In a really bad year, this can amount to an epidemic, but it's impossible to predict how much flu there'll be every year.

If I had the jab last year, do I need it again now?

Yes. The viruses that cause flu change every year, which means the flu this winter will be different from last winter's, and the vaccine will be different as well.

Why shouldn't everyone have a flu jab?

For most people, flu is nasty but not usually serious. The vaccine is offered only to people who are at high risk from the serious complications of flu.

How long will the jab protect me?

The vaccine provides protection for about a year.

How does the vaccine work?

Your body starts making antibodies to the vaccine virus about a week to ten days after the injection. The antibodies help protect you against any similar viruses you then come into contact with.

Will it stop me from getting ill?

Flu vaccinations only protect against flu: they won't stop you catching the many other viruses that appear every winter. But because flu is generally more serious, it makes sense to have a flu jab.

Can the flu jab actually cause flu?

No. The vaccine doesn't contain any live virus, so it can't cause flu.

Will there be any side effects?

Side effects should be expected. Some people get a slight temperature and aching muscles for a couple of days afterwards, and your arm may feel a bit sore where you were injected, but that's about all. Any other reactions are very rare.

How effective is the vaccine?

No vaccine is 100% effective. Most people who've been vaccinated will not get the flu. If you do catch flu, it's likely to be milder than if you hadn't been vaccinated.

When are flu vaccines given?

The best time is between September and early November, ready for the winter. Don't wait until there's a flu epidemic.

Is there anyone who shouldn't get a flu jab?

If you have a serious allergy to hens' eggs, you shouldn't get vaccinated. If in doubt, ask your doctor. And you shouldn't have the vaccine if you have ever had a serious allergic reaction to the flu vaccine, or to any of its ingredients, which needed urgent medical treatment. If you're not sure please ask your doctor for advice.

Can I have the flu vaccine if I am pregnant?

Yes. If you are in one of the risk groups mentioned above, talk to your GP about this. No problems have been reported in giving the vaccine to pregnant women.

How do I go about getting immunised?

If you think you need a flu vaccination, check with your doctor or the practice nurse – or if a nurse visits you regularly, you can ask them. Alternatively, ask your local pharmacist. Most doctors organise special vaccination sessions in the autumn.

Are you aged 65 or over?

Ask your GP whether you need the pneumo jab to protect you against serious forms of pneumococcal infection. It is available for everyone aged 65 years or over and for younger people with certain serious medical conditions. You won't need it each year – for most it is a one-off vaccination. It is OK to have the pneumo jab at the same time as your flu jab.

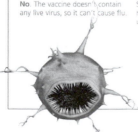

NHS

(Department of Health, 1998). On the whole, how effective environmentally based interventions are is not necessarily determined by whether the people who are to benefit from the measures are aware of the measures or are required to engage with the intervention. For instance, people do not have to be aware that foodstuff ingredients are regulated for them to receive benefits from this process, namely by not being exposed to potentially harmful ingredients in foods through statutory legislation.

Interventions based on behaviour, in contrast, are dependent on the actions of individuals and groups. Interventions which aim to raise awareness of and knowledge about health risks and health hazards (through focused education), such as those concerned with HIV prevention or drink-driving, are examples of this type of promotion. Unlike environmentally based interventions, for behavioural types to be effective requires that people are actively involved and cooperate in the intervention programme. For this to occur necessitates that the intervention needs to be designed so as to maximize engagement with the focus of the intervention and must be delivered in such a way that any individual or group will be subject to maximal persuasion (see persuasion processes concept – this chapter).

According to Marks et al. (2005) there are basically three main approaches that can be thought of as informing health promotion initiatives – the **behaviour change approach**, the **self-empowerment approach** and the **collective action/ community development approach**. The behaviour change perspective argues that the alteration of thinking processes (cognitions such as beliefs about the efficacy of behaviour) should be the central focus of health promotion (education) activities (see Rutter and Quine, 2002). Models based on social cognitive principles have been developed to understand decision-making processes and the link between thought and action (namely, behaviour). These models include the theories of reasoned action and planned behaviour, the health belief model, and protection motivation theory, among others (see Chapter 3 for a detailed discussion of these models). By knowing the beliefs an individual holds about protective action and the perceived risks associated with a behaviour, we are able to identify which types of belief sets need to be changed to result in behavioural change (Conner and Norman, 2005). While these models specify the types of thoughts that need to change in order for behaviour to alter in the desired direction, they do not address fully how to explicitly change these thoughts (Sutton, 2002). Models proposed to address this conundrum operate within the realms of the persuasion process (see persuasion processes concept – this chapter).

The self-empowerment perspective argues that health promotion activities can be designed and implemented most efficiently if the individual is in control of their social and internal environments. Increased self-empowerment is proposed to influence the decisions we make in relation to all aspects of our everyday being, including health-related matters. Self-empowerment occurs through engagement and involvement with health-related activities whether at an individual or community-based level. For example, in a review of the literature for encouraging safer sex practice (namely condom use) and decreasing the risk of HIV infection, Abraham and Sheeran (1994) argued that interventions directed at self-appraisal and behavioural reflection, such as the rehearsal of negotiation and communications strategies and peer education initiatives, engender self-empowerment by raising behaviour specific self-efficacy beliefs.

The collective action or community development approach differs from the behaviour change and self-empowerment perspectives by emphasizing the relationship between individual health status and the social/health context within which the individual lies. This perspective argues that individual health status is dependent upon, for example, environmental causes of illness, and it is these causes that require intervention for the individual's health to be manipulated. It is also proposed that people act collectively to change their physical and social environment.

Evidence assessing the impact of health promotion campaigns, including community-based interventions, has on the whole been rather inconclusive. For example, the Minnesota Heart Health Programme sought to change the coronary heart disease risk status of population members by combining media advice and awareness strategies, screening programmes, community-based workshops and environmental measures (such as the labelling of food as 'low fat', and so on). Results showed little effect on health behaviours and actual health among the population studied (Jacobs et al., 1986). However, peer education programmes have demonstrated significant effects on the HIV risk behaviours of at risk populations. For example, Williamson et al. (2001) report a study of the effect of the so-called Gay Men's Task Force – a trained group of peers who made contact with and discussed safe sex practices with other gay men in their community. Results showed that participants who had contact with a member of the team of peer education facilitators reported more protective safe sex practices than those who had not had any exposure.

SIGNIFICANCE TO HEALTH PSYCHOLOGY Health promotion activities have been the mainstay of public health policy and intervention for many years in many countries. Health promotion activities can be delivered at the individual level, the group level or even the population level. Various mechanisms have been proposed to understand how best to conceptualize health promotion. One perspective is based on changing individual action, another locates that health promotion is served best by developing self-empowerment in individuals, while the third argues for the importance of the social and environmental context and that health benefits will accrue when people act collectively to develop a healthy status through community action.

Further reading

Bennett, P. and Murphy, S. (1997) *Psychology and Health Promotion*. Buckingham: Open University Press.
A detailed examination of the conceptual basis for health promotion activities and its relationship to important psychological components.

Norman, P., Abraham, C. and Conner, M. (2000) *Understanding and Changing Health Behaviour: From Health Beliefs to Self-Regulation*. Amsterdam: Harwood Academic.
Explores various models of health behaviour and how such theoretical approaches have been conceptualized, developed and tested in health-related behavioural interventions.

Rutter, D.R. and Quine, L. (2002) *Changing Health Behaviour.* Buckingham: Open University Press.
Excellent volume that details specific examples of interventions based on clear theoretical principles.

See also **health promotion and intervention and persuasion processes; health promotion and intervention and adherence; health promotion and intervention and fear appeals**

HEALTH PROMOTION AND INTERVENTION
and: PERSUASION PROCESSES

MEANING

For social and health psychologists, persuasion refers to how attitudes or beliefs change as a result of exposure to messages and information about an attitude object, or something we have an opinion about (Petty and Cacioppo, 1996; Bohner and Schwartz, 2003). Persuasive messages are everywhere. We are continually exposed to these from the television screen, the radio, on billboards, in newspapers and magazines, as well as from other people around us. These messages come in the form of advertising campaigns and also health promotion campaigns. These messages are designed to alter our attitudes towards an object or about a behaviour, such that for something we have been in favour of originally we are now disfavourable towards having been exposed to a persuasive communication. The persuasive communication has changed our 'thinking' about the attitude/belief object. The assumption behind understanding persuasion is that a change in an attitude or belief in a desired direction will result in a behavioural change in line with the new attitude or belief (Bohner and Wänke, 2002). For health psychologists understanding how to persuade people,

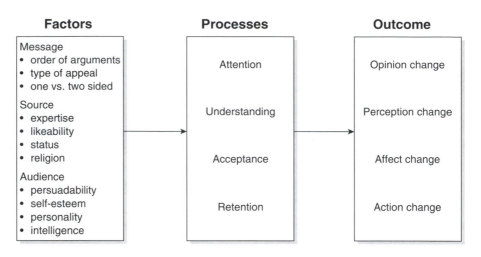

Figure 10.2   The Yale model of persuasive communication (adapted from Fishbein and Ajzen,1975)

to abandon original risky beliefs about health-compromising behaviours in favour of those that result in health protective behaviour, is a fundamental issue.

ORIGINS   Over the years, psychologists have been interested in which cognitive processes are important for understanding how attitudes change after exposure to a persuasive communication and how we can design persuasive communications that are likely to evoke long-lasting attitude change and behavioural change. Early work on **persuasion processes** at Yale University identified a number of factors that are important for describing the conditions necessary for a persuasive communication to be effective or not (Hovland and Janis, 1959) (see Figure 10.2). These factors are the message *source* (who is doing the persuading?), aspects of the *message* itself (e.g. does scaring people persuade them to change?), the message *recipient* (who is being persuaded?), and the *context* of the persuasion attempt (under what conditions is the person being persuaded?).

CURRENT USAGE   This early work did not identify specific cognitive processes that are fundamental for manipulating attitudes or beliefs and then behaviour through persuasive communication. More recently models that propose two modes of cognitive processing (so-called 'dual route models') have been influential in understanding such cognitive conditions of persuasion. The routes proposed by these models differ in the extent to which a person uses more effortful thinking about the information and arguments included in a persuasive message. The most influential of these dual route models are the **elaboration likelihood model** (ELM) (e.g. Petty and Cacioppo, 1996) and the **heuristic systematic model** (HSM) (Bohner et al., 1995;

Chen and Chaiken, 1999). These approaches have been the focus of much persuasion work since the late 1970s and were based on earlier work from the so-called 'cognitive response approach' to persuasion (see Greenwald, 1968).

In the ELM the modes of thinking or routes of cognitive processing that create changes in attitudes and subsequently behaviour after exposure to a persuasive communication are called the 'central route' and the 'peripheral route' (see Figure 10.3). These routes describe the poles of a cognitive processing continuum characterized by levels of cognitive effort (Petty and Cacioppo, 1986).

For the central route to be in operation the persuasive message recipient has to be fully engaged with the content of the message and the information it contains. They are engaged in effortful cognitive processing. In contrast, the peripheral route or mode is dependent on resources that require very little cognitive effort. So, for instance, heuristics, which are general rules of thumb used in decision making (e.g. 'what experts say is always correct'), may be one tool used as part of peripheral processing. The ELM proposes that to achieve central route processing requires that people elaborate on the details of the message and, in this way, engage in a cognitively effortful way. Cacioppo et al. (1981) identify the thought-listing technique as a mechanism through which elaboration can occur – during exposure to a persuasive message participants are required to report any relevant thoughts that come to mind. However, since individuals have limited processing capacity (see Fiske and Taylor, 1991), they cannot elaborate every persuasive message encountered. In this way, it could be that less effortful peripheral processing is the default mechanism used when an individual is initially exposed to a persuasive message.

Other work within the framework of the ELM has examined which factors determine whether a person elaborates on the message or not. Evidence shows that motivation to process received information, such as being personally involved with the message content or accountability for a behavioural decision based on message content, are important factors (Petty and Wegener, 1998). In addition, actual ability to process the information (e.g. the presentation of strong versus weak arguments – Petty et al., 1981) may be important. In effect, a person who is motivated and able to engage with a message is more likely to elaborate the message and use the central processing route, while decreased motivation and ability result in less cognitive effort and subsequent peripheral processing.

In general, attitude or belief sets developed or altered through central route processing appear to be more persistent, harder to change, and are also good predictors of behaviour. Processing via the peripheral route appears to result in more temporary belief change and is also less likely to result in long term behaviour change. In effect, it seems that one of the aims of any persuasive communication is to provide the conditions in which central route processing is likely to occur, because it is this level of 'thinking' that leads to more profound attitude and subsequent behaviour change.

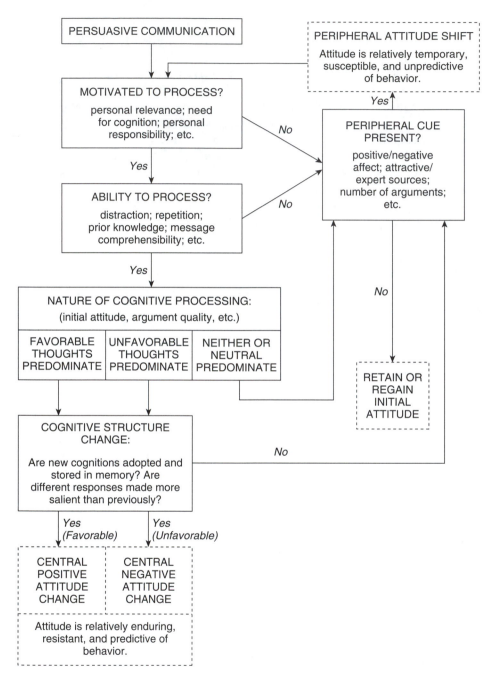

Figure 10.3   The elaboration likelihood model of persuasion (*Source*: Eagly and Chaiken (1993) *The Psychology of Attitudes*, p. 308. Originally presented in Petty and Cacioppo, 1986, p. 126)

The ELM has been used in trying to change attitudes and behaviour in applied contexts including health-related behaviours (e.g. Jones et al., 2003). For example, Quine et al. (2002) used the ELM to deliver a persuasive communication based on the theory of planned behaviour and directed at persuading schoolchildren to use cycle helmets when riding. Ninety-seven children aged between 11 and 15 years, who stated they did not use a cycle helmet, were randomly assigned to receive a persuasive communication in the form of an intervention booklet, or a control booklet. The intervention booklet contained persuasive messages based on behavioural beliefs (e.g. 'protecting one's head'), normative beliefs (e.g. 'the expectations of parents for wearing a cycle helmet') and control beliefs (e.g. 'overcoming the barriers to helmet use'). While being presented with the persuasive communication, participants were asked to elaborate on the information by, for example, listing any thoughts that came to mind while studying the message. The control group was given a booklet that was concerned with attending a cycling proficiency course. Twenty-five per cent of the intervention group wore a helmet when riding five months after the intervention, compared to none in the control group. In addition, participants subjected to the persuasive message also showed more positive beliefs about wearing cycle helmets when riding. See Figure 10.4 for Quine et al.'s persuasive communication.

A second currently influential model is the heuristic-systematic model of persuasion (HSM) (Chen and Chaiken, 1999). The HSM, like the ELM, comprises two modes of processing – an effortless heuristic mode and a cognitively demanding systematic mode. The HSM also assumes a 'processing continuum', and that processing mode is dependent upon a person's motivation and ability to process the persuasive message encountered. Systematic processing is characterized by an analytical appraisal of the message when forming a judgment. In the heuristic processing mode general rules of thumb (or heuristics) which are stored in the long-term memory, like 'if an expert thinks that it must be right', are used in decision making. Little cognitive effort is required to use this processing mode. Activation in memory and the use of this mode depend upon an heuristic cue contained in the format or content of the message. For example, delivery of a message by a perceived-to-be-an-expert source may act as an heuristic cue. In much the same way as the peripheral route of the ELM, heuristic processing is argued to be the default when presented with persuasive messages.

The HSM makes different assumptions to the ELM in terms of what effects fluctuations in motivation and cognitive activity have on processing type and persuasion effectiveness. For instance, the HSM allows for the operation of both systematic and heuristics processing simultaneously – the so called 'co-occurrence hypotheses' (Bohner et al., 1995). For instance, if a message is ambiguous in that it contains both strong and weak points, initial default heuristic processing of the information will bias and inform subsequent systematic processing. The HSM also suggests a number of factors that may be important for predicting levels of

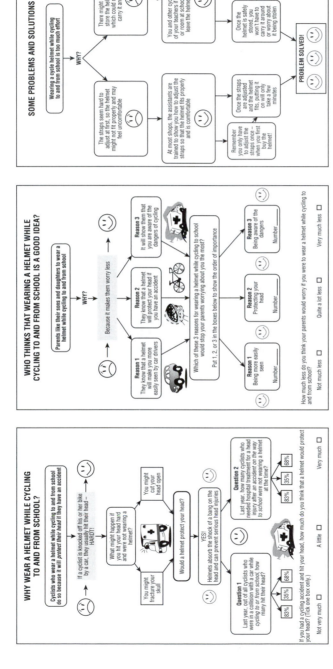

Figure 10.4   Quine et al.'s (2002) communication to persuade young cyclists to wear cycle helmets (*Source:* Quine et al., 2002, p. 179)

motivation related to either heuristic or systematic modes. One example here is called the 'sufficiency principle' which assumes that individuals want to have confidence in their attitudes but that this confidence has to be sufficient and is dependent on the sufficiency threshold (or desired confidence) and actual confidence. When actual confidence is less than desired confidence the motivation to process information at the systematic level is increased, and the wider the difference between desired and actual confidence the greater will be the processing required for narrowing the gap. Other factors such as accountability and the relevance of a message to the individual have also been found to be important for desired confidence or sufficiency thresholds (see Eagly and Chaiken, 1993: 326–346). For instance, a highly personally relevant and persuasive communication is likely to result in a person trying to achieve greater certainty in the judgment being formed.

Understanding the conditions under which people are more easily persuaded in a prioritized direction is essential if health promotion activities are to result in behavioural change via attitude/belief realignment or development. This applies to media-based and advertising-based general health campaigns directed at large populations of individuals, and also to individualized and intensive interventions (e.g. such as delivered in smoking cessation clinics). Evidence over the years has shown which factors are likely to result in a more sustained attitude change, as well as demonstrating the relationship between types of 'thinking' or levels of cognitive processing that increase the likelihood of receiving, analysing and comprehending a persuasive message.

SIGNIFICANCE TO HEALTH PSYCHOLOGY

Further reading

Bohner, G. and Schwartz, N. (2003) Attitudes, persuasion and change. In A. Tesser and N. Schwartz (eds), *Blackwell Handbook of Social Psychology: Intraindividual Processes*. Oxford: Blackwell. pp. 413–435.
Provides an overview of psychological principles and models involved in understanding attitude change and persuasion. Gives some nice examples of such processes in an applied context.

Petty, R.E. and Wegener, D. (1998) Attitude change: multiple roles for persuasion variables. In D.T. Gilbert, S.T. Fiske and G. Lindzey (eds), *Handbook of Social Psychology* (4th edition). New York: McGraw-Hill. pp. 323–390.
Provides an interesting account of a number of persuasion processes, including the elaboration likelihood model, which are effective in maximizing belief-based and behavioural change.

See also **health promotion and intervention and fear appeals; health promotion and intervention and health promotion**

HEALTH PROMOTION AND INTERVENTION
and: FEAR APPEALS

MEANING   One approach to persuasion that has been the focus of much work over the past 50 or so years is that based on what are called **fear appeals**. Doubtless you can recall many examples of fear appeals that you have encountered that were intended to make you think about a particular behaviour that may be potentially detrimental to your health and should be acted upon. These include appeals such as those related to mortality in relation to driving too fast or after having consumed alcohol, the threat of contracting HIV or other sexually transmitted diseases if condoms are not used, and so on. Figure 10.5 gives two examples of persuasive communications that can be thought of as eliciting arousal or fear in the individual. The idea behind this approach is that the fear aroused in a person by the appeal will motivate them to change their attitudes and behaviour. However, some evaluations of these fear appeals suggest that they are not always successful (Witte, 1992) and these have even questioned the effectiveness of evoking fear when attempting to persuade individuals to change (Ruiter et al., 2001).

ORIGINS   Early work proposed that fear has a persuasive impact on current attitudes, beliefs and behaviour because the emotional arousal evoked, in response to fear, acts as a motivational source for the appraisal of current beliefs and attitudes (McGuire, 1968). In other words, if a persuasive communication evokes fear the individual will be motivated to reduce this unpleasant psychological state by altering their beliefs and/or behaviour towards some attitude object (Sutton, 1982). Therefore, there is a relationship between fear and a drive to reduce this experienced fear through belief or behavioural modification.

CURRENT USAGE   The relationship between the level of fear experienced (or arousal) and the likelihood of behaviour change is not linear in nature. There does not seem to be a proportionate increase in the likelihood of behaviour change with increasing arousal level. As well as motivating an individual to actively search for ways of reducing the fear or perceived threat by, for example, changing behaviour, arousal may also lead to more deliberative processing of the recommended action and as such will act as an interference to change. The observation is that as the level of fear increases facilitation effects are hypothesized to increase at a greater rate than interference effects, but that this relationship is only relevant up to an optimal level of fear arousal. Once this optimal level is reached, interference effects created by fear increase at a greater velocity than facilitation effects and as such the U-shaped representation results. McGuire (1968) conducted many studies in which he altered the levels of fear invoked by different messages. He found that the relationship

One recent (Department of Transport, Think campaign poster) Road Safety Image

Figure 10.5   Two fear appeals

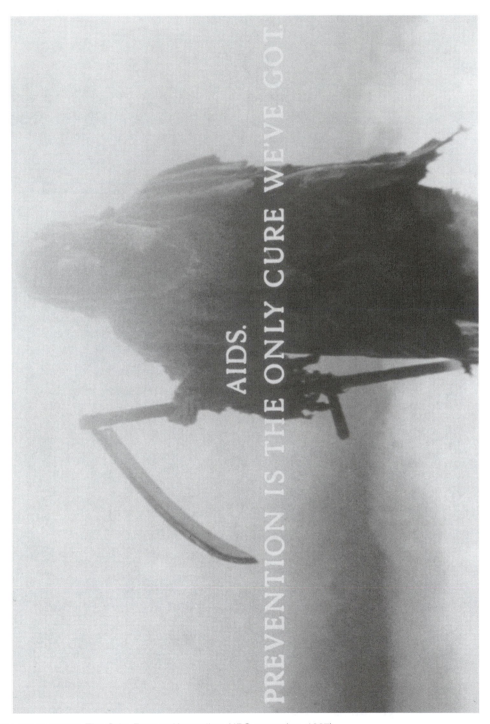

… and one not so recent. The Grim Reaper (Australian AIDS campaign, 1987)

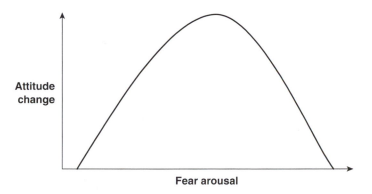

Figure 10.6   McGuire's inverted U curve hypothesis for describing the relationship between levels of fear and attitude change

between the amount of fear aroused and the degree of attitude change was best represented by this inverted U-shaped curve (see Figure 10.6).

When too little or too much fear is invoked there is weak attitude or behaviour change, whereas moderate doses of fear bring optimal levels of change. It is argued that this is because when little fear is aroused the message fails to grab the attention of the perceiver, and when fear is extreme attention to the message will again decrease. But what explains this attentional process? In effect, it seems that the individual is diverting cognitive resources (or thinking resources) towards dealing with the negative arousal (e.g. the anxiety invoked through the experience of fear). If the fear-arousal hypothesis is correct, the best course of action for those designing fear-based appeals is to produce messages that involve neither too much nor too little fear. This should result in the perceiver attending to the content of the message and does not allow for the diversion of resources away from the message to deal with the arousal experienced.

One social cognition approach that has already addressed which cognitive and emotional processes are important when a person is experiencing arousal through fear is **protection motivation theory** (Rogers, 1983; see also Norman et al., 2005) (see protection motivation theory concept – Chapter 3). PMT argues that a number of key factors are fundamental for understanding the mechanisms by which a person reduces the threat of an event and stimulates the motivation to protect themself from potential negative outcomes associated with the threat. These are the degree of perceived severity of an event, the perceived likelihood of an event or outcome occurring if no adaptive response is made to the threat event, and finally, how efficacious the response made to the threat is perceived to be.

Individuals are argued to undertake two parallel cognitive appraisal processes when presented with a source of information that invokes fear or negative arousal. These appraisal processes contain cognitive mediators in the relationship between the experience of threat and behavioural enactment. One process is labelled **threat appraisal**. Perceived severity of threat and perceived vulnerability to the threat are central components in this appraisal process and are proposed to inhibit maladaptive responses. So, for example, an individual may be motivated to take self-protective action and, as such, to inhibit maladaptive responses if they perceive themselves as vulnerable to a severe health threat. PMT also makes the important point that for any given person there may be intrinsic rewards, such as expectancies related to positive mood if a course of action is taken, or extrinsic rewards, such as expectancies related to social approval in undertaking a behaviour, that operate to promote the adoption of a maladaptive behaviour.

The second appraisal process is called **coping appraisal**. Three cognitive factors are outlined as important for coping efficiently with a perceived threat and altering the likelihood of an adaptive response. **Response efficacy** refers to personal beliefs that self-protective action would decrease the health threat arousal experienced, while **self-efficacy** concerns personal beliefs associated with whether the recommended action can be undertaken by the individual (see the social cognition theory concept – Chapter 3; self-efficacy concept – Chapter 5). High response efficacy and high self-efficacy increase the likelihood of an adaptive behaviour being undertaken (Milne et al., 2000). This coping appraisal process also proposes that there are response costs, or barriers to behaviour, that inhibit the likely performance of a self-protective action, and these are perceived by an individual when formulating a decision to act in a protective way.

The final core factor in PMT is called 'protection motivation' and is the result of the thinking processes a person engages in during threat appraisal and coping appraisal. Protection motivation is positively associated with perceptions of severity and vulnerability, response efficacy and self-efficacy. It is negatively associated with rewards for maladaptive responses and perceived costs of adaptive responses. PMT proposes that protection motivation is high when severity and vulnerability to a health threat outweigh the rewards related to acting in an unhealthy way, and also when response and self-efficacy are increased relative to the costs of taking adaptive action (see the protection motivation theory key concept in Chapter 3 for greater detail). Whether health promotion professionals utilize this knowledge in the design of public health interventions is questionable. For instance, a content analysis of the nature of a large number of health promotion leaflets showed that severity and vulnerability beliefs are detailed very frequently whereas efficacy perceptions are not (Kline and Mattson, 2000). If PMT is correct, this should not result in increased protection motivation since only threat appraisal processes are being manipulated.

Fear appeals operate to emphasize specifically beliefs or attitudes that can be thought of as addressing the risks of undertaking a maladaptive behavioural pattern. It is common to stress the negative outcomes that are more likely to occur if a person does not act in a protective way. This is called 'negative framing of messages'. An alternative to this method is to frame the message by reinforcing the positive aspects of behaving in a self-protective manner – called 'positive framing'. It has been argued that the positive framing of messages encourages and enhances the processing of information, especially when people are not motivated to engage with the message. The evidence for the effectiveness of the positive versus negative framing of health communications is inconsistent. Some research has shown that positive messages are more likely to lead to health protective behaviour (e.g. for sunscreen purchasing – Detweiler et al., 1999). Other research has shown that negative framing shows greater effects (mammography attendance – Banks et al., 1995), while recent work has shown no differences in the type of framing on attendance for screening (Finney and Iannotti, 2003).

Another approach which has been recently adopted to study the effects of fear appeals of health behaviours has been conceptualized within **terror management theory** (TMT). One characteristic of fear appeals is that they focus on the mortality-related risks connected to the performance (or not) of the risky behaviour in question. We are exposed very regularly to adverts or other media-based interventions that emphasize the risk of dying or some other health outcome associated with behaviours we may undertake. TMT suggests that when people are reminded of their own mortality (such as through information provided in fear appeals) they use proximal defensive strategies like denial or distancing, but after some delay when thoughts of one's own mortality have become accessible but are not in focal attention, an individual will engage distal defence strategies (Pyszczynski et al., 1999, 2004).

The **mortality salience hypothesis** of TMT proposes that two types of distal defence strategies are used to reduce the state of 'terror' caused by the saliency of mortality. The first is that people make cognitive and behavioural efforts to protect their cultural worldview, which are views shared among individuals about the nature of reality (see Greenberg et al., 1997). Secondly, cognitive and behavioural attempts may be made to maintain or increase personal self-esteem by reinforcing the values sanctioned by these cultural worldviews. Studies have shown that when mortality is made salient individuals who perceive a behaviour to be relevant for their self-esteem will actually engage in more maladaptive health behaviour than those who do not view the behaviour as important for their self-esteem (e.g. Arndt et al., 2006). People are striving to maintain their self-esteem such that when this is threatened they undertake actions that serve to bolster self-esteem. For example, Taubman Ben-Ari et al. (1999, 2000) have shown that in drivers for whom driving per se is important for their self-esteem, having their mortality made salient has led to an increase in risky driving-related intentions and risky driving in a simulator (see Figure 10.7). Importantly, in another study they showed that giving positive feedback eliminated this effect because the individuals had already found a mechanism for protecting or enhancing personal self-esteem. This work is of potential significance because it details a mechanism based on the need to protect or enhance self-esteem that could account for large individual differences in behavioural response to fear appeals when mortality is made salient. In effect, it could be the case that when a behaviour is important for self-esteem any attempt to change a person's behaviour may be compromised because they use more maladaptive

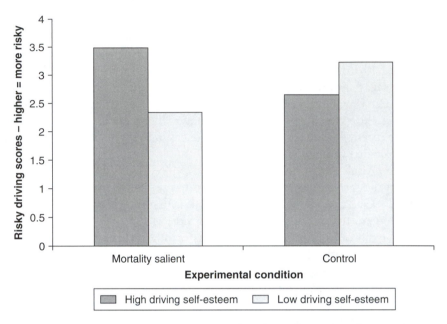

Figure 10.7   Terror management theory in practice: the effects of mortality salience and driving self-esteem on risky driving intention (Adapted from Taubman Ben-Ari et al., 1999)

Note: Mortality salience is induced by requiring half the participants to write down what will happen to them when they physically die and the emotions that the thought of their own death arouses in them. The other participants wrote about what will happen to them when they visit a restaurant. For drivers with high driving as relevant to self-esteem scores mortality salience had the effect of increasing the likelihood of reporting risky driving behaviours relative to the control group. For those low in driving self-esteem mortality salience resulted in a decreasing likelihood of reporting risky driving compared to the control group.

behavioural responses to defend their self-esteem. The question then becomes, are certain interventions actually producing more risky behaviour – the opposite of that intended – for some individuals? This is an empirical question for which evidence is sparse at the moment.

SIGNIFICANCE TO HEALTH PSYCHOLOGY While fear appeals are used in health promotion campaigns and the fear-arousal relationship has been consistently proposed as a potential mechanism for understanding belief change via the effects of emotional arousal, studies that have aimed to examine the relationship have not provided a measure of the levels of fear aroused in an individual (see Sutton, 1982). Nevertheless, researchers have used fear appeals (of one sort or another) to manipulate key factors inherent in a number of models of health behaviour (see Rutter and Quine, 2002, for a number of examples). However, the exact nature of the interaction between the message given and the arousal experienced in the message recipient has not been the focus of this work.

Further reading

Ruiter, R.A.C., Abraham, C.A. and Kok, G. (2001) Scary warnings and rational precautions: a review of the psychology of fear appeals. *Psychology and Health*, 16, 613–630.
Excellent contemporary review of how fear appeals may be beneficial in persuading people to change their health behaviour.

Sutton, S. (1982) Fear arousing communications: a critical examination of theory and research. In J.R. Eiser (eds), *Social Psychology and Behavioural Medicine*. London: Wiley. pp. 303–337.
Considers components of fear appeals and how psychological approaches have utilized such processes in understanding behaviour and behaviour change.

See also **health promotion and intervention and health promotion; health promotion and intervention and persuasion processes; health promotion and intervention and adherence**

HEALTH PROMOTION AND INTERVENTION
and: DOCTOR-PATIENT COMMUNICATION

At some point in your life you have probably been to see a doctor (or another health professional) about a medical complaint you have identified and are suffering from. What do you remember about these encounters? Were they beneficial? Did you understand what was being said to you? Did you take the advice of the professional and act upon it, namely, were you compliant with the recommendations? And were you in general satisfied with the interaction and outcome of the consultation? Communication between a patient and a health professional is usually the only way that knowledge about the physical and mental well being of a person can be examined and addressed. Because most consultations take place in a face-to-face manner (or more recently, in telephone conversations with appropriate professionals), communication is interpersonal (that is, between people). Given this, knowledge about a health problem is initially given verbally by the patient to the professional, as are the recommendations for action given by the professional. The effects of the interaction between doctor and patient can result in dissatisfaction and ultimately non-compliance/non-adherence with any treatment recommendations proposed (Stewart, 1995).

MEANING

ORIGINS

Doctor-patient communication is about those factors that both the patient and doctor bring to the interpersonal communication in a consultation setting. Some work has focused on the communication skills required for an effective consultation. For instance, Hall et al. (1988) identified that satisfaction with a consultation was best associated with occasions when the health professionals used positive social conversation and non-verbal communication strategies. Other work has identified a number of fundamental elements for effective communication in the consultation process, including information giving in combination with emotional support, checking for understanding of the details of the information given, the recognition of the expectations and concerns of the patient by the doctor, and that the health professionals themselves may not be therapeutically committed to working with certain patient groups (Stewart, 1995; Albery et al., 1996; Roter et al., 1997; Albery et al., 2003).

CURRENT USAGE

Psychologists have been particularly interested in studying the relationship between various factors inherent in the doctor-patient communication setting and compliance to recommended courses of action. A plethora of evidence has shown that a significant proportion of patients had stated that they were not satisfied with the medical consultations they had experienced (Ong et al., 1995; Marteau and Weinman, 2004), which may be reflected in elevated rates of partial compliance or non-compliance in some instances. Ley (1988) proposed the cognitive model hypothesis of compliance to conceptualize and form the basis for a research programme examining those psychological factors that are important for manipulating satisfaction and compliance in patients as a result of the medical consultation (see Figure 10.8).

Ley (1988) was specifically interested in the operation of various cognitively based mechanisms – understanding processes and memory processes – that affect satisfaction and compliance. Studies have shown that in general the success of the consultation in terms of reported satisfaction was dependent upon consultation content. Factors such as how the practitioner conveyed information (in terms of memorability), emotional support, the 'personalization' of information, using language that was easily comprehended, checking for understanding in the patient, among others, have all been shown to be positively related to satisfaction and ultimately compliance (e.g. Ley, 1998; Berry et al., 2003). In terms of maximizing understanding of the information conveyed, studies have shown that requiring patients to 'think through' the types of issues or clarifications that they want to be discussed in the consultation (such as preparing lists of questions or using prompt sheets) produced greater satisfaction in both doctors and patients (e.g. Bruera et al., 2003). Other research has shown that the expectations brought to the consultation by the patients in combination with information-giving style predict satisfaction (Rutter et al., 1996; Iconomu and Rutter, 2001). While it seems that communication skills in the consultation are an important factor for satisfaction and compliance, evidence suggests that these skills are not consistently present (e.g. Campion et al., 2002). However, it has been demonstrated that such skills can be learned through

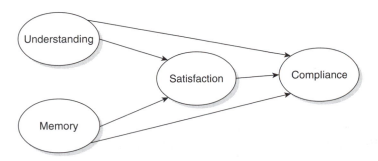

Figure 10.8   The cognitive model hypothesis of compliance (*Source*: Ley, 1988)

training and intervention and can then subsequently be used in practice (e.g. Fallowfield et al., 2002).

While patients bring beliefs and expectations to the medical consultation, so do health professionals. Beliefs about illness, causes of ailments and courses of treatment held by the doctor may guide the information given to the patient, the information asked for by the patient and ultimately the recommendations made for intervention. For example, research has shown that in terms of clinical decision making doctors use both their expectations of patients' wishes and needs, as well as their beliefs about the effectiveness of treatment outcomes and the seriousness of the illness (Weinman, 1987; Grunfeld et al., 2001). Work has also shown that the characteristics of the health professionals themselves affect the kind of intervention given or the communication encountered. Hoppe and Ogden (1997) showed that the type of advice given to obese patients by overweight practice nurses was different than for thinner practice nurses. With this in mind it seems that the interaction between doctor and patient is multifaceted and subject to powerful motivational and cognitive factors brought by both the practitioner and patient.

SIGNIFICANCE TO HEALTH PSYCHOLOGY

The significance of understanding the role of doctor-patient communication, and those psychological processes that are fundamental for describing communication effectiveness, is that these factors are likely to influence compliance which is an essential component for the adoption of health protective behaviours. Compliance in patients may be dependent upon satisfaction with the content of the medical consultation, which in turn, it is argued, is generated from how much the patient can understand and recall of the information given and received in the consultation.

Further reading

Marteau, T.M. and Weinman, J. (2004) Communicating about health threats and treatments. In S. Sutton, A. Baum and M. Johnston (eds), *The Sage Handbook of Health Psychology*. London: Sage. pp. 270–298.
Useful and exhaustive review of key factors involved in practitioner-patient interactions. Includes a detailed synthesis of such factors.

Stewart, M.A. (1995) Effective physician-patient communication and health outcomes: a review. *Canadian Medical Association Journal*, 152, 1423–1433.
Identifies and reviews relevant evidence to describe beneficial and harmful communication strategies between the doctor and patient.

See also **health promotion and intervention and adherence; health promotion and intervention and health promotion**

HEALTH PROMOTION AND INTERVENTION
and: ADHERENCE

MEANING In the context of health psychology, **adherence** refers to the situation when the behaviour of an individual matches the recommended action or advice proposed by a health practitioner or information derived from some other information source (such as advice given in a health promotion leaflet or via a mass media campaign). One example of adherence is following a course of medication whereby the patient takes the prescribed dose at a recommended time. Another example is the self-medication of insulin in a Type 1 diabetic patient. Psychologists are interested in establishing what sorts of cognitive and affective factors are important for predicting adherence and, importantly, non-adherence behaviour. In recent times, the term 'adherence' has been used as an alternative to 'compliance', since it reflects a more active management or self-regulation of treatment advice. **Compliance**, on the other hand, implies a more passive role for the individual of just following the advice of a prescriber with little engagement and possession of treatment by that patient.

ORIGINS To be adherent is not the rule. In fact, non-adherence rates are high in many treatment programmes including those for chronic illnesses (Petrie et al., 1996; Hand, 1998), as well as for primary intervention strategies such as diet and exercise regimes (Christensen, 2004). As such, the fact that people are and remain non-adherent to intervention regimes designed not only to reduce the risks of experiencing a negative outcome but also to overcome or manage chronic conditions is a significant issue in healthcare and policy. Marteau and Weinman (2004) categorize non-adherence into two types – passive non-adherence and active non-adherence. The former refers to non-adherence that is unintentional, such as is created by miscomprehension of treatment advice. The latter concerns occasions when the patient deliberately and intentionally makes a decision not to follow a treatment regime.

While the objective measurement of adherence or non-adherence is not without difficulties (Myers and Midence, 1998), there is strong evidence to suggest that increased adherence is related to positive health outcomes (DiMatteo et al., 2002) and non-adherence to negative health outcomes (e.g. Horwitz et al., 1990). In addition, there is little to suggest that adherence rates are associated with a plethora of socio-demographic (e.g. socio-economic status) (Sackett and Haynes, 1976) and individual difference type factors (e.g. personality) (Bosley et al., 1995).

More recent research has focused on specific cognitive and affective psychological factors for the prediction of adherence and non-adherence to treatment regimes (see Horne, 1998). Researchers have utilized a number of key factors from social cognition theory to understand the belief-based differences between those who adhere to treatment regimes and those who do not. Evidence from work based on the predictions of models like the health belief model and the theory of planned behaviour (see the concepts in Chapter 3) have shown a relationship between, for instance, adherence rates and the perceived susceptibility to those outcomes related to not taking the recommended action, emphasizing the barriers to action over the benefits, and the perceived beliefs of significant others (e.g. Cummings et al., 1981; Reid and Christensen, 1988; Conner and Norman, 2005).

CURRENT USAGE

Other studies have utilized attention paradigms in studying the non-verbal responses of participants suffering from chronic illness to stimuli associated with their ailment and its relationship with adherence. In one study Jessop et al. (2004) used the modified Stroop paradigm to study differences in attentional bias to asthma-related stimuli among people with asthma categorized as adherers or non-adherers. The modified Stroop task requires participants to ignore the actual word itself and respond as quickly as possible to the ink colour of a word presented on a computer screen. Words related to the illness condition (in this example, asthma-related words) are matched in terms of verbal frequency and word length to a set of neutral (or control) words. The idea is that the content of the word grabs the attention of the participants and reaction times to concern-related words will be slower than for neutral words (see Albery et al., 2006; Munafò and Albery, 2006). This has been found in a number of other areas such as alcohol use (Sharma et al., 2001), gambling (McCusker and Gettings, 1997) and smoking (Munafò et al., 2003). Jessop et al. (2004) found that those asthma sufferers who reported the highest and lowest levels of adherence showed the greatest interference from asthma-related stimuli. This evidence suggests that for some individuals the activation of a cognitive representation associated with asthma is related to whether or not they adhere to treatment.

Finally, adherence behaviour has been studied using the self-regulatory model (or illness representations model) (Leventhal et al., 1992). This model outlines cognitive and affective processes that operate to interpret any symptoms experienced, coping with the perceived symptoms and appraising how effective any response applied to the interpretation is. (Leventhal's approach is detailed in the self-regulation model key concept in Chapter 6.) In terms of adherence behaviour research has shown that, for instance, people who believe their condition to be controllable or curable (a type of illness representation) were more likely to attend for rehabilitation after myocardial infarction (Petrie et al., 1996). In addition, people who showed more concern with respect to the long-term consequences of taking medication for chronic conditions showed decreased adherence (Horne et al., 1999).

SIGNIFICANCE TO HEALTH PSYCHOLOGY Understanding the psychological processes involved in adherence and non-adherence to a prescribed course of action to overcome illness is important if interventions are to be designed to maximize the likelihood that people or patients will benefit from treatment. Research has shown that, in general, adherence is facilitated according to a number of factors including how a person cognitively represents their illness in terms of curability, controllability, perceived susceptibility to negative outcomes (if they do not enact appropriate behaviour), emphasizing perceived benefits to action over any barriers, as well as perceiving that important others would wish them to behave in the recommended manner.

Further reading

DiMatteo, M.R., Giordani, P.J., Lepper, H. and Croghan, T.W. (2002) Patient adherence and medical treatment outcomes. *Medical Care*, 40, 794–811.
Useful paper that identifies a number of key components in adherence that predict different treatment outcomes.

Myers, L. and Midence, K. (1998) *Adherence to Treatment in Medical Conditions*. London: Harwood Academic.
Excellent volume that draws together evidence from a number of health-related fields to explore the key factors involved in adherence and compliance to medical and health-related interventions.

See also **health promotion and intervention and doctor-patient communication; health promotion and intervention and health promotion**

GLOSSARY

ACE models Genetic models which indicate the proportion of additive genetic (A), common environmental (C) and unique environmental (E) variance which accounts for observed phenotypic variance.

Acquired Immunodeficiency Syndrome A serious (often fatal) disease of the immune system transmitted through bodily fluids, and in particular blood products, especially by sexual contact or contaminated needles in intravenous drug users.

Acute A condition having a short or rapid onset and lasting for a distinct and typically short period. As distinct from **chronic**.

Acute pain Pain which is short-lasting and clearly related to an underlying physical pathology (e.g., tissue damage), and which resolves relatively quickly as the injury causing it heals.

Addiction A chronic, relapsing condition characterized by compulsive drug-seeking and drug-taking, possibly related to long-term changes in the brain.

Adherence The active process whereby the behaviour of an individual reflects that recommended action or advice proposed by a health practitioner or through information derived from some other information source.

Alcohol A colourless, volatile, flammable liquid produced by the fermentation of sugars or starches. Generally taken to mean ethanol, when consumed by humans, which produces psychoactive and intoxicating effects.

Alcohol abuse The excessive consumption of alcohol in a manner which may cause physical, psychological or social harm, and which may be related to **alcohol dependence.**

Alcohol dependence Reliance on alcohol, typically as a result of the withdrawal symptoms that arise when alcohol consumption ceases in those who have used alcohol to excess over an extended period. Resumption of alcohol consumption removes withdrawal symptoms, thereby leading to further alcohol use through negative reinforcement processes.

Alcoholism Increasingly rarely used term (**alcohol abuse** and **alcohol dependence** are now preferred, as they refer to distinct components of the syndrome) which refers to the **addiction** to **alcohol**.

Allele   Alternative form of a genetic locus; a single allele for each locus is inherited separately from each parent.

Alzheimer's disease   A progressive form of dementia that is similar to senile dementia except that it usually starts earlier in life; first symptoms are impaired memory which is followed by impaired thought and speech and finally complete helplessness.

Anchoring   The classification and naming of unfamiliar objects by comparing that which is experienced against the collection of familiar classes of event or protoypes.

Appraisal   A judgment, in psychology typically referring to another person or external events, and made in terms of the impact of oneself, potential threat, etc.

Association   In molecular genetics, a technique for identifying whether or not variation in a specific gene is related to a behaviour or disease, by determining whether a specific variant occurs in a given population at a greater than chance frequency.

Attentional bias   Refers to the selective attention to, or processing of, material of specific personal relevance. For example, heavy drinkers appear to demonstrate attentional bias towards alcohol-related cues compared to neutral cues.

Attitude   A general feeling or evaluation, in a positive (favour) or a negative (disfavour) direction, about a person, object or issue.

Attrition   The loss of participants in a study. If this in non-random (for example, attrition is higher in a treatment group compared to the control group), this may lead to **bias**.

Automaticity   A process or behaviour that operates outside of conscious awareness, is very difficult to control, is unintentional (not consciously planned) and is mentally efficient such that it can operate when cognitive resources are also being used to do other tasks.

Aversion therapy   The pairing of a behaviour (e.g., drug taking) with an unpleasant or aversive consequence, in an attempt to reduce the specific behaviour through learning processes.

Behaviour change approach   A health promotion perspective that argues that the alteration of thinking processes should be the central focus in the development of health promotion activities.

Behaviour genetics   The study of the relative contribution of genetic and environmental influences on various outcomes such as behaviours and risk of disease. Typically involves the study of twins or other related family members.

Behavioural addiction   An addictive-like behaviour which occurs in the absence of a substance of pharmacological agent (e.g., gambling addiction). There is some debate regarding whether such behaviours genuinely constitute an addiction.

Behavioural intention   Prior to behaviour enactment people form a cognitively based intention to behave in that way. Intention is formed from attitudes, beliefs, normative values and perceived control over doing the behaviour. From the theory of planned behaviour.

Behavioural models   Models which emphasize the relationship between behaviours and their consequences in sustaining these behaviours, usually through learning processes such as operant conditioning. Have been widely used in attempting to understand the maintenance of pain behaviours in chronic pain.

Behavioural support   In therapeutic interventions, the use of motivational counselling, group therapy and other therapies which do not include a pharmacological component.

Benign   In cancer, tumours which are not malignant – an abnormal growth that is not cancerous and does not spread to other areas of the body.

Bias   In research, a statistical sampling or testing error, either intentional or unintentional, caused by systematically favouring some outcomes over others. This can limit the interpretability of generalizability of research findings.

Binge   Excessive consumption of alcohol in a single episode, although there is no clear consensus regarding what constitutes a binge. Some have argued that five drinks or more in a single episode constitutes a binge, but other definitions place higher or lower limits on the amount of alcohol which must be consumed to be regarded as a binge.

Biofeedback   The use of biological information (e.g., heart rate or blood pressure) to teach patients how to relax and exert volitional control of the body's systems.

Bio-medical model   A model of health, disease and illness which emphasizes the role of biological agents, and a mechanistic view of the body, so that disease and illness reflect interruptions on the normal functioning of the body.

Biopsychosocial model   A model of health, disease and illness which extends the bio-medical model and places importance on the role of social and psychological factors, and their interaction with biological factors (e.g., the relationship between stress and health).

Blinding In a research study, the process of keeping participants and researchers uninformed about the specific aim of a study which they are in, in order to minimize the potential effects of **bias** which may arise if the treatment which is being received is known.

Cancer Any malignant growth or tumour caused by abnormal and uncontrolled cell division; it may spread to other parts of the body through the lymphatic system or the blood stream.

Candidate gene A specific gene which is of a priori interest in relation to the phenotype which is being studied, for example because it is involved in a neurobiological pathway known to be important in regulating the phenotype.

Carbon monoxide A colourless, odourless, poisonous gas, produced by incomplete burning of carbon-based organic products. When carbon monoxide gets into the body, for example through inhalation, the carbon monoxide combines with chemicals in the blood and prevents the blood from bringing oxygen to cells, tissues, and organs.

Case-control A research study design, used widely in epidemiology, which matches groups of individuals on the basis of the presence or absence of a certain characteristic (e.g., a specific disease), in order to identify other factors (e.g., exposure to an environmental factor) associated with the specific characteristic.

Causation The act or mechanism by which an effect or outcome is produced. In research, this refers to factors which cause an outcome (e.g., a disease state) to occur. Certain study designs (e.g., experimental designs) are better able to provide evidence of causation than others.

Central nervous system The brain and spinal cord, which receives signals from the peripheral nervous system and exerts control over the body.

Central neural plasticity The capacity of the central nervous system to be modified, for example through learning processes, giving rise to functional and structural changes which may be permanent or semi-permanent.

Chippers Smokers who do not appear to be dependent on nicotine, and smoke socially and at irregular intervals, compared with nicotine dependence smokers who consume cigarettes at regular intervals to maintain circulating levels of nicotine.

Chronic A condition having a slow, progressive onset and lasting for an extended period, sometimes (although not necessarily) in the absence of any identifiable physical pathology. Cure is sometimes not possible and treatment may be focused on the amelioration of symptoms. As distinct from **acute**.

Chronic obstructive pulmonary disease   A progressive lung disease process characterized by difficulty breathing, wheezing and a chronic cough. Complications include bronchitis, pneumonia and lung cancer.

Chronic pain   Pain which is long lasting, may not be related to any identifiable physical pathology or tissue damage, and which does not resolve over time. Often resistant to pain-relieving medication.

Chronic pain syndrome   A behavioural syndrome consisting of high levels of reported pain, as well as **chronic** anxiety and depression, anger and changed lifestyle. Often occurs in the absence of identifiable physical pathology or tissue damage, and may be maintained in part by learning processes related to **gain**.

Cigarettes   Finely ground or cut tobacco, rolled in paper, for smoking. Usually manufactured but may be hand-rolled using loose tobacco. Provides very rapid delivery of nicotine to the central nervous system, and therefore have high **addiction** potential.

Classical conditioning   A learning process whereby an initially neutral stimulus is repeatedly paired with a natural reinforcer so that, over time, the initially neutral stimulus comes to elicit the same reaction as the natural reinforcer.

Cohort   A research study design which follows a group of participants over an extended period (i.e., longitudinally) in order to identify factors which predict change in status or some outcome (e.g., disease onset).

Collective action/community development approach   A health promotion perspective that argues that individual health status is dependent upon environmental causes of illness and that people should act collectively to change their physical and social environment.

Comparative optimism, optimistic bias or **unrealistic optimism**   The processes characterized by the observation that people consider themselves to be less likely to experience negative events and more likely to experience positive events in the future when comparing themselves to others.

Compliance   The passive processes whereby the individual follows the advice of a prescriber with little engagement and possession of treatment by the patient.

Conditioned response   In **classical conditioning**, the learned response to the initially neutral stimulus.

Conditioned stimulus   In **classical conditioning**, the name given to an initially neutral stimulus which has acquired the capacity to elicit a **conditioned response**.

Constructivism   Qualitative research perspective which argues that 'reality' is constructed from the interactions of individuals and the meaning placed on events and phenomena by individuals and society.

Control   In research study design, the use of a comparison group (e.g., in a case-control study, or a randomized controlled trial) to determine factors which are associated with an outcome of interest (e.g., disease status, or response to treatment).

Coping appraisal   A component of protection motivation theory that proposes that coping efficiently with a perceived threat and altering the likelihood of an adaptive response is dependent upon response efficacy, self-efficacy and response costs, or barriers to behaviour.

Coping strategy   A set of actions or a plan related to ways of addressing issues relating to overcoming difficulties or/and securing well being. May be internal (e.g., changing the way in which one perceives or appraises specific situations) or external (e.g., involving specific activities or behavioural responses).

Coronary heart disease   Damage to the heart that occurs because its blood supply is reduced. Fatty deposits build up on the linings of the blood vessels that supply the heart muscles with blood, causing them to narrow. The narrowing reduces the blood supply to the heart muscles and causes pain known as angina.

Cross-over   In research study design, the allocation of participants in an experimental study to both treatment conditions, given sequentially so that each participant crosses over from one treatment condition to the other, usually with a wash out period in between.

Cross-sectional   In research study design, the study of a group of participants at a single point in time (as distinct from a **cohort** study, where a group of individuals is followed-up and investigated repeatedly over time).

Cue exposure   In addiction research, the use of a set of techniques which involve presenting drug users with stimuli (cues) which are typically present when the drug is consumed. Because of the learned associations between the drug and these cues, the cues alone can elicit marked subjective and physiological responses in the user.

Cues to action   Factors, or triggers, that are likely to stimulate the activation of health behaviour when certain belief sets are held. From the health belief model.

Decisional balance   The weighing up of the pros and cons of behaviour change as conceptualized in the transtheoretical model.

Deoxyribonucleic acid (DNA)   The material inside the nucleus of cells that carries genetic information.

Depression   A mental state characterized by chronic low mood, a pessimistic sense of inadequacy and a lack of activity.

Design   In research, the methods which will be used to address a specific research question (e.g., case-control versus experimental). Certain research designs are better suited to answering specific research questions than others.

Disability   The absence or impairment of specific physical or mental functions, usually permanently.

Discourse analysis   An analytical technique in which the researcher seeks to undertake a 'reading' or 'interpretative account' of a text or conversation by isolating a number of strategies used by participants in their language to describe an event or experience.

Discursive psychology   The approach that proposes that experience is predominantly social in nature and is concerned not with inferred, unobservable and static beliefs (as in social cognitive approaches), but with how language and discourse is used to describe experience. This approach emphasizes that what people say should be interpreted in terms of both current and historical context.

Disease   An impairment of health or a condition associated with abnormal functioning of a bodily system.

Disease model   A conception of addiction which emphasizes the biological effects of substance use, and assumes that addictive behaviours can be best understood as a disease state resulting from chronic substance use.

Dispositional optimism   A generalized expectancy that good things will happen in the future and bad things will not irrespective of how these outcomes occurred.

Dizygotic   In genetics, the non-identical twins which result from the separate fertilization of two separate eggs, and who shared 50% of their genotype as a result.

Doctor-patient communication   Those factors that both the patient and doctor bring to the interpersonal communication in the consultation setting and which may predict satisfaction with the consultation, understanding and adherence to advice for recommended health behaviour.

Documentary analysis   In qualitative research, the analysis of documentary and other written records.

Dopamine   A monoamine neurotransmitter, or chemical, that transmits signals between nerve cells, which has been suggested to play a role in a number of psychiatric conditions, including addictive behaviours.

Double blind   In research study design, the condition whereby both the research participant and the researcher are **blind** to the specific experimental condition to which the participant has been allocated.

Elaboration likelihood model   Petty and Cacioppo's model of attitude change in which when people attend carefully to the persuasive message they engage in central processing, otherwise they engage in peripheral processing.

Electrodermal activity   The electrical conductivity of the skin, resulting from sweat gland activity. Changes in this conductivity reflect changes in sweat gland activity.

Electroencephalogram   The recording of electrical activity of the brain by positioning electrodes on the scalp.

Endorphins   Any of a group of peptide hormones (endogenous opioids) that bind to opiate receptors and are found mainly in the brain. They play a role in the regulation of the pain response to injury.

Environmental tobacco smoke   Also known as secondhand smoke or **passive smoking**. The ambient tobacco smoke which results from cigarette smoking and which can be inhaled by those not smoking cigarettes themselves but in the close vicinity of those who are.

Epidemiology   The study of the patterns, causes and control of disease in groups of people or populations.

Equivalence   In research study design, the attempt to demonstrate that the effects of a medication are at least as beneficial as those of an established, proven treatment for the same disease or condition.

Error   In research, the uncertainty associated with any measurement, due to imperfections in the measurement instrument or the methods used. Error may be unsystematic (i.e., random) or systematic (i.e., non-random).

Event-related potentials   Electroencephalogram activity, produced in response to some environmental sensory stimulus (e.g., a noise), and obtained by averaging data recorded after presentation of the stimulus.

Expectancy-value   The idea that people hold expectancies about what outcomes they should get if they behave in a particular way and at the same time their beliefs about the value of that outcome for themselves which is related to decision making and behaviour choice.

Experimental   In research study design, the manipulation of a condition in order to determine the effects of that condition on the outcome of interest. For example, a new treatment may be compared with a placebo to determine the efficacy of that treatment. This study design offers the strongest evidence regarding **causation**.

Explanatory style   The dispositional manner in which an individual attributes particular causes to observed events.

Fear appeals   Types of persuasive communications that try to motivate people to change their attitudes or behaviour by inducing fear in the recipient.

Fight or flight response   An instinctual response when the organism perceives that its survival is threatened, characterized by increased sympathetic nervous system activation.

Figuration   The use of metaphorical images in language to give an abstract notion a more concrete flavour (e.g. butter mountains for overproduction of foodstuffs).

Focus Groups   A group or team formed for the purpose of either resolving a given problem within a larger group or (more often) simply identifying the spread of opinions and feeling on the issue.

Functional magnetic resonance imaging   A non-invasive tool used to observe functioning in the brain or other organs by detecting changes in chemical composition, blood flow or both.

Gain   In disability, the advantages which may be achieved by certain behaviours, such as sympathy, reassurance, financial benefit, in addition to the immediate benefits of those behaviours such as reducing pain and promoting healing.

Galvanic skin response   A change in the ability of the skin to conduct electricity (i.e., skin conductance response), caused by an environmental stimulus (typically an emotional stimulus, such as fright).

Gambling addiction   Excessive gambling which appears to share many of the characteristics of archetypal chemical addictions. Often cited as an example of a behavioural addiction which can occur in the absence of a psychoactive substance.

Gate Control Theory   Theory of pain perception which hypothesizes that a neural structure at the base of the spinal cord governs the transmission of pain information from the peripheral nervous system to the central nervous system, and which can be influenced by descending signals from the central nervous system that may 'close' the gate (rendering the individual less sensitive to pain).

Gene   A hereditary unit consisting of a sequence of DNA that occupies a specific location on a chromosome and determines production of a particular protein. Two copies of each gene are inherited, one from the father and one from the mother.

Gene x environment interaction   An effect of the environment which serves to modify the effects of a genetic variant on an outcome. For example, life stress may influence the impact of a specific gene on the risk of developing major depression. Most genetic effects are likely to be modified in some way by the environment.

General Adaptation Syndrome   A general description of the body's short-term and long-term response to environmental stress, which assumes that the response is broadly similar irrespective of the nature of the environmental stress.

Genetic marker   A gene or DNA sequence having a known location on a chromosome.

Genetics   The study of the inherited basis of human characteristics, traits, behaviours, diseases and so on.

Genome   The entire genetic sequence, comprising the entirety of genetic information about an individual.

Genotype   The specific combination of genetic variants (**alleles**) possessed by an individual, which give rise to genetic variation between individuals.

Grounded Theory   In qualitative research, a method of data collection and analysis which involves the recursive use of themes that emerge through the course of the research to refine the research question and methods of investigation.

Group therapy   Any therapeutic intervention which involves an interaction between individuals in a group setting, where the group setting itself is considered to be an integral part of the therapeutic component (e.g., because of the support offered by other group members).

Habit   The process characterized by learning through the repetition of a behaviour under the same environmental conditions such that over time exposure to a particular cue or stimulus will activate an automatic cognitive process which guides behaviour. Negative and positive reinforcement processes may serve to maintain habitual behaviours.

Hardiness   A personality type characterized by commitment (a sense of purpose in life events and activities), control (the belief of personal influence over situations) and challenge (seeing adaptation and change as a 'normal' and positive experience).

Health action process approach   A stage based model specifying that both a motivational phase and a volition phase have to be passed through in order for a person to adopt, initiate and maintain health protective behaviour.

Health belief model   Focuses on threat perception and health-related behavioural evaluation as the primary aspects concerned with understanding how a person represents health action. Behavioural decisions are based on beliefs about susceptibility to and severity of an illness threat (i.e. threat perception) and the benefits of change and barriers to undertaking a recommended behaviour (i.e. behavioural evaluation).

Health locus of control   The perception that one's health is either under the control of the individual themselves, controlled by powerful others, or by external factors such as chance.

Health promotion   Any activity, event or process that facilitates the improvement of the health status of individuals and groups or which stimulates behavioural change to protect against harm associated with maladaptive health behaviour.

Health psychology   The scientific study of psychologically based factors and processes that are involved in the health, illness and healthcare.

Heritability   The proportion of variability in a trait (phenotype) that is due to additive genetic influences.

Heuristic systematic model   Chaiken's model of attitude change in which when people attend carefully to the persuasive message they engage in systematic processing, otherwise they process the information using heuristics or cognitive short-cuts.

Hospitalization   The act of placing a person in a hospital as a patient. The condition of being hospitalized.

Hostility   A pattern of behaviour characterized by thoughts and behaviours based on the expression of anger, cynical views of the world, and negative expectations of others.

Human Immunodeficiency Virus   The retrovirus that causes AIDS – the acquired immunodeficiency syndrome.

Illness representations   Mental models that operate in long-term memory and comprise a number of beliefs associated with the identity, onset, progression, cause, expectancies and outcome of illness.

Implementation intentions   The processes by which formed behavioural intentions are likely to manifest themselves in actual behaviour and the striving for goal intentions based on recognition that a response that will lead to the successful completion of a goal, and also the situation in which that response would be possible.

Infertility   A diminished or absent ability to produce offspring. Diminished ability is sometimes referred to as **subfertility**.

Inpatients   An individual who is admitted to hospital overnight, usually for a period not less than 24 hours, in order to receive treatment or services.

Interpretative phenomenological analysis   An analytical approach that is concerned with personal perception or account of an event and does not attempt to produce an objective statement of the object or event itself. It assumes that there is an association between what people say and how they think and feel about an object in their social worlds.

Interpretative repertoires   The types of metaphors and images used in everyday talk to 'construct' an object. They are used in contradictory ways by the same person in differing contexts such as the goals that people bring to their interactions.

Interviews   In qualitative research, the technique of conducting a research interview in person in the field by a trained individual in order to ask a series of structured or semi-structured questions related to the research question of interest.

Korsakoff's syndrome   A syndrome of severe mental impairment characterized by confusion, disorientation and amnesia, often resulting from excessive and chronic alcohol abuse.

Linkage   In molecular genetics, a technique for identifying a region of a chromosome which may contain a genetic variant related to the phenotype of interest. Due to the tendency for genetic markers to be inherited together because of their location near one another.

Locus of control   A personality based factor that emphasizes the distinction between the internal control of an event and the external attribution of an event.

Longitudinal   In research study design, the measurement of outcomes at repeated intervals over time in a **cohort** of individuals. Allows the identification of factors related to outcomes of interest before those outcomes have become apparent or have developed.

Lung cancer   The uncontrolled growth of abnormal cells in lung tissue. The disease tends to progress extremely rapidly, and life expectancy following diagnosis is typically short.

Malignant   In cancer, a progressive and uncontrolled growth, caused by abnormal cell division, which spreads to other body parts.

Meta-analyses   The combination, review and re-analysis of existing datasets that provides a large sample size and high statistical power for analysis.

Molecular genetics   The study of the relationship between specific genetic variants, using either **association** or **linkage** techniques, with any phenotype of interest, including behavioural traits, risk of disease, and so on.

Monozygotic   In genetics, the identical twins which result from the simultaneous fertilization of a single egg by two sperms, and who shared 100% of their genotype as a result.

Moral model   In addiction, the perspective that addictive behaviours are a matter of choice, deserving of punishment rather than treatment. This view was widely held in the past but is not in current conceptions of addictive behaviour.

Morbidity rates   The numbers of cases of people in a population who suffer costs associated with a particular illness or disease such as disability or injury.

Mortality rates   The numbers of cases of people in a population who die from a particular illness or disease.

Mortality salience hypothesis   Derived from terror management theory. Identifies that two types of distal defence strategies are used to reduce the state of 'terror' caused by the saliency of mortality, by making cognitive and behavioural efforts to protect their cultural worldview (views shared among individuals about the nature of reality) or to maintain or increase personal self-esteem by reinforcing the values sanctioned by their cultural worldviews.

Motivational phase   A pre-intentional stage proposed by the health action process approach which proposes that behavioural intention is predicted by perceived self-efficacy, outcome expectancies and risk perception processes.

Myocardial infarction   A heart attack, which occurs when the blood supply to part of the heart is cut off. If the blood flow to the heart is not restored, that part of the heart will die, causing disability or death.

Narrative   In qualitative research, the analysis of (usually textual) accounts of individuals who are the focus of research, and the detailed description of the findings of this research (as distinct from the numerical findings of quantitative research).

Natural reinforcer   In learning theory, a reinforcer which occurs naturally (e.g., food, water) and has reinforcing properties that do not arise from association with other reinforcers. Can act as an unconditioned stimulus, giving rise to an unconditioned response, in **classical conditioning**, for example.

Negative affectivity   A tendency to experience persistent and pervasive negative mood and negative self-concept. As distinct from **positive affect**.

Negative reinforcement   In learning theory, the increase in the frequency of a response or behaviour resulting from the removal of an aversive event immediately after the response or behaviour is performed. As distinct from **positive reinforcement**.

Neoplasms   New growth or tumour which may be **benign** or **malignant**.

Neuroadaptation   A permament or semi-permanent structural or functional change in the central nervous system, for example as a result of learning processes.

Neurobiological model   In addiction, the view that addictive behaviours have a biological basis, with learning processes and the resulting changes in the central nervous system thought to play a central role in the maintenance of these behaviours.

Neuroimmune system   Comprised of the immune system and those components of the central and peripheral nervous system that modulate immune response.

Neurological models   In pain, the view that subjective experiences of pain can be understood in terms of activity in the central and peripheral nervous system.

Neuropathic pain   Pain that originates from damage to a nerve or the nervous system.

Nicotine replacement therapy   Pharmaceutical products used in smoking cessation which work by replacing the nicotine usually consumed in cigarette smoke, via patches, gum, lozenges, or other delivery devices. These roughly double the chances of successfully stopping smoking.

Nociception   Activity in specific nerve pathways resulting from tissue damage which is felt subjectively as pain.

Objectification   The mechanism by which unfamiliar (or abstract) events are changed into concrete realities and may result in the use of metaphor in everyday language to explain and understand abstract concepts.

Objectivity   The extent to which a measurement is impartial and impervious to influence by the participant or experimenter in a research study.

Observational   In research study design, a method of collecting data which does not involve an **experimental** manipulation. **Case-control** and **cohort** studies may both be observational in nature.

Ontologizing   The processes in which physical characteristics are attributed to some concept or idea or how the immaterial becomes materialized.

Operant conditioning   The learning process by which behaviours that result in positive outcomes (or the removal of negative outcomes) increase in frequency, and those that result in negative outcomes decrease in frequency.

Opioid   Narcotic drugs that resemble naturally occurring opiates and are used to treat moderate to severe pain. Opioids are similar to opiates such as morphine and codeine.

Outcome expectancies   Beliefs that undertaking a particular behaviour will result in an anticipated outcome.

Outpatients   A patient who visits a healthcare facility for diagnosis or treatment without spending the night. Sometimes called a day patient.

Pain   An unpleasant sensation, either related to tissue damage or defined in terms of such damage, that can range from mild, localized discomfort to agony. Pain has both physical and emotional components.

Parkinson's disease   A progressive nervous disease occurring in later life, associated with the destruction of brain cells that produce dopamine, and characterized by muscular tremours, slowing of movement, partial facial paralysis, distortions of gait and posture, and physical weakness.

Passive smoking   The inhalation of tobacco smoke produced by someone else – a consequence of exposure to **environmental tobacco smoke**.

Pathological gambling   An impulse control disorder associated with gambling. It is a chronic and progressive mental illness similar in many respects to substance use disorders. Often cited as an example of a **behavioural addiction**.

Patient controlled analgesia   A system that allows people to control the amount of pain medication that they receive. The person pushes a button and a machine delivers a dose of pain medicine into the bloodstream through a vein.

Perceived barriers   Beliefs related to the likely barriers to undertaking a recommended course of action in response to a health threat. From the health belief model.

Perceived behavioural control   Beliefs that relate to how much control a person thinks they have over a certain behaviour. From the theory of planned behaviour.

Perceived benefits   Beliefs related to the likely positive consequences associated with undertaking a healthy behaviour. From the health belief model.

Perceived severity   Beliefs about the severity of the consequences of becoming ill or not undertaking a behaviour on one's health. From the health belief model.

Perceived susceptibility   Beliefs about how likely one is to suffer a negative (or positive) health outcome. From the health belief model.

Personality   An area of psychology that is about individual differences and what makes us unique as human beings by emphasizing how psychological systems (i.e. traits) are organized within an individual and how this causes behaviours and ways of thinking that are characteristic of the individual.

Personification   The perceived connection between a concept and some person or group (e.g. Skinner and behaviourism) in order to provide for the concept a concrete existence.

Persuasion processes   Attitude formation or change process. Occurs usually after exposure to arguments or other information about the attitude object.

Phantom limb pain   Pain or discomfort felt by an amputee in the area of the missing limb.

Phenotype   The observable physical or behavioural characteristics of an organism, as determined by both genetic and environmental influences.

Physical dependence   An adaptive physiological state that occurs over time with regular drug use and results in a **withdrawal syndrome** when drug use is stopped; usually occurs with **tolerance**. As distinct from **psychological dependence**.

Placebo effect   The beneficial effect in a patient following a particular treatment that arises from the patient's expectations concerning the treatment, rather than any active properties of the treatment itself.

Polymorphic   Occurring in multiple forms. In genetics, refers to the fact that certain genes may exist in multiple forms, sometimes resulting in differences in function.

Positive affect   Broad term describing elevated mood, happiness and other positive emotional states. As distinct from **negative affect**.

Positive imagery   A therapeutic intervention which involves the maintenance of positive thoughts and mental images.

Positive reinforcement   In learning theory, the increase in the frequency of a response or behaviour resulting from the acquisition of a positive event or outcome immediately after the response or behaviour is performed. As distinct from **negative reinforcement**.

Positron emission tomography A neuroimaging technique that uses signals emitted by radioactive tracers to construct images of the distribution of the tracers in the human body (usually the brain).

Precaution adoption process model Weinstein's model that identifies seven stages that people progress through in a defined sequence from being unaware of a potential health threat to the maintenance of behaviour designed to remove this threat, and processes that are influential for transition from one stage to the next.

Prevalence The proportion of individuals in a population having a disease.

Primary gain The relief of emotional conflict and distress by the patient which can be achieved by ascribing emotional conflict (e.g., resulting from job loss) to an organic illness as a coping mechanism. As distinct from **secondary gain** and **tertiary gain**.

Problem drinking Pattern of drinking that is potentially harmful and association with lifestyle factors, but has not yet resulted in a diagnosis of alcohol dependence.

Problem gambling Participation in any form of gambling to the extent that it creates any negative consequences to the gambler, their family, place of employment, or others. Related to **pathological gambling**.

Prohibition A law forbidding the sale of alcoholic beverages, established in 1920 in the USA and later repealed.

Prospective In research study design, where one or more groups (**cohorts**) of individuals who have not yet had the outcome of interest are monitored for the number of such events which occur over time.

Protection motivation theory Rogers' approach for the understanding of mechanisms by which a person reduces the threat of an event and stimulates the motivation to protect oneself from potential negative outcomes associated with the threat based on the degree of perceived severity of an event, the perceived likelihood of an event or outcome occurring if no adaptive response is made to the threat event, and how efficacious the response made to the threat is perceived to be.

Prototypes Those cases of an event which are used to compare an unfamiliar event against. If the unfamiliar object is similar to the prototype it is assigned the characteristics of the prototype. If the unfamiliar is dissimilar to the prototype it is adjusted so as to fit the characteristics of the prototype.

Pseudo-longitudinal   In research study design, the **cross-sectional** collection of data on groups of individuals of, for example, different ages, to allow the (imperfect) study of changes over time (e.g., related to age).

Psychological dependence   A compulsion to use a drug for its pleasurable effects (see **positive reinforcement**) or for its removal of unpleasant effects or moods (see **negative reinforcement**). As distinct from **physical dependence**.

Psychometric   The design, administration and interpretation of quantitative tests for the measurement of psychological variables such as intelligence, aptitude and personality traits.

Psychoneuroimmunology   The branch of psychology concerned with the study of the interaction of psychological, behavioural, neural and endocrine factors and the functioning of the immune system.

Psychophysiology   The branch of psychology that is concerned with the biological and physiological bases of psychological processes.

Psychosocial risk factors   Those psychological and social factors (such as belief sets and behaviours) that put an individual at an increased risk of experience of suffering a negative health outcome.

Psychosomatic medicine   A view that considers that psychological causes can not only be the consequences of an illness but may also be the cause of physical illness.

Public health   The approach to medicine that is concerned with the health of the community as a whole (as opposed to individual patient health).

Quality of life   The overall enjoyment of life, including an individual's sense of well being and ability to perform various tasks, as well as simple longevity.

Randomization   A method based on chance by which study participants are assigned to a treatment group. Randomization minimizes the differences among groups by equally distributing people with particular characteristics among all the trial arms.

Randomized clinical trial   A study in which the participants are assigned by chance to separate groups that compare different treatments; neither the researchers nor the participants can choose which group. Using **randomization** to assign people to groups means that the groups will be similar and that the treatments they receive can be compared objectively.

Relapse   The return of signs and symptoms of a disease after a patient has enjoyed a remission. This can include behavioural symptoms, such as an abstinent smoker relapsing to regular cigarette consumption.

Relative risk ratio   The calculation of the likelihood of a certain event occurring equally for two population groups. A relative risk ratio of 1 means that the event is equally likely in both groups; a ratio of above one that the event is more likely in the first group; and a risk ratio below 1 that the event is less likely in the first group.

Relaxation   A therapeutic intervention using simple relaxation and breathing exercises to enable an individual to relax.

Reliability   The extent to which a measurement instrument yields consistent, stable and uniform results over repeated observations or measurements under the same conditions each time. Freedom from measurement error.

Replacement therapy   In addiction, the use of pharmaceutical grade drugs (e.g., nicotine for smoking cessation) or alternatives (e.g., methadone for heroin dependence) to ameliorate **withdrawal symptoms** in abstinent drug users while minimizing the harmful effects of the drug.

Response efficacy   A component of protection motivation theory that refers to personal beliefs that self-protective action will decrease the arousal experienced as a result of a health threat.

Retrospective   A study looking back in time, so the outcomes have occurred to the participants before the study commences. **Case-control** studies are always retrospective, **cohort** studies can be, and **randomized clinical trials** are never retrospective.

Risk factor   A characteristic of personal behaviour, lifestyle or inherited factor that is associated with the experience of health-related outcomes.

Schizophrenia   A mental illness in which the person suffers from distorted thinking, hallucinations and a reduced ability to feel normal emotions.

Secondary gain   The acquisition of (often unanticipated) positive outcomes by the patient, such as personal attention and service, monetary gains, disability benefits, and release from unpleasant responsibilities, resulting from an organic illness. As distinct from **primary gain** and **tertiary gain**.

Self-efficacy   Beliefs about the perceived degree to which people have control over outcomes associated with doing a particular behaviour, or how confident a person is in their ability to perform a certain action and attain anticipated outcomes.

Self-empowerment approach   A health promotion perspective that argues for the emphasis in activities to be on self-empowerment derived by engagement and involvement with health-related activities at an individual or community based level.

Self-monitoring   The process of maintaining an awareness of one's own actions and intentions. Can be applied broadly to describe personality traits (some people are high 'self-monitors') or therapeutic interventions (where greater awareness is encouraged for some therapeutic benefit).

Self-regulation   The process by which an individual monitors their behaviour, emotions and thoughts to maintain an equilibrium in psychological and physical functioning.

Self-regulation model of illness cognition and behaviour   Outline of the process by which people monitor and respond to changes in experience behaviour, thinking and emotion by utilising the illness representations and emotional representations derived from an illness experience to generate coping responses aimed at re-establishing healthy equilibrium. The system involves appraisal of the effectiveness of the coping responses applied for re-establishing equilibrium.

Sexually transmitted disease   Any disease (e.g., gonorrhoea, syphilis, herpes, Chlamydia) that is transmitted through sexual contact.

Sexually transmitted infection   An infection that can be transferred from one person to another through sexual contact.

Single blind   In research study design, the condition whereby *either* the research participant *or* the researcher are **blind** to the specific experimental condition to which the participant has been allocated.

Single photon emission computed tomography   A type of **neuroimaging** using nuclear imaging that shows how blood flows to tissues and organs.

Smokeless tobacco   Tobacco that is not burned or smoked but used in another form such as chewing tobacco or snuff.

Social cognition models   Models which emphasize the way in which our cognitions, thoughts and emotions are affected by the immediate social context, and in turn how these affect social behaviour through learning processes.

Social Cognitive Theory   A widely used approach that emphasizes the role social modelling, or vicarious learning, on human motivation, thinking and behaviour. Motivation and behaviour are regulated through reasoned pre-actional thinking and behavioural change is determined by a sense of personal control over the environment.

Social comparison theory   The argument that individuals are motivated to seek self understanding and self knowledge by evaluating themselves in their social worlds, and attempting to understand whether the beliefs and opinions they hold are correct by 'looking' at others and how others' behaviour or belief sets differs from their own.

Social constructionism   An approach that argues that as social experiences are forever changing, we can only examine how the world appears at the time at which we are looking at it, and that knowledge and experience of the social world is created (or constructed) by language, culture and history. Reality is argued to be socially constructed through interactions in the social world.

Social context   The social context or social environment is the set of social positions and social roles which an individual participates in and interacts with.

Social inequalities   The observation that there are real differences in the health status of individuals according to socio-demographic characteristics.

Social learning theory   The argument that social behaviour is learned by observing and imitating the behaviours of others and also by receiving reinforcement for their own social behaviours. Behaviour is shaped by perceived outcome expectancies and self-efficacy beliefs related to an event.

Social model   In disability, the argument that barriers, prejudice and exclusion by society (purposely or inadvertently) are the ultimate factors defining disability, rather than any inherent characteristics of the individual.

Social representations   The values, thoughts, knowledge and images that a collective share in which a person's own identity is found in the collectivity of others and own experience.

Social support   The availability and use of emotional and instrumental advice in coping with currently experienced environmental stressors.

Socio-economic status   A broad term that is used to describe factors about a person's lifestyle including occupation, income and education.

Spinothalamic tract   The sensory pathway in the body that transmits pain, temperature, itch and touch information from the peripheral nervous system to the central nervous system.

Stages of change model   see **transtheoretical model**

Stress-health relationship   The effects of subjective stress and the resulting **stress reaction** on psychological and physical health, in particular as a consequence on long-term exposure to **stressors**.

Stress management   Interventions designed to reduce the impact of stressors in the workplace and environment more generally. These can have an individual focus, aimed at increasing an individual's ability to cope with stressors.

Stress reaction   Any physiological or psychological reaction to physical, mental or emotional stress that disturbs the organism's homeostasis.

Stressor   Internal or external factors or stimuli that produce stress. These can be physical, biological, environmental or psychological. They share the capacity to elicit a common **stress reaction**.

Subfertility   A state of reduced fertility, resulting in a less than normal capacity for reproduction.

Subjective norm   Beliefs we have about how other people we perceive as being important to us would like us to behave (normative beliefs) and the value we hold about behaving that way in line with other's wishes (motivation to comply). From the theory of planned behaviour.

Substance   In addiction, any agent with psychoactive properties which has the potential to be abused because of **physical dependence** or **psychological dependence** liability.

Superiority   In research study design, the attempt to demonstrate that the effects of a medication are superior to a placebo medication. As distinct from **equivalence** trials.

Tar   The term used to describe the particular (as opposed to gaseous) chemicals (mostly toxic) found in cigarette smoke produced by the burning of tobacco.

Tension-reduction hypothesis   In addiction, the hypothesis that substance use is maintained in part by **negative reinforcement** processes related to the ability of the substance to reduce subjective tension and stress.

Tertiary gain   The acquisition of (often unanticipated) positive outcomes by the *caregiver*, such as gratitude, monetary gains, disability benefits, resulting from an organic illness in the patient for whom he or she is caring. As distinct from **primary gain** and **secondary gain**.

Textual accounts   In qualitative research, written or transcripted interview material used as the object of study for analysis.

Thematic methods   In qualitative research, the identification of themes (for examples in interview exchanges), which may be used to guide the development of theoretical perspectives and, in some cases, subsequent data collection (see **Grounded Theory**).

Theory of planned behaviour   Ajzen's extension of the **theory of reasoned action**. States that the immediate antecedent of actual behaviour is behavioural intention. Behavioural intention is predicted by perceived behavioural control, attitude and subjective norm.

Theory of reasoned action   Fishbein and Ajzen's theory that proposes that the immediate antecedent of actual behaviour is behavioural intention. Behavioural intention is predicted by attitude and subjective norm.

Terror management theory   An approach to the study of the effects of fear appeals. When people are reminded of their own mortality they use proximal defensive strategies like denial or distancing. After delay when thoughts of one's own mortality are accessible but not in focal attention, distal defence strategies such as bolstering self-esteem will be used.

Threat appraisal   A component of protection motivation theory that proposes that the inhibition of maladaptive responses is dependent upon the perceived severity of a threat and perceived vulnerability to the threat.

Tobacco   Leaves of the tobacco plant, of the genus Nicotiana, dried and prepared for smoking or oral ingestion.

Tolerance   In addiction, the condition that occurs over time when the body gets used to a substance so that increasing doses are required to achieve the same effect.

Transtheoretical model   Prochaska and DiClemente's model that proposes five stages through which a person progresses in sequence from not thinking about undertaking a behaviour change, through the decision to change to maintenance of the change. Developed from an amalgamation of a number of key psychological and psychotherapeutic theories of processes in change.

Triple blind   In research study design, the condition whereby the research participant, the researcher and a third-party (e.g., the statistician analysing the resulting data) are **blind** to the specific experimental condition to which the participant has been allocated.

Tumour   A mass of abnormally growing cells that serve no useful bodily function. Tumours can be either **benign** or **malignant**.

Type A behaviour   A constellation of factors including competitiveness, achievement-orientated behaviour, impatience, being easily annoyed, hostility and anger, trying to achieve too much in too little time and a vigorous speech pattern that has been used to study the aetiology of various health outcomes (e.g. coronary heart disease). It was first described as an important risk factor in coronary disease in the 1950s by Friedman.

Type C personality   A personality type characterized by the personal attributes of cooperation, appeasement, compliance, passivity, stoicism, unassertiveness, being self-sacrificing and the inhibition of negative emotions. Suggested as a risk factor in cancer.

Type D personality type   A personality type characterized by inhibition of expression of negative emotions and avoidance of social interaction so as to avoid feelings of disapproval.

Unconditioned response   In classical conditioning, the **unconditioned response** is the unlearned (i.e., innate) response that occurs naturally in response to the **unconditioned stimulus**.

Unconditioned stimulus   In classical conditioning, a stimulus that evokes an **unconditioned response**.

Validity   The ability of a test to measure what it was designed to measure, and the degree to which the results of a experimental method lead to robust and clear conclusions (see **Psychometrics**).

Volition phase   A post-intentional stage proposed by the health action process approach which describes factors that are important for translating intention into action such as specific types of efficacy beliefs and planning processes.

Withdrawal symptoms   Abnormal physical or psychological symptoms that follow the abrupt discontinuation of a drug that has the capability of producing **physical dependence**.

REFERENCES

Abood, D.A., Black, D.R. and Feral, D. (2003) Smoking cessation in women with cardiac risk: a comparative study of two theoretically based therapies. *Journal of Nutrition Education and Behavior*, 35, 260–267.

Abraham, C. and Sheeran, P. (1994) Modelling and modifying young heterosexuals' HIV preventative behaviour: a review of theories, findings and educational implications. *Patient Education and Counselling*, 23, 173–186.

Abraham, C. and Sheeran, P. (2004) Implications of goal theories for the theories of reasoned action and planned behaviour. *Current Psychology*, 22, 219–233.

Abraham, C. and Sheeran, P. (2005) The health belief model. In M. Conner and P. Norman (eds), *Predicting Health Behaviour (2nd edition)*. Buckingham: Open University Press. pp. 28–80.

Abraham, C., Sheeran, P., Abrams, D. and Spears, R. (1996) Health beliefs and teenage condom use: a prospective study. *Psychology and Health*, 11, 641–655.

Abraham, C., Sheeran, P., Norman, P., Conner, M., de Vries, N. and Otten, W. (1999) When good intentions are not enough: modelling post-intention cognitive correlates of condom use. *Journal of Applied Social Psychology*, 29, 2591–2612.

Adler, N.E., Boyce, T., Chesney, M.A., Cohen, S., Folkman, S., Kahn, R. and Syme, S.L. (1994) Socioeconomic status and health: the challenge of the gradient. *American Psychologist*, 49, 15–24.

Adler, N.E. and Matthews, K.A. (1994) Health psychology: why do some people get sick and some stay well? *Annual Review of Psychology*, 45, 229–259.

Ajzen, I. (1991) The theory of planned behaviour. *Organizational Behavior and Human Decision Processes*, 50, 179–211.

Ajzen, I. (2002a) Perceived behavioural control, self-efficacy, locus of control and the theory of planned behaviour. *Journal of Applied Social Psychology*, 32, 1–20.

Ajzen, I. (2002b) Residual effects of past on future behaviour: habituation and reasoned action perspectives. *Personality and Social Psychology Review*, 6, 107–122.

Albery, I.P. and Guppy, A. (1995) Drivers' differential perceptions of legal and safe driving consumption. *Addiction*, 90, 245–254.

Albery, I.P., Heuston, J., Durand, M.A., Groves, P., Gossop, M. and Strang, J. (1996) Training primary healthcare workers about drugs: a national survey of UK trainers' perceptions towards training. *Drug and Alcohol Review*, 15, 343–355.

Albery, I.P., Heuston, J., Ward, J., Groves, P., Durand, M.A., Gossop, M. and Strang, J. (2003) Measuring therapeutic attitude among drug workers. *Addictive Behaviors*, 28, 995–1005.

Albery, I.P. and Messer, D.M. (2005) Comparative optimism about health and nonhealth events in 8– and 9–year old children. *Health Psychology*, 24, 316–320.

Albery, I.P., Sharma, D., Niyazi, A. and Moss, A.C. (2006) Theoretical perspectives and approaches. In M. Munafò and I.P. Albery (eds), *Cognition and Addiction*. Oxford: Oxford University Press. pp. 1–30.

Allport, G.W. (1961) *Pattern and Growth in Personality*. New York: Holt, Rinehart and Winston.

Altman, D.G. (1991) *Practical Statistics for Medical Research*. London: Chapman & Hall.

American Psychiatric Association (2000) *Diagnostic and Statistical Manual of Mental Disorders (4th edition, text revision)*. Washington, DC: American Psychiatric Association.

Anagnostopoulos, F. and Spanea, E. (2005) Assessing illness representations of breast cancer: a comparison of patients with healthy and benign controls. *Journal of Psychosomatic Research*, 58, 327–334.

Anagnostopoulou, T. (2005) Health psychology: a critical review of the field. *Hellenic Journal of Psychology*, 2, 114.

Anderson, G. (1996) The benefits of optimism: a meta-analytic review of the Life Orientation Test. *Personality and Individual Differences*, 21, 719–725.

Armitage, C.J. (2004) Implementation intentions and eating a low fat diet: a randomized controlled trial. *Health Psychology*, 23, 319–323.

Armitage, C.J. and Conner, M. (1999) Distinguishing perceptions of control from self-efficacy: predicting consumption of a low fat diet using the theory of planned behaviour. *Journal of Applied Social Psychology*, 29, 72–90.

Armitage, C.J. and Conner, M. (2001) Efficacy of the theory of planned behaviour: a meta-analytic review. *British Journal of Social Psychology*, 40, 471–499.

Armitage, C.J. and Conner, M. (2002) Reducing fat intake: interventions based on the Theory of Planned Behaviour. In D. Rutter and L. Quine (eds), *Changing Health Behaviour*. Buckingham: Open University Press. pp. 87–104.

Armstrong, D. (1987) Theoretical tensions in the biopsychosocial medicine. *Social Science and Medicine*, 25, 1213–1218.

Arndt, J., Routledge, C. and Goldenberg, J. A. (2006) Predicting proximal health responses to reminders of death: the influence of coping style and health optimism. *Psychology and Health*, 25, 593–614.

Aveyard, P., Griffin, C., Lawrence, T. and Cheng, K.K. (2003) A controlled trial of an expert system and self-help manual intervention based on the stages of change versus standard self-help materials in smoking cessation. *Addiction*, 98, 345–354.

Bailis, D.S., Chipperfield, J.G. and Perry, R. P. (2005) Optimistic social comparisons of older adults low in primary control: a prospective analysis of hospitalization and mortality. *Health Psychology*, 24, 393–401.

Bandura, A. (1977) Self-efficacy: toward a unifying theory of behavioural change. *Psychological Review*, 84, 191–215.

Bandura, A. (1986) *Social Foundations of Thought and Action*. Englewood Cliffs, NJ: Prentice-Hall.

Bandura, A. (1997) *Self-efficacy: The Exercise of Control*. New York: Freeman.

Bandura, A. (2000) Exercise of human agency through collective agency. *Current Directions of Psychological Science*, 9, 75–78.

Banks, S.M., Salovey, P. and Greener, S. (1995) The effects of message framing on mammography utilization. *Health Psychology*, 14, 178–184.

Bargh, J.A. (1994) The four horsemen of automaticity: awareness, intention, efficiency, and control in social cognition. In R.S. Wyer and T.K. Srull (eds), *Handbook of Social Cognition: Volume 1*. Hillsdale, NJ: Lawrence Erlbaum. pp. 1–40.

Bargh, J.A. (1997) The automaticity of everyday life. In R.S. Wyer (ed.), *Advances in Social Cognition: Volume X*. Hillsdale, NJ: Lawrence Erlbaum.

Bargh, J.A. and Chartrand, T.L. (1999) The unbearable automaticity of being. *American Psychologist*, 54, 462–479.

Bargh, J.A. and Ferguson, M.J. (2000) Beyond behaviorism: on the automaticity of higher mental processes. *Psychological Bulletin*, 126, 925–945.

Bartels, M., Van den Berg, M., Sluyter, F., Boomsma, D.I. and de Geus, E.J. (2003) Heritability of cortisol levels: review and simultaneous analysis of twin studies. *Psychoneuroendocrinology*, 28, 121–137.

Becker, M.H., Drachman, R.H. and Kirscht, P. (1974) A new approach to explaining sick-role behaviour in low income populations. *American Journal of Public Health*, 64, 205–216.

Becker, M.H., Haefner, D.P., Kasl, S.V., Kirscht, J.P., Maiman, L.A. and Rosenstock, I.M. (1977) Selected psychosocial models and correlates of individual health-related behaviours. *Medical Care*, 18, 348–366.

Beecher, H.K. (1946) Pain in men wounded in battle. *Annals of Surgery*, 123 (1), 95–105.

Bennett, P. and Murphy, S. (1997) *Psychology and Health Promotion*. Buckingham: Open University Press.

Berry, D.C., Michas, I.C. and Bersellini, E. (2003) Communicating information about medication: the benefits of making it personal. *Psychology and Health*, 18, 127–139.

Biesheuvel, C.J., Grobbee, D.E. and Moons, K.G. (2006) Distraction from randomization in diagnostic research. *Annals of Epidemiology*, 16, 540–544.

Black, D. (1980) *Inequalities in Health*. London: DHSS.

Blalock, S.J., DeVillis, R.F., Giogino, K., DeVellis, B.M., Gold, D.T. and Dooley, M. (1996) Osteoporosis prevention in premenopausal women: using a stage model approach to examine predictors of behaviour. *Health Psychology*, 15, 84–93.

Bohner, G., Moskowitz, G. and Chaiken, S. (1995) The interplay of heuristic and systematic processing of social information. *European Review of Social Psychology*, 6, 33–68.

Bohner, G. and Schwartz, N. (2003) Attitudes, persuasion and change. In A. Tesser and N. Schwartz (eds), *Blackwell Hanbbook of Social Psychology: Intraindividual Processes*. Oxford: Blackwell. pp. 413–435.

Bohner, G. and Wänke, M. (2002) *Attitudes and Attitude Change*. Hove: Psychology Press.

Bolam, B., Murphy, S. and Gleeson, K. (2006) Place-identity and geographical inequalities in health: a qualitative study. *Psychology and Health*, 21, 399–420.

Booth-Kewley, S. and Friedman, H.S. (1987) Psychological predictors of heart disease: a quantitative review. *Psychological Bulletin*, 101, 343–362.

Bosley, C.M., Fosbury, J.A. and Cochrane, G.M. (1995) The psychological factors associated with poor compliance with treatment in asthma. *European Respiratory Journal*, 8, 899–904.

Bridle, C., Riemsma, R.P., Pattenden, J., Sowden, A.J., Mather, L., Watt, I.S. and Walker, A. (2005) Systematic review of the effectiveness of health behaviour interventions based on the transtheoretical model. *Psychology and Health*, 20, 283–301.

Brocki, J.M. and Wearden, A.J. (2006) A critical evaluation of the use of interpretative phenomenological analysis (IPA) in health psychology. *Psychology and Health*, 21, 87–108.

Brown-Peterside, P., Redding, C.A. and Leigh, R. (2000) Acceptability of a stage-matched expert system intervention to increase condom use among women at high risk of HIV infection in New York. *AIDS Education and Prevention*, 12, 171–181.

Bruera, E., Sweeney, C., Wiley, J., Palmer, J.L., Tolley, S., Rosales, M. and Ripamonti, C. (2003) Breast cancer patient perception of the helpfulness of a prompt sheet versus a general information sheet during outpatient consultation: a randomized controlled trial. *Journal of Pain and Symptom Management*, 25, 412–419.

Budd, R. and Rollnick, S. (1996) The structure of the readiness to change questionnaire: a test of Prochaska and DiClemente's transtheoretical model. *British Journal of Health Psychology*, 1, 365–376.

Buunk, B.P. and Gibbons, F.X. (eds) (1997) *Health, Coping and Well-Being*. Hillsdale, NJ: Lawrence Erlbaum.

Cacioppo, J.T., Harkins, S.G. and Petty, R.E. (1981) The nature of attitudes and cognitive responses and their relationships to behavior. In R. Petty, T. Ostrom and T. Brock (eds), *Cognitive Responses in Persuasion*. Hillsdale, NJ: Lawrence Erlbaum. pp. 31–54.

Cameron, L.D. and Leventhal, H. (eds) (2003) *The Self-Regulation of Health and Illness Behaviour*. London: Routledge.

Cameron, L.D. and Moss-Morris, R. (2004) Illness-related cognition and behaviour. In A. Kaptein and J. Weinman (eds), *Health Psychology*. Oxford: BPS Blackwell. pp. 84–110.

Campbell, L.C., Clauw, D.J. and Keefe, F.J. (2003) Persistent pain and depression: a biopsychosocial perspective. *Biological Psychiatry*, 54, 399–409.

Campion, P., Foulkes, J., Neighbour, R. and Tate, P. (2002) Patient centredness in the MRCGP video examination: analysis of a large cohort. *British Medical Journal*, 325, 691–692.

Carlisle, A.C.S., John, A., Fife-Shaw, C. and Lloyd, M. (2005) The self-regulatory in women with rheumatoid arthritis: relationships between illness representations, coping strategies, and illness outcome. *British Journal of Health Psychology*, 10, 571–587.

Carlson, N.R. (2006) *Physiology of Behavior (9th edition)*. Needham Heights: Allyn and Bacon.

Carroll, D., Davey Smith, G. and Bennett, P. (2002) Some observations on health and socioeconomic status. In D. Marks (ed.), *The Health Psychology Reader*. London: Sage. pp. 140–162.

Carver, C.S., Pozo, C., Harris, S.D., Noriega, V., Scheier, M.F., Robinson, D.S., Ketcham, A.S., Moffat, F.L. and Clark, A.C. (1993) How coping mediates the effects of optimism on distress: a study of women with early stage breast cancer. *Journal of Personality and Social Psychology*, 65, 375–390.

Carver, C.S., Scheier, M.F and Weintraub, J.K. (1989) Assessing coping strategies: a theoretically based approach. *Journal of Personality and Social Psychology*, 56, 267–283.

Caspi, A., Sugden, K., Moffitt, T.E., Taylor, A., Craig, I.W., Harrington, H., McClay, J., Mill, J., Martin, J., Braithwaite, A. and Poulton, R. (2003) Influence of life stress on depression: moderation by a polymorphism in the 5-HTT gene. *Science*, 301, 386–389.

Champion, V.L. (1984) Instrument development for health belief model constructs. *Advances in Nursing Science*, 6, 73–85.

Chen, S. and Chaiken, S. (1999) The heuristic-systematic model in its broader context. In S. Chaiken and Y. Trope (eds), *Dual Process Theories in Social Psychology*. New York: Guilford. pp. 73–96.

Chippindale, S. and French, L. (2001) HIV counselling and the psychosocial management of patients with HIV or AIDS. *British Medical Journal*, 322, 1533–1535.

Christensen, A.J. (2004) *Patient Adherence to Medical Treatment Regimens: Bridging the Gap Between Behavioral Science and Biomedicine*. New Haven, CT: Yale University Press.

Christiansen, M., Vik, P.W. and Jarchow, A. (2002) College student heavy drinking in social contexts versus alone. *Addictive Behaviors*, 27, 393–404.

Clemow, L., Costanza, M.E., Haddad, W.P., Luckmann, R., White, M. and Klaus, D. (2000) Underutilizers of mammography screening today: characteristics of women planning, undecided about, and not planning mammogram. *Annals of Behavioral Medicine*, 22, 80–88.

Concato, J. (2004) Observational versus experimental studies: what's the evidence for a hierarchy? *NeuroRx*, 1, 341–347.

Conner, M. and Armitage, C. (1998) Extending the theory of planned behaviour: a review and avenues for further research. *Journal of Applied Social Psychology*, 28, 1430–1464.

Conner, M. and Norman, P. (2005) *Predicting Health Behaviour (2nd edition)*. Buckingham: Open University Press.

Conner, M. and Sparks, P. (2005) Theory of planned behaviour and health behaviour. In M. Conner and P. Norman (eds), *Predicting Health Behaviour (2nd edition)*. Buckingham: Open University Press. pp. 170–222.

Contrada, R.J. and Goyal, T.M. (2004) Individual differences, health and illness: the role of emotional traits and generalised expectancies. In S. Sutton, A. Baum and M. Johnston (eds), *The Sage Handbook of Health Psychology*. London: Sage. pp. 143–168.

Cox, K.L., Gorely, T.J., Puddey, I., Burke, V. and Beilin, L. (2003) Exercise behaviour change in 40 to 65 year old women: the SWEAT study (Sedentary Women Exercise Adherence Trial). *British Journal of Health Psychology*, 8, 477–495.

Cox, W.M., Fadardi, J.S. and Pothos, E.M. (2006) The addiction-Stroop test: theoretical considerations and procedural recommendations. *Psychological Bulletin*, 132, 443–476.

Cummings, K.M., Becker, M.H., Kirscht, J.P. and Levin, N.W. (1981) Intervention strategies to improve compliance with medical regimes by ambulatory haemodialysis patients. *Journal of Behavioral Medicine*, 4, 111–127.

Dalgard, O.S. and Haheim, L.L. (1998) Psychosocial risk factors and mortality: a prospective study with special emphasis on social support, social participation and locus of control in Norway. *Journal of Epidemiology and Community Health*, 52, 476–481.

Dembrowski, T.M., MacDougall, J.M., Costa, P.T. and Grandits, G.A. (1989) Components of hostility as predictors of sudden death and myocardial infarction in the Multiple Risk Factor Intervention Trial. *Psychosomatic Medicine*, 51, 514–522.

Denollet, J. (1998) Personality and coronary heart disease: the type-D scale 16 (DS16). *Annals of Behavioral Medicine*, 20, 209–215.

Department of Health (1998) *Our Healthier Nation: A Contract for Health*. London: HMSO.

Detweiler, J.B., Bedell, B.T., Salovet, P., Pronin, E. and Rothamn, A.J. (1999) Message framing and sunscreen use: gain framed message motivates beachgoers. *Health Psychology*, 18, 189–196.

DeVillis, B.M. and DeVillis, R.F. (2000) Self-efficacy and health. In A. Baum, T.A. Revenson and J.E. Singer (eds), *Handbook of Health Psychology*. Mahwah, NJ: Erlbaum. pp. 235–247.

Dickenson, A.H. (2002) Gate control theory of pain stands the test of time. *British Journal of Anaesthesia*, 88, 755–757.

DiClemente, C.C. and Prochaska, J.O. (1982) Self-change and therapy change of smoking behaviour: a comparison of processes of change in cessation and maintenance. *Addictive Behaviors*, 7, 133–142.

Dijkstra, A., Bakker, M. and DeVries, H. (1997) Subtypes within a pre-contemplating sample of smokers: a preliminary extension of the stages of change. *Addictive Behaviors*, 22, 327–337.

Dijkstra, A., Conijn, B. and De Vries, H. (2006) A match–mismatch test of a stage model of behaviour change in tobacco smoking. *Addiction*, 101, 1035–1043.

Dijkstra, A., DeVries, H., Kok, G. and Roijackers, J. (1999) Self-evaluation and motivation to change: social cognitive constructs in smoking cessation. *Psychology and Health*, 14, 747–759.

DiMatteo, M.R., Giordani, P.J., Lepper, H. and Croghan, T.W. (2002) Patient adherence and medical treatment outcomes. *Medical Care*, 40, 794–811.

Doll, R. and Hill, A.B. (1950) Smoking and carcinoma of the lung. *British Medical Journal*, 2, 739–748.

Doll, R. and Hill, A.B. (1956) Lung cancer and other causes of death in relation to smoking: a second report on the mortality of British doctors. *British Medical Journal*, 2, 1071.

Doll, R. and Peto, R. (1981) *The Causes of Human Cancer*. Oxford: Oxford University Press.

Doll, R., Peto, R., Hall, E. and Gray, R. (1994) Mortality in relation to drinking: 13 years observations on male British doctors. *British Medical Journal*, 309, 911–918.

Donovan, B. (2004) Sexually transmissible infections other than HIV. *Lancet*, 363, 545–556.

Donovan, D.M. (1988) Assessment of addictive behaviors: implications of an emerging *biopsychosocial* model. In D.M. Donovan and G.A. Marlatt (eds), *Assessment of Addictive Behaviors*. New York: Guilford Press. pp. 3–48.

Drummond, D.C. (2001) Theories of drug craving, ancient and modern. *Addiction*, 96, 33–46.

Durkheim, E. (1897/1951) *Suicide: A Study in Sociology*. Glencoe, IL: Free Press.

Eagly, A.H. and Chaiken, S. (1993) *The Psychology of Attitudes*. New York: Harcourt Brace.

Ebrahim, S. (1995) Clinical and public health perspectives and applications of health-related quality of life measurement. *Social Science and Medicine*, 41, 1383–1394.

Egbert, L.D., Battit, G.E., Welch, C.E. and Bartlett, M.K. (1964) Reduction of postoperative pain by encouragement and instruction of patients: a study of doctor-patient rapport. *New England Journal of Medicine*, 270, 825–827.

Eiser, J.R., Eiser, C. and Pauwels, P. (1993) Skin cancer: assessing perceived risk and behavioural attitudes. *Psychology and Health*, 8, 393–404.

Engel, G.L. (1977) The need for a new medical model: a challenge for biomedicine. *Science*, 196, 129–136.

Engel, G.L. (1980) The clinical application of the biopsychosocial model. *American Journal of Psychiatry*, 137, 535–544.

Engels, F. (1845/1958) *The Condition of the Working Class in England*. London: Lawrence and Wishart.

Enoch, M.A. (2006) Genetic and environmental influences on the development of alcoholism: resilience vs. risk. *Annals of the New York Academy of Sciences*, 1094, 193–201.

Erblich, J., Montgomery, G.H., Valdimarsdottir, H.B., Cloitre, M. and Bovbjerg, D.H. (2003) Biased cognitive processing of cancer-related information among women with family histories of breast cancer: evidence from a cancer Stroop task. *Health Psychology*, 22, 235–244.

Evans, D. and Norman, P. (2002) Improving pedestrian road safety among adolescents: an application of the theory of planned behaviour. In D.R. Rutter and L. Quine (eds), *Changing Health Behaviour*. Buckingham: Open University Press. pp. 153–171.

Evans, S., Ferrando, S.J., Rabkin, J.G. and Fishman, B. (2000) Health locus of control, distress and utilization of protease inhibitors among HIV-positive men. *Journal of Psychosomatic Research*, 49, 157–162.

Evers, A.W., Kraaimaat, F.W., Geenen, R., Jacobs, J.W. and Bijlsma, J.W. (2003) Pain coping and social support as predictors of long-term functional disability and pain in early rheumatoid arthritis. *Behaviour Research and Therapy*, 41, 1295–1310.

Eysenck, H.J. (1982) *Personality, Genetics and Behaviour*. New York: Praeger.

Eysenck, H.J. (1988) The respective importance of personality, cigarette smoking and interaction effects for the genesis of cancer and coronary heart disease. *Personality and Individual Differences*, 9, 453–464.

Fallowfield, L., Jenkins, W., Farwell, V., Saul, J., Duffy, A. and Eves, R. (2002) Efficacy of a cancer research UK communication skills training model for oncologists: a randomized controlled trial. *Lancet*, 359, 650–656.

Fazio, R.H. (1990) Multiple processes by which attitudes guide behavior: the MODE model as an integrative framework. *Advances in Experimental Social Psychology*, 23, 75–109.

Fekete, E.M., Antoni, M.H. and Schneiderman, N. (2007) Psychosocial and behavioral interventions for chronic medical conditions. *Current Opinion in Psychiatry*, 20, 152–157.

Festinger, L. (1954) A theory of social comparison processes. *Human Relations*, 7, 117–140.

Field, M. (2006) Attentional biases in drug use and addiction: cognitive mechanisms, causes, consequences and implications. In M. Munafò and I.P. Albery, *Cognition and Addiction*. Oxford: Oxford University Press. pp. 73–100.

Field, M. and Eastwood, B. (2005) Experimental manipulation of attentional bias increases the motivation to drink alcohol. *Psychopharmacology (Berl)*, 183, 350–357.

Finney, L.J. and Iannotti, R.J. (2003) Message framing and mammography screening: a theory driven intervention. *Behavioral Medicine*, 28, 5–14.

Fishbein, M. and Ajzen, I. (1975) *Belief, Attitude, Intention and Behavior*. Reading, MA: Addison-Wesley.

Fiske, S.T. (2004) *Social Beings: A Core Motives Approach to Social Psychology*. Hoboken, NJ: John Wiley and Sons.

Fiske, S.T. and Taylor, S.E. (1991) *Social Cognition (2nd edition)*. New York: McGraw-Hill.

Floyd, D.L., Prentice-Dunn, S. and Rogers, R.W. (2000) A meta-analysis of protection motivation theory. *Journal of Applied Social Psychology*, 30, 407–429.

Fontaine, K.R. and Smith, S. (1995) Optimistic bias in cancer risk perception: a cross-national study. *Psychological Reports*, 77, 143–146.

Fordyce, W.E. (1976) *Behavioral Methods for Chronic Pain and Illness*. St Louis, MO: C.V. Moseby.

Fortune, G., Barrowclough, C. and Lobban, F. (2004) Illness representations in depression. *British Journal of Clinical Psychology*, 43, 347–364.

Franken, I.H.A. (2003) Drug craving and addiction: integrating psychological and neuropsychopharmacological approaches. *Progress in Neuro-Psychopharmacology and Biological Psychiatry*, 27, 563–579.

Friedman, M. and Rosenman, R.H. (1959) Association of specific overt behavior pattern with blood and cardiovascular findings: blood cholesterol level, blood clotting time, incidence of arcus senilis, and clinical coronary artery disease. *Journal of the American Medical Association*, 169, 1286–1296.

Gergen, K. (1973) Social psychology as history. *Journal of Personality and Social Psychology*, 26, 309–320.

Gerits, P. and De Brabander, B. (1999) Psychosocial predictors of psychological, neurochemical and immunological symptoms of acute stress among breast cancer patients. *Psychiatry Research*, 85, 95–103.

Gerrard, M., Gibbons, F.X. and Bushman, B.J. (1996) The relation between perceived vulnerability to HIV and precautionary sexual behavior. *Psychological Bulletin*, 119, 390–409.

Gillies, V. and Willig, C. (1997) 'You get nicotine and that in your blood' – constructions of addiction and control women's accounts of cigarette smoking. *Journal of Community and Applied Social Psychology*, 7, 285–301.

Godin, G. and Kok, G. (1996) The theory of planned behaviour: a review of its application to health-related behaviours. *American Journal of Health Promotion*, 11, 87–98.

Goetz, A.T. and Shackelford, T.K. (2006) Modern application of evolutionary theory to psychology: key concepts and clarifications. *American Journal of Psychology*, 119, 567–584.

Gollwitzer, P.M. (1990) Action phases and mind sets. In E.T. Higgins and J.R. Sorrentino (eds), *The Handbook of Motivation and Cognition*. New York: Guilford. pp. 53–92.

Gollwitzer, P.M. (1993) Goal achievement: the role of intentions. In W. Stroebe and M. Hewstone (eds), *European Review of Social Psychology Volume 4*. Chichester: Wiley. pp. 141–185.

Gollwitzer, P.M. (1999) Implementation intentions: strong effects of simple plans. *American Psychologist*, 54, 493–503.

Gollwitzer, P.M., Bayer, U.C. and McCulluch, K.C. (2005) The control of the unwanted. In R.R. Hassin, J.S. Uleman and J.A. Bargh (eds), *The New Unconscious*. New York: Oxford University Press. pp. 485–515.

Gollwitzer, P.M. and Branstätter, V. (1997) Implementation intentions and effective goal pursuit. *Journal of Personality and Social Psychology*, 73, 186–199.

Gough, B. and McFadden, M. (2001) *Critical Social Psychology: An Introduction*. Basingstoke: Palgrave.

Graham, J.E., Christian, L.M. and Kiecolt-Glaser, J.K. (2006) Stress, age, and immune function: toward a lifespan approach. *Journal of Behavioural Medicine*, 29, 389–400.

Greenberg, J., Solomon, S. and Pyszczynski, T. (1997) Terror management theory of self-esteem and cultural worldviews: empirical assessments and conceptual refinements. In M. P. Zanna (ed.), *Advances in Experimental Social Psychology, Volume 29*. San Diego, CA: Academic Press. pp. 61–141.

Greenwald, A.G. (1968) Cognitive learning, cognitive response to persuasion and attitude change. In A.G. Greenwald, T. Brock and T. Ostrom (eds), *Psychological Foundations of Attitudes*. New York: Academic Press. pp. 148–170.

Grunfeld, E.A., Ramirez, A.J., Maher, E.J., Peach, D., Albery, I.P. and Richards, M.A. (2001) Chemotherapy for advanced breast cancer: what factors influence oncologists' decision making? *British Journal of Cancer*, 84, 1172–1178.

Habra, M.E., Linden, W., Anderson, J.C. and Weinberg, J. (2003) Type D personality is related to cardiovascular and neuroendocrine reactivity to acute distress. *Journal of Psychosomatic Research*, 55, 235–245.

Hagger, M., Chatzisarantis, N. and Biddle, S. (2002) A meta-analytic review of the theories of reasoned action and planned behaviour in physical activity: predictive validity and the contribution of additional variables. *Journal of Sport and Exercise Psychology*, 24, 3–32.

Hagger, M.S. and Orbell, S. (2005) A confirmatory factor analysis of the revised illness perception questionnaire (IPQ-R) in a cervical screening context. *Psychology and Health*, 20, 161–173.

Hagger, M.S. and Orbell, S. (2006) Illness representations and emotion in people with abnormal screening results. *Psychology and Health*, 21, 183–209.

Hall, J.A., Roter, D.L. and Katz, N.R. (1988) Meta-analysis of provider behavior in medical encounters. *Medical Care*, 26, 657–675.

Hampson, S.E. (1988) *The Construction of Personality: An Introduction (2nd edition)*. London: Routledge.

Hand, C. (1998) Adherence and asthma. In L.B. Myers and K. Midence (eds), *Adherence To Treatment in Medical Conditions*. Amsterdam: Harwood Academic Publishers. pp. 383–421.

Hariri, A.R., Mattay, V.S., Tessitore, A., Kolachana, B., Fera, F., Goldman, D., Egan, M.F. and Weinberger, D.R. (2002) Serotonin transporter genetic variation and the response of the human amygdala. *Science*, 297, 400–403.

Harris, P. (1996) Sufficient grounds for optimism?: the relationship between perceived controllability and optimistic bias. *Journal of Social and Clinical Psychology*, 15, 9–52.

Harris, P., Middleton, W. and Joiner, R. (2000) The typical student as an in-group member: eliminating optimistic bias by reducing social distance. *European Journal of Social Psychology*, 30, 235–253.

Harrison, J.A., Mullen, P.D. and Green, L.W. (1992) A meta-analysis of studies of the health belief model with adults. *Health Education Research*, 7, 107–116.

Hayes, J.A., Black, N.A., Jenkinson, C., Young, J.D., Rowan, K.M., Daly, K. and Ridley, S. (2000) Outcome measures for adult critical care: a systematic review. *Health Technology Assessment*, 4, 1–111.

Haynes, S.G., Feinleib, M. and Kannel, W.B. (1980) The relationship of psychosocial factors to coronary heart disease in the Framingham study. III. Eight year incidence of coronary heart disease. *American Journal of Epidemiology*, 111, 37–58.

Heath, A.C., Martin, N.G., Lynskey, M.T., Todorov, A.A. and Madden, P.A. (2002) Estimating two-stage models for genetic influences on alcohol, tobacco or drug use initiation and dependence vulnerability in twin and family data. *Twin Research*, 5, 113–124.

Heine, S.J. and Lehman, D.R. (1995) Cultural variation in unrealistic optimism: does the West feel more vulnerable than the East? *Journal of Personality and Social Psychology*, 68, 595–607.

Henderson, B.N. and Baum, A. (2004) Biological mechanism of health and disease. In S. Sutton, A. Baum and M. Johnston (eds), *The Sage Handbook of Health Psychology*. London: Sage. pp. 89–93.

Herzlich, C. (1973) *Health and Illness: A Social Psychological Approach*. London: Academic Press.

Heurtin-Roberts, S. (1993) 'High-pertension' – the uses of a chronic folk illness for personal adaptation. *Social Science and Medicine*, 37, 285–294.

Hewstone, M. (1986) *Understanding Attitudes to the European Community: A Social Psychological Study in Four Member States*. Cambridge/Paris: Cambridge University Press/Maison des Sciences de l'Homme.

Higgins, A. and Conner, M. (2003) Understanding adolescent smoking: the role of the theory of planned behaviour and implementation intentions. *Psychology, Health and Medicine*, 8, 177–190.

Holland, C.A. (1993) Self-bias in older drivers' judgements of accident likelihood. *Accident Analysis and Prevention*, 25, 431–441.

Holroyd, K.A. and Coyne, J. (1987) Personality and health in the 1980s: psychosomatic medicine revisited? *Journal of Personality*, 55, 359–376.

Hoppe, R. and Ogden, J. (1997) Practice nurses' beliefs about obesity and weight-related interventions in primary care. *International Journal of Obesity*, 21, 141–146.

Horne, R. (1998) Adherence to medication: a review of existing literature. In L. Myers and K. Midence (eds), *Adherence to Treatment in Medical Conditions*. London: Harwood Academic. pp. 285–309.

Horne, R., Weinman, J. and Hankins, M. (1999) The Beliefs about Medicines Questionnaire (BMQ): the development and evaluation of a new method for assessing the cognitive representation of medication. *Psychology and Health*, 14, 1–24.

Horwitz, R., Viscoli, C.M., Berkman, L., Donaldson, R.M., Horwitz, S., Murray, C., Ransohoff, D. and Sindelar, J. (1990) Adherence treatment and risk of death after a myocardial infarction. *Lancet*, 336, 852–855.

Hovland, C.I. and Janis, I.L. (eds) (1959) *Personality and Persuasibility*. New Haven, CT: Yale University Press.

Hudcova, J., McNicol, E., Quah, C., Lau, J. and Carr, D.B. (2006) Patient controlled opioid analgesia versus conventional opioid analgesia for postoperative pain. *Cochrane Database Syst Rev. CD003348.*

Hunter, M., Grunfeld, E. and Ramirez, A.R. (2003) Help-seeking intentions for breast cancer symptoms: a comparison of self-regulation model and the theory of planned behaviour. *British Journal of Health Psychology*, 8, 319–334.

Iconomu, G. and Rutter, D.R. (2001) Communication and satisfaction with the consultation in a general practice: a prospective examination. *Psychology: The Journal of the Hellenic Psychological Society*, 8, 401–410.

Jacobs, D.R., Luepker, R., Mittelmark, M., Folsom, A., Pirie, P., Mascioli, S., Hannan, P., Pechacek, T., Bracht, N., Carlaw, R., Kilne, F. and Blackburn, H. (1986) Community wide prevention strategies: evaluation design of the Minnesota Heart Health Program. *Journal of Chronic Diseases*, 39, 775–788.

Janis, I.L. (1958) *Psychological Stress*. Wiley: New York.

Janis, I.L. (1967) Effects of fear arousal on attitude change: recent developments in theory and experimental research. In L. Berkowitz (ed.), *Advances in Experimental Social Psychology (Volume 3)*. New York: Academic Press. pp. 166–224.

Janz, N. and Becker, M.H. (1984) The health belief model: a decade later. *Health Education Quarterly*, 11, 1–47.

Jessop, D. and Rutter, D.R. (2003) Adherence to asthma medications: the role of illness representations. *Psychology and Health*, 18, 595–612.

Jessop, D.C., Rutter, D.R., Sharma, D. and Albery, I.P. (2004) Do individuals with asthma display colour naming interference for asthma symptom words, and are such attentional biases related to adherence to treatment? *British Journal of Psychology*, 95, 127–147.

Joffe, H. (1996) AIDS research and prevention: a social representational approach. *British Journal of Medical Psychology*, 69, 169–191.

Joffe, H. (2003) Social representations and health psychology. *Social Science Information*, 41, 559–580.

Joffe, H. and Bettega, N. (2004) Social representations of AIDS among Zambian adolescents. *Journal of Health Psychology*, 8, 616–631.

Jones, L.W., Sinclair, R.C. and Courneya, K.S. (2003) The effects of source credibility and message framing on exercise intentions, behaviors, and attitudes: an integration of the elaboration likelihood model and prospect theory. *Journal of Applied Social Psychology*, 33, 179–196.

Jorgensen, A.W., Hilden, J. and Gotzsche, P.C. (2006) Cochrane reviews compared with industry supported meta-analyses and other meta-analyses of the same drugs: systematic review. *British Medical Journal*, 333, 782.

Kadden, R.M. (2001) Behavioral and cognitive-behavioral treatments for alcoholism: research opportunities. *Addictive Behaviors*, 26, 489–507.

Kamen-Siegel, L., Rodin, J., Seligman, M. and Dwyer, J. (1991) Explanatory style and cell-mediated immunity in elderly men and women. *Health Psychology*, 10, 229–235.

Kaptchuk, T.J. (2002) Acupuncture: theory, efficacy, and practice. *Annals of Internal Medicine*, 136, 374–383.

Kaptein, A. and Weinman, J. (2004) Health psychology: some introductory remarks. In A. Kaptein and J. Weinman (eds), *Health Psychology*. Oxford: BPS Blackwell. pp. 3–18.

Keefe, F.J., Abernethy, A.P. and Campbell, L.C. (2005) Psychological approaches to understanding and treating disease-related pain. *Annual Review of Psychology*, 56, 601–630.

Kelly, J.A., St. Lawrence, J.S., Brasfield, I.L. and Lemke, A. (1990) Psychological factors that predict AIDS high-risk vs. AIDS precautionary behaviour. *Journal of Consulting and Clinical Psychology*, 58, 117–119.

Kendler, K.S. (2005) Psychiatric genetics: a methodologic critique. *American Journal of Psychiatry*, 162, 3–11.

Kiecolt-Glaser, J.K., Page, G.G., Marucha, P.T., MacCallum, R.C. and Glaser, R. (1998) Psychological influences on surgical recovery: perspectives from psychoneuroimmunology. *American Psychologist*, 53, 1209–1218.

Kivimäki, M., Elovainio, M., Kokko, K., Pulkinnen, L., Kortteinen, M. and Tuomikoski, H. (2003) Hostility, unemployment and health status: testing three theoretical models. *Social Science and Medicine*, 56, 2139–2152.

Kivimäki, M., Vahtera, J., Elovainio, M., Helenius, H., Singh-Manoua, A. and Pentti, J. (2005) Optimism and pessimism as predictors of change in health after death or onset of severe illness in family. *Health Psychology*, 24, 413–421.

Klein, W.M. and Weinstein, N.D. (1997) Social comparison and unrealistic optimism about personal risk. In B.P. Buunk and F.X. Gibbons (eds), *Health, Coping and Well-being*. London: Lawrence Erlbaum. pp. 25–61.

Kline, K.N. and Mattson, M. (2000) Breast self-examination pamphlets: a content analysis grounded in fear appeals research. *Health Communication*, 12, 1–21.

Kline, P. (1999) *A Psychometric Primer*. London: Free Association Books.

Kobasa, S.C. (1979) Stressful life events, personality and health: an inquiry into hardiness. *Journal of Personality and Social Psychology*, 37, 1–11.

Kobasa, S.C., Maddi, S. and Kahn, S. (1982) Hardiness and health: a prospective study. *Journal of Personality and Social Psychology*, 42, 168–177.

Koestner, R., Lekes, N., Powers, T.A. and Chicoine, E. (2002) Attaining personal goals: self-concordance plus implementation intentions equals success. *Journal of Personality and Social Psychology*, 83, 231–244.

Kok, G., Deb Boer, D., DeVries, H., Gerards, F., Hospers, H.J. and Mudde, A.N. (1992) Self-efficacy and attribution theory in health education. In R. Schwarzer (ed.), *Self-efficacy: Thought Control of Action*. Washington, DC: Hemisphere. pp. 245–262.

Krantz, D.S. and McCeney, M.K. (2002) Effects of psychological and social factors on organic disease: a critical assessment of research on coronary heart disease. *Annual Review of Psychology*, 53, 341–369.

Larson, M.R., Duberstein, P.R., Talbot, N.L., Caldwell, C. and Moynihan, J.A. (2000) A presurgical psychosocial intervention for breast cancer patients: psychological distress and the immune response. *Journal of Psychosomatic Research*, 48, 187–194.

Lawson, V.L., Bundy, C., Lyne, P.A. and Harvey, J.N. (2004) Using the IRQ and PMDI to predict regular diabetes care-seeking among patients with type 1 diabetes. *British Journal of Health Psychology*, 9, 241–252.

Levenson, H. (1974) Activism and powerful others: distinctions within the concept of internal/external control. *Journal of Personality Assessment*, 38, 377–383.

Leventhal, H., Benyamini, Y., Brownlee, S., Diefenbach, M., Leventhal, E. A., Patrick-Miller, L. and Robitaille, C. (1997) Illness representations: theoretical foundations. In K. Petrie and J. Weinman (eds), *Perceptions of Health and Illness: Current Research and Applications*. Amsterdam: Harwood Academic Publishers. pp. 19–45.

Leventhal, H., Brisette, I. and Leventhal, E.A. (2003) The common-sense of self-regulation of health and illness. In L.D. Cameron and H. Leventhal (eds), *The Self-Regulation of Health and Illness Behaviour*. London: Routledge.

Leventhal, H., Diefenbach, M. and Leventhal, E. (1992) Illness cognition: using common sense to understand treatment adherence and effect cognitive interactions. *Cognitive Therapy and Research*, 16, 143–163.

Leventhal, H., Nerenz, D.R. and Steele, D.J. (1984) Illness representations and coping with health threats. In A. Baum, S.E. Taylor and J.E. Singer (eds), *Handbook of Psychology and Health*. Hillsdale, NJ: Lawrence Erlbaum. pp. 219–252.

Ley, P. (1988) *Communication with Patients: Improving Communication, Satisfaction and Compliance*. London: Croom Helm.

Ley, P. (1998) The use and improvement of written *communication* in mental healthcare and promotion. *Psychology, Health and Medicine*, 3, 19–53.

Ludwick, R. and Garczlowski, T. (2001) Breast self-exams among teenagers: outcome of a teaching program. *Cancer Nursing*, 24, 315–319.

Luszczynska, A. (2004) Change of breast self-examination: the effects of intervention on enhancing self-efficacy. *International Journal of Behavioral Medicine*, 11, 95–103.

Luszczynska, A. and Schwarzer, R. (2003) Planning and self-efficacy in the adoption and maintenance of breast self-examination: a longitudinal study on regulatory cognitions. *Psychology and Health*, 18, 93–108.

Luszczynska, A. and Schwarzer, R. (2005) Social cognitive theory. In M. Conner and P. Norman (eds), *Predicting Health Behaviour (2nd edition)*. Buckingham: Open University Press. pp. 127–169.

Lyvers, M. (1998) Drug addiction as a physical disease: the role of physical dependence and other chronic drug-induced neurophysiological changes in compulsive drug self-administration. *Experimental and Clinical Psychopharmacology*, 6, 107–125.

McCrae, R. and Stone, S. (1997) Personality. In A. Baum, S. Newman, J. Weinman, R. West and C. McManus (eds), *Cambridge Handbook of Psychology, Health and Medicine*. Cambridge: Cambridge University Press. pp. 29–35.

McCusker, C.G. (2001) Cognitive biases and addiction: an evolution in theory and method. *Addiction*, 96, 47–56.

McCusker, C.G. and Gettings, B. (1997) Automaticity of cognitive bias in addictive behaviours: further evidence with gamblers. *British Journal of Clinical Psychology*, 36, 543–554.

McDermott, M. (2002) Redefining health psychology: Matarazzo revisited. In D. Marks (ed.), *The Health Psychology Reader*. London: Sage. pp. 40–49.

McGhee, P. (2001) *Thinking Psychologically*. Basingstoke: Palgrave.

McGuire, W.J. (1968) The nature of attitudes and attitude change. In G. Lindzey and E. Aronson (eds), *The Handbook of Social Psychology (2nd edition)*. Reading, MA: Addison-Wesley. pp. 136–314.

McKenna, F.P. (1993) It won't happen to me: unrealistic optimism or illusion of control? *British Journal of Psychology*, 84, 39–50.

McKenna, F.P. and Albery, I.P. (2001) Does unrealistic optimism change following negative experience? *Journal of Applied Social Psychology*, 31, 1146–1157.

McKenna, F.P and Myers, L. (1997) Can accountability reduce or reverse existing illusory self-assessments? *British Journal of Psychology*, 88, 39–51.

McKenna, F.P., Warburton, D.M. and Winwood, M. (1993) Exploring the limits of optimism: the case of smokers' decision making. *British Journal of Psychology*, 84, 389–394.

McMillan, B. and Conner, M. (2003) Applying an extended version of the theory of planned behaviour to illicit drug use among students. *Journal of Applied Social Psychology*, 33, 1662–1683.

Maddux, J.E. and Rogers, R.W. (1983) Protection motivation and self efficacy: a revised theory of fear appeals and attitude change. *Journal of Experimental Social Psychology*, 19, 469–479.

Mahler, H. and Kulik, J.M. (1990) Preferences for healthcare involvement, perceived control and surgical recovery: a prospective study. *Social Science and Medicine*, 31, 743–751.

Manolio, T.A., Bailey-Wilson, J.E. and Collins, F.S. (2006) Genes, environment and the value of prospective cohort studies. *Nature Review Genetics*, 7, 812–820.

Marks, D.F., Murray, M., Evans, B., Willig, C., Woodall, C. and Sykes, C.M. (2005) *Health Psychology: Theory, Research and Practice*. London: Sage.

Marlatt, G.A., Baer, J.S., Donovan, D.M. and Kivlahan, D.R. (1988) Addictive behaviors: etiology and treatment. *Annual Review of Psychology*, 39, 223–252.

Marlatt, G.A. and Gordon, J.R. (1985) *Relapse Prevention*. New York: Guilford Press.

Marmot, M.G., Davey Smith, G., Stansfeld, S., Patel, C., North, F., Head, J., White, I., Brunner, E. and Feenay, A. (1991) Health inequalities among British civil servants. *Lancet*, 337, 1387–1393.

Marmot, M.G. and McDowell, M.E. (1986) Mortality decline and widening social inequalities. *Lancet*, 2 August, 274–276.

Marshall, S.J. and Biddle, S. (2001) The transtheoretical model of behaviour change: a meta-analysis of applications to physical activity and exercise. *Annals of Behavioral Medicine*, 23, 229–246.

Marteau, T.M., Kinmouth, A.L., Pyke, S. and Thompson, S.G. (1995) Readiness for lifestyle advice: self-assessments of coronary risk prior to screening in the British Family Heart study. *British Journal of General Practice*, 45, 5–8.

Marteau, T.M. and Weinman, J. (2004) Communicating about health threats and treatments. In S. Sutton, A. Baum and M. Johnston (eds), *The Sage Handbook of Health Psychology*. London: Sage. pp. 270–298.

Matarazzo, J.D. (1980) Behavioural health and behavioural medicine: frontiers for a new health psychology. *American Psychologist*, 35, 807–817.

Matarazzo, J.D. (1982) Behavioral health's challenge to academic, scientific and professional psychology. *American Psychologist*, 37, 1–14.

Matthews, K.A. (2005) Psychological perspectives on the development of coronary heart disease. *American Psychologist*, 60, 783–796.

Melzack, R. and Wall, P.D. (1965) Pain mechanisms: a new theory. *Science*, 150, 971–979.

Meyer, T.J. and Mark, M.M. (1995) Effects of psychosocial interventions with adult cancer patients: a meta-analysis of randomized experiments. *Health Psychology*, 14, 101–108.

Michie, S. (2004) Professional practice and issues in health psychology. In A. Kaptein and J. Weinman (eds), *Health Psychology*. Oxford: Blackwell. pp. 384–406.

Middleton, W., Harris, P.R. and Surman, M. (1996) Give 'em enough rope: perception of health and safety risks in bungee jumpers. *Journal of Social and Clinical Psychology*, 15, 68–79.

Miles, S. and Scaife, V. (2003) Optimistic bias and food. *Nutrition Research and Reviews*, 16, 3–19.

Miller, T.Q., Smith, T.W., Turner, C.W., Guijarro, M.L. and Hallet, A.J. (1996) A meta-analytic review of research on hostility and physical health. *Psychological Bulletin*, 119, 322–348.

Milne, S., Orbell, S. and Sheeran, P. (2002) Combining motivational and volitional interventions to promote exercise participation: protection motivation theory and implementation intentions. *British Journal of Health Psychology*, 7, 163–184.

Milne, S., Sheeran, P. and Orbell, S. (2000) Protection and intervention in health-related behaviour: a meta-analytic review of protection motivation theory. *Journal of Applied Social Psychology*, 30, 106–143.

Moscovici, S. (1981) On social representations. In J.P Forgas (ed.), *Social Cognition: Perspectives on Everyday Understanding*. London: Academic Press. pp. 181–209.

Moscovici, S. (1984) The phenomenon of social representations. In R.M. Farr and S. Moscovici (eds), *Social Representations*. Cambridge: Cambridge University Press. pp. 3–70.

Moscovici, S. (1988) Notes towards a description of social representations. *European Journal of Social Psychology*, 18, 211–250.

Moscovici, S. and Hewstone, M. (1983) Social representations and social explanation: from the 'naive' to the 'amateur' scientist. In M. Hewstone (ed.), *Attribution Theory: Social and Functional Extensions*. Oxford: Blackwell. pp. 98–125.

Moss-Morris, R., Petrie, K.J. and Weinman, J. (1996) Functioning in chronic fatigue syndrome: do illness perceptions play a regulatory role? *British Journal of Health Psychology*, 1, 15–25.

Moss-Morris, R., Weinman, J. and Petrie, K.J. (2002) The revised illness perception questionnaire (IPQ-R). *Psychology and Health*, 17, 1–16.

Munafò, M. and Albery, I.P. (eds) (2006) *Cognition and Addiction*. Oxford: Oxford University Press.

Munafò, M.R., Clark, T.G., Johnstone, E.C., Murphy, M.F.G. and Walton, R. (2004) The genetic basis for smoking behaviour: a systematic review and meta-analysis. *Nicotine and Tobacco Research*, 6, 583–597.

Munafò, M., Mogg, K., Roberts, S., Bradley, B. P. and Murphy, M. (2003). Selective processing of smoking-related cues in current smokers, ex-smokers and never-smokers on the modified Stroop task. *Journal of Psychopharmacology*, 7, 310–316.

Munafò, M.R. and Stevenson, J. (2001) Anxiety and surgical recovery: reinterpreting the literature. *Journal of Psychosomatic Research*, 51, 589–596.

Munafò, M. and Stevenson, J. (2003) Selective processing of threat-realted cues in day surgery patients and prediction of post-operative pain. *British Journal of Health Psychology*, 8, 439–449.

Murgraff, V., McDermott, M. and Walsh, J. (2003) Self-efficacy and behavioural enactment: the application of Schwarzer's Health Action Process Approach to the prediction of low-risk, single occasion drinking. *Journal of Applied Social Psychology*, 33, 339–361.

Murgraff, V., White, D. and Philips, K. (1996) Moderating binge drinking: is it possible to change behaviour if you plan in advance? *Alcohol and Alcoholism*, 6, 577–582.

Murgraff, V., White, D. and Philips, K. (1999) An application of protection motivation theory to riskier single occasion drinking. *Psychology and Health*, 14, 339–350.

Murray, M. (1997) A narrative approach to health psychology. *Journal of Health Psychology*, 2, 9–20.

Murray, M. (ed.) (2004) *Critical Health Psychology*. London: Palgrave.

Myers, L. and Frost, S. (2002) Smoking and smoking cessation: modifying perceptions of risk. In D. Rutter and L. Quine (eds), *Changing Health Behaviour*. Buckingham: Open University Press. pp. 49–65.

Myers, L. and Midence, K. (1998) *Adherence to Treatment in Medical Conditions*. London: Harwood Academic.

Myint, P.K., Luben, R.N., Welcj, A.A., Bingham, S.A., Wareham, N.J. and Khaw, K-T. (2006) Effect of age on the relationship of occupational social class with prevalence of modifiable cardiovascular risk factors and cardiovascular diseases. *Gerontology*, 52, 51–58.

Norman, P., Abraham, C. and Conner, M. (2000) *Understanding and Changing Health Behaviour: From Health Beliefs to Self-Regulation*. Amsterdam: Harwood Academic.

Norman, P. and Bennett, P. (1996) Health locus of control. In M. Conner and P. Norman (eds), *Predicting Health Behaviour*. Buckingham: Open University Press. pp. 62–94.

Norman, P., Bennett, P., Smith, C. and Murphy, S. (1997) Health locus of control and leisure time exercise. *Personality and Individual Differences*, 23, 769–774.

Norman, P., Boer, H. and Seydel, E.R. (2005) Protection motivation theory. In M. Conner and P. Norman (eds), *Predicting Health Behaviour (2nd edition)*. Buckingham: Open University Press. pp. 81–126.

Norman, P. and Brain, K. (2005) An application of the extended health belief model to the prediction of breast self-examination among women with a family history of breast cancer. *British Journal of Health Psychology*, 10, 1–16.

Norman, P. and Conner, M. (1993) The role of social cognition models in predicting attendance at health checks. *Psychology and Health*, 8, 447–462.

Norman, P., Searle, A., Harrard, R. and Vedhara, K. (2003) Predicting adherence to eye patching in children with amblyopia: an application of protection motivation theory. *British Journal of Health Psychology*, 8, 67–82.

O'Carroll, R.E., Smith, K.B., Grubb, N.R., Fox, K.A. and Masterton, G. (2001) Psychological factors associated with delay in attending hospital following a myocardial infarction. *Journal of Psychosomatic Research*, 51, 611–614.

Ogden, J., Clementi, C. and Aylwin, S. (2006) The impact of obesity surgery and the paradox of control: a qualitative study. *Psychology and Health*, 21, 273–293.

Ong, L.M., de Haes, J.C., Hoos, A.M. and Lammes, F.B. (1995) Doctor-patient communication: a review of the literature. *Social Science and Medicine*, 40, 903–918.

Orbell, S. and Sheeran, P. (1998) 'Inclined abstainers': a problem for predicting health behaviour. *British Journal of Social Psychology*, 37, 151–165.

Orford, J. (2001) Addiction as excessive appetite. *Addiction*, 96, 15–31.

Ormel, J., Kempen, G., Penninx, B.W., Brilman, E.I., Beekmam, A.T. and van Sonderen, E. (1997) Chronic medical conditions and mental health in older people: disability and psychosocial resources mediate specific mental health effects. *Psychological Medicine*, 27, 1065–1077.

Osborn, M. and Smith, J. (1998) The personal experience of chronic benign lower back pain: an interpretative phenomenological analysis. *British Journal of Health Psychology*, 3, 65–84.

Ouellette, J.A. and Wood, W. (1998) Habit and intention in everyday life: the multiple processes by which the past predicts the future. *Psychological Bulletin*, 124, 54–74.

Pallesen, S., Mitsem, M., Kvale, G., Johnsen, B.H. and Molde, H. (2005) Outcome of psychological treatments of pathological gambling: a review and meta-analysis. *Addiction*, 100, 1412–1422.

Pearce, J.M. (2002) Psychosocial factors in chronic disability. *Medical Science Monitor*, 8, RA275–281.

Peate, I. (1999) Testicular cancer: helping to promote self-examination. *Community Nurse*, 5(1), 32–33.

Peterson, C. and Seligman, M. (1987) Explanatory style and illness. *Journal of Personality*, 55, 237–265.

Petrie, K.J., Cameron, L., Ellis, C.J., Buick, D. and Weinman, J. (2002) Changing illness perceptions after myocardial infarction: and early intervention randomized controlled trial. *Psychosomatic Medicine*, 64, 580–586.

Petrie, K. and Weinman, J. (eds) (1997) *Perceptions of Health and Illness*. Reading: Harwood Academic.

Petrie, K.J., Weinman, J., Sharpe, N. and Buckley, J. (1996) Role of patients' view of their illness in predicting return to work and functioning following myocardial infarction. *British Medical Journal*, 312, 1191–1194.

Petty, R.E. and Cacioppo, J.T. (1986) The elaboration likelihood model of persuasion. *Advances in Experimental Social Psychology*, 19, 124–203.

Petty, R.E. and Cacioppo, J.T. (1996) *Attitudes and Persuasion: Classic and Contemporary Approaches*. Oxford: Westview.

Petty, R.E., Cacioppo, J.T. and Goldman, R. (1981) Personal involvement as a determinant of argument-based persuasion. *Journal of Personality and Social Psychology*, 41, 847–855.

Petty, R.E. and Wegener, D. (1998) Attitude change: multiple roles for persuasion variables. In D.T. Gilbert, S.T. Fiske and G. Lindzey (eds), *Handbook of Social Psychology (4th edition)*. New York: McGraw-Hill. pp. 323–390.

Plotnikoff, R.C. and Higginbottom, N. (2002) Protection motivation and exercise behaviour change for the prevention of coronary heart disease in a high risk, Australian representative community sample of adults. *Psychology, Health and Medicine*, 7, 87–98.

Potenza, M.N. (2006) Should addictive disorders include non-substance-related conditions? *Addiction*, 101, 142–151.

Potter, J. and Wetherell, M. (1987) *Discourse and Social Psychology: Beyond Attitudes and Behaviour.* Thousand Oaks, CA: Sage.

Pressman, S.D. and Cohen, S. (2005) Does positive affect influence health? *Psychological Bulletin*, 131, 925–971.

Prochaska, J.O. and DiClemente, C.C. (1983) Stages and processes of self-change of smoking: towards an integrative model of change. *Journal of Consulting and Clinical Psychology*, 51, 390–395.

Prochaska, J.O., DiClemente, C.C. and Norcross, J.C. (1992) In search of how people change: applications to addictive behaviours. *American Psychologist*, 47, 1102–1114.

Prochaska, J.O. and Velicer, W.F. (1997) The transtheoretical model of health behavior change. *American Journal of Health Promotion*, 12, 38–48.

Pyszczynski, T., Greenberg, J. and Solomon, S. (1999) A dual-process model of defense against conscious and unconscious death-related thoughts: an extension of terror management theory. *Psychological Review*, 106, 835–845.

Pyszczynski, T., Greenberg, J., Solomon, S., Arndt, J. and Schimel, J. (2004) Why do people need self-esteem? A theoretical and empirical review. *Psychological Bulletin*, 130, 435–468.

Quadrel, M.J., Fischoff, B. and Davis, W. (1993) Adolescent (in)vulnerability. *American Psychologist*, 48, 102–117.

Quadrel, M.J. and Lau, R. (1989) Health promotion, health locus of control, and health behaviour: two field experiments. *Journal of Applied Social Psychology*, 19, 1497–1521.

Quine, L., Rutter, D.R. and Arnold, L. (2002) Increasing cycle helmet use in school-age cyclists: an intervention based on the theory of planned behaviour. In D.R. Rutter and L. Quine (eds), *Changing Health Behaviour*. Buckingham: Open University Press. pp. 172–192.

Radley, A. (1994) *Making Sense of Illness: The Social Psychology of Health and Diseases.* London: Sage.

Radtke, H.R. and van Mens-Verhulst, J. (2001) Being a mother and living with asthma: an exploratory analysis of discourse. *Journal of Health Psychology*, 6, 379–391.

Rawl, S., Champion, V., Menon, U., Loehrer, P.J., Vance, G.H. and Skinner, C.S. (2001) Validation of scales to measure benefits of and barriers to colorectal cancer screening. *Journal of Psychosocial Oncology*, 19, 47–63.

Reddy, D.M., Fleming, R. and Adesso, V.J. (1992) Gender and health. In S. Maes, H. Leventhal and M. Johnstone (eds), *International Review of Health Psychology*. Chichester: Wiley.

Reid, L.D. and Christensen, D.B. (1988) A psychosocial perspective in the explanation of patients' drug taking behaviour. *Social Science and Medicine*, 27, 277–285.

Reime, B., Ratner, P.A., Tomaselli-Reime, S.N., Kelly, A., Schuecking, B.A. and Wenzlaff, P. (2006) The role of mediating factors in the association between social deprivation and low birth weight in Germany. *Social Science and Medicine*, 62, 1731–1734.

Renner, B. and Schwarzer, R. (2003) Social cognitive factors in health behaviour change. In J. Suls and K. Wallston (eds), *Social Psychological Foundations of Health and Illness*. Oxford: Blackwell. pp. 169–196.

Renner, B. and Schwarzer, R. (2005) The motivation to eat a healthy diet: how intenders and nonintenders differ in terms of risk perception, outcome expectancies, self-efficacy, and nutrition behavior. *Polish Psychological Bulletin*, 36, 7–15.

Richard, R., van der Pligt, J. and de Vries, N. (1996) Anticipated affect and behavioural choice. *Basic and Applied Social Psychology*, 18, 111–129.

Rise, J., Strype, J. and Sutton, S. (2002) Comparative risk ratings and lung cancer among Norwegian smokers. *Addiction Research*, 10, 313–320.

Robinson, T.E. and Berridge, K.C. (2000) The psychology and neurobiology of addiction: an incentive-sensitization view. *Addiction*, 95, S91–117.

Robinson, T.E. and Berridge, K.C. (2003) Addiction. *Annual Review of Psychology*, 54, 25–53.

Robinson-Whelen, S., Kim, C. and MacCallum, R.C. (1997) Distinguishing optimism from pessimism in older adults: is it more important to be optimistic or not to be pessimistic? *Journal of Personality and Social Psychology*, 73, 1345–1353.

Rodgers, W.M., Hall, C.R., Blanchard, C.M., McAuley, E. and Munroe, K.J. (2002) Task and scheduling self-efficacy as predictors of exercise behaviour. *Psychology and Health*, 27, 405–416.

Rogers, R.W. (1975) A protection motivation theory of fear appeals and attitude change. *Journal of Psychology*, 91, 93–114.

Rogers, R.W. (1983) Cognitive and physiological processes in fear appeals attitude change: a revised theory of protection motivation. In J.T. Cacioppo and R.E. Petty (eds), *Social Psychophysiology: A Source Book*. New York: Guilford Press. pp. 153–176.

Rosen, C.S. (2000) Is the sequencing of change processes by stage consistent across health problems? *Health Psychology*, 19, 593–604.

Rosenberger, P.H., Jokl, P. and Ickovics, J. (2006) Psychosocial factors and surgical outcomes: an evidence-based literature review. *Journal of the American Academy of Orthopaedic Surgeons*, 14, 397–405.

Rosenman, R.H. (1978) Role of Type A pattern in the pathogenesis of ischaemic heart disease and modification for prevention. *Advances in Cardiology*, 25, 34–46.

Rosenstock, I.M. (1974) Historical origins of the health belief model. *Health Education Monographs*, 2, 1–8.

Roter, D.L., Stewart, M., Putman, S.M., Lipkin, M., Stiles, W. and Inui, T.S. (1997) Communication patterns of primary care physicians. *Journal of the American Medical Association*, 277, 350–356.

Rotter, J.B. (1966) Generalised expectancies for internal vs. external control of reinforcement. *Psychological Monographs*, 80, 1–28.

Rotter, J.B. (1982) *The Development and Applications of Social Learning Theory: Selected Papers*. Brattleboro, VA: Praeger.

Rugulies, R. (2002) Depression as a predictor of coronary heart disease: a review and meta-analysis. *American Journal of Preventive Medicine*, 23, 51–61.

Rugulies, R., Aust, R. and Syme, S.L. (2004) Epidemiology of health and illness: a socio-psycho-physiological perspective. In S. Sutton, A. Baum and M. Johnston (eds), *The Sage Handbook of Health Psychology*. London: Sage. pp. 27–68.

Ruiter, R.A.C., Abraham, C.A. and Kok, G. (2001) Scary warnings and rational precautions: a review of the psychology of fear appeals. *Psychology and Health*, 16, 613–630.

Rutter, D.R., Iconomou, G. and Quine, L. (1996) Doctor-patient communication and outcome in cancer patients: an intervention. *Psychology and Health*, 12, 57–71.

Rutter, D.R. and Quine, L. (1996) Social psychological mediators of the relationship between demographic factors and health outcomes: a theoretical model and some preliminary data. *Psychology and Health*, 11, 5–22.

Rutter, D.R. and Quine, L. (2002) *Changing Health Behaviour.* Buckingham: Open University Press.

Rutter, D.R., Quine, L. and Albery, I.P. (1998) Perceptions of risk in motorcyclists: unrealistic optimism, relative realism, and predictions of behaviour. *British Journal of Psychology*, 89, 681–696.

Rutter, D.R., Quine, L. and Chesham, D. (1993) *Social Psychological Approaches to Health.* Hemel Hempstead: Harvester Wheatsheaf.

Sackett, D.L. and Haynes, R.B. (1976) *Compliance with Therapeutic Regimes.* Baltimore: Johns Hopkins University Press.

Scarr, S. and McCartney, K. (1983) How people make their own environment: a theory of genotype > environment effects. *Child Development*, 54, 424–430.

Scheier, M.F. and Carver, C.S. (1985) Optimism, coping and health: assessment and implications of generalised outcome expectancies. *Health Psychology*, 4, 219–247.

Scheier, M.F. and Carver, C.S. (1992) Effects of optimism on psychological and physical well-being: theoretical overview and empirical update. *Cognitive Therapy Research*, 16, 201–228.

Scheier, M.F., Carver, C.S. and Bridges, M.W. (1994) Distinguishing optimism from neuroticism (and trait anxiety, mastery and self-esteem): a reevaluation of the Life Orientation Test. *Journal of Personality and Social Psychology*, 67, 1063–1078.

Schultz, R., Bookwala, J., Knapp, J.E., Scheier, M.F. and Williamson, G.M. (1996) Pessimism, age and cancer mortality. *Psychology and Ageing*, 11, 304–309.

Schwarzer, R. (1992) Self-efficacy in the adoption and maintenance of health behaviours: theoretical approaches and a new model. In R. Schwarzer (ed.), *Self-efficacy: Though Control of Action.* Washington, DC: Hemisphere. pp. 217–243.

Schwarzer, R. (2004) *Modeling Health Behaviour Change: The Health Action Process Approach (HAPA).* Retrieved 24 October 2006 from http://userpage.fuberlin.de/~health/hapa.htm.

Schwarzer, R., Jerusalem, M. and Hahn, A. (1994) Unemployment, social support and health complaints: a longitudinal study of stress in East German refugees. *Journal of Community and Applied Social Psychology*, 4, 31–45.

Schwarzer, R. and Schroder, K.E. (1997) Social and personal coping resources as predictors of quality of life in cardiac patients. *European Review of Social Psychology*, 47, 131–135.

Sebregts, E.H., Falger, P.R. and Bar, F.W. (2000) Risk factor modification through nonpharmacological interventions in patients with coronary heart disease. *Journal of Psychosomatic Research*, 48, 425–441.

Selye, H. (1946) The general adaptation syndrome and the diseases of adaptation. *Journal of Clinical Endocrinology*, 6, 117–231.

Senior, V., Smith, J.A. and Michie, S. (2002) Making sense of risk: an interpretative phenomenological analysis of vulnerability to heart disease. *Journal of Health Psychology*, 7, 157–168.

Sesardic, N. (2005) *Making Sense of Heritability.* Cambridge: Cambridge University Press.

Shaffer, J.W., Graves, P.L., Swank, R.T. and Pearson, T.A. (1987) Clustering of personality traits in youth and the subsequent development of cancer among physicians. *Journal of Behavioral Medicine*, 10, 441–447.

Sharma, D., Albery, I.P. and Cook, C.C.H. (2001) Selective attentional bias to alcohol related stimuli in problem drinkers and non-problem drinkers. *Addiction*, 96, 285–295.

Sharp, T.J. (2001) Chronic pain: a reformulation of the cognitive-behavioural model. *Behavioral Research and Thereapy*, 39, 787–800.

Sheeran, P. (2002) Intention-behavior relations: a conceptual and empirical review. In W. Strobe and M. Hewstone (eds), *European Review of Social Psychology. Volume 12.* Chichester: Wiley. pp. 1–30.

Sheeran, P., Aarts, H., Custers, R., Rivis, A., Webb, T.L. and Cooke, R. (2005) The goal-dependent automaticity of drinking habits. *British Journal of Social Psychology*, 44, 47–63.

Sheeran, P., Milne, S., Webb, T.L. and Gollwitzer, P. (2005) Implementation intentions and health behaviour. In M. Conner and P. Norman (eds), *Predicting Health Behaviour (2nd edition)*. Buckingham: Open University Press. pp. 276–323.

Sheeran, P. and Orbell, S. (1996) How confidently can we infer health beliefs from questionnaire responses? *Psychology and Health*, 11, 273–290.

Sheeran, P., Trafimow, D. and Armitage, C. (2003) Predicting behaviour from perceived behavioural control: tests of the accuracy assumption of the theory of planned behaviour. *British Journal of Social Psychology*, 42, 393–410.

Sheeran, P., Webb, T.L. and Gollwitzer, P.M. (2005) The interplay between goal intentions and implementation intentions. *Personality and Social Psychology Bulletin*, 31, 87–98.

Shepperd, J., Mototo, J. and Pbert, L. (1996) Dispositional optimism as a predictor of health changes among cardiac patients. *Journal of Personality and Social Psychology*, 59, 517–532.

Siegrist, J. and Marmot, M.G. (2004) Health inequalities and the psychosocial environment – two scientific challenges. *Social Science and Medicine*, 58, 1463–1473.

Sluka, K.A. and Walsh, D. (2003) Transcutaneous electrical nerve stimulation: basic science mechanisms and clinical effectiveness. *Journal of Pain*, 4, 109–121.

Smith, J.A. (1996) Beyond the divide between cognition and discourse: using interpretative phenomenological analysis in health psychology. *Psychology and Health*, 11, 261–271.

Smith, J.A. (ed.) (2003) *Qualitative Psychology: A Practical Guide to Research Methods*. London: Sage.

Smith, J.A., Michie, S. and Stephenson, M. (2002) Risk perception and decision-making processes in candidates for genetic testing for Huntington's disease: an interpretative phenomenological analysis. *Journal of Health Psychology*, 7, 131–144.

Smith, J.A. and Osborn, M. (2003) Interpretative phenomenological analysis. In J.A. Smith (ed.), *Qualitative Psychology: A Practical Guide to Research Methods*. Thousand Oaks, CA: Sage. pp. 51–80.

Smith, M.S., Wallston, K.A. and Smith, C.A. (1995) The development and validation of the Perceived Health Competence Scale. *Health Education Research: Theory and Practice*, 10, 51–64.

Sniehotta, F.F., Scholz, U. and Schwarzer, R. (2005) Bridging the intention-behaviour gap: planning, self-efficacy and action control in the adoption and maintenance of physical exercise. *Psychology and Health*, 20, 143–160.

Spielberger, C.D., Gorsuch, R.L., Lushene, R., Vagg, P. and Jacobs, G. A. (eds) (1983) *Manual For the State-Trait Anxiety Inventory*. Palo Alto, CA: Consulting Psychological Press.

Stacy, A.W., Newcomb, M.D. and Ames, S.L. (2000) Implicit cognition and HIV risk behaviour. *Journal of Behavioral Medicine*, 23(5), 475–499.

Stanley, M.A. and Maddux, J.E. (1986) Cognitive processes in health enhancement: investigation of a combined protection motivation and self-efficacy model. *Basic and Applied Social Psychology*, 7, 101–113.

Steadman, L. and Quine, L. (2004) Encouraging young males to perform testicular self-examination: a simple, but effective, implementation intentions intervention. *British Journal of Health Psychology*, 9, 479–487.

Steadman, L., Rutter, D.R. and Field, S. (2002) Individually elicited versus modal normative beliefs in predicting adherence at breast cancer screening: examining the role of belief salience in the theory of planned behaviour. *British Journal of Health Psychology*, 7, 317–330.

Sternbach, R.A. (1987) *Mastering Pain: A Twelve StepProgram for Coping with Chronic Pain.* New York: Ballantyne Books.

Sterne, J.A. and Davey Smith, G. (2001) Sifting the evidence – what's wrong with significance tests? *British Medical Journal*, 322, 226–231.

Steptoe, A. and Wardle, J. (2001) Locus of control and health behaviour revisited: a multivariate analysis of young adults from 18 countries. *British Journal of Psychology*, 92, 659–672.

Stewart, M.A. (1995) Effective physician-patient communication and health outcomes: a review. *Canadian Medical Association Journal*, 152, 1423–1433.

Strecher, V.J., Kreuter, M., DenBoer, D.J., Kobrin, S., Hospers, H.J. and Skinner, C.S. (1994) The effects of computer-tailored smoking cessation messages in family practice settings. *Journal of Family Practice*, 39, 262–270.

Strecher, V.J. and Rosenstock, L.M. (1997) The health belief model. In A. Baum, S. Newman, J. Weinman, R. West and C. McManus (eds), *Cambridge Handbook of Psychology, Health and Medicine*. Cambridge: Cambridge University Press. pp. 113–117.

Suarez, E.C., Kuhn, C.M., Schanberg, S.M., Williams, R.B. and Zimmermann, E.A. (1998) Neuroendocrine, cardiovascular and emotional responses of hostile men: the role of interpersonal challenge. *Psychosomatic Medicine*, 60, 78–88.

Sulloway, J. (1980) *Freud: Biologist of the Mind*. London: Fontana.

Sutton, S. (1982) Fear arousing communications: a critical examination of theory and research. In J.R. Eiser (eds), *Social Psychology and Behavioural Medicine*. London: Wiley. pp. 303–337.

Sutton, S. (1994) The past predicts the future: interpreting behaviour-behaviour relationships in social psychological models of health behaviour. In D.R. Rutter and L. Quine (eds), *Social Psychology and Health: European Perspectives*. Aldershot: Avebury. pp. 71–88.

Sutton, S.R. (1996) Can 'stages of change' provide guidance in the treatment of addictions? A critical examination of Prochaska and DiClemente's model. In G. Edwards and C. Dare (eds), *Psychotherapy, Psychological Treatments and the Addictions*. Cambridge: Cambridge University Press. pp. 189–205.

Sutton, S. (1998) Explaining and predicting intentions and behaviour: how well are we doing? *Journal of Applied Social Psychology*, 28, 1318–1319.

Sutton, S. (2002) Using social cognition models to develop health behaviour interventions: problems and assumptions. In D. Rutter and L. Quine (eds), *Changing Health Behaviour*. Buckingham: Open University Press. pp. 193–208.

Sutton, S. (2005) Stage theories of health behaviour. In M. Conner and P. Norman (eds), *Predicting Health Behaviour (2nd edition)*. Buckingham: Open University Press. pp. 223–275.

Taubman Ben-Ari, O., Florian, V. and Mikulincer, M. (1999) The impact of mortality salience on reckless driving: a test of terror management mechanisms. *Journal of Personality and Social Psychology*, 76, 35–45.

Taubman Ben-Ari, O., Florian, V. and Mikulincer, M. (2000) Does a threat appeal moderate reckless driving? A terror management theory perspective. *Accident Analysis and Prevention*, 32, 1–10.

Taylor, S.E. and Brown, J.D. (1988) Illusion and well-being: a social psychological perspective on mental health. *Psychological Bulletin*, 103, 193–210.

Taylor, S.E., Kemeny, M.E., Aspinwall, L.G., Schneider, S.G., Rodriguez, R. and Herbert, M. (1992) Optimism, coping and psychological distress, and high risk sexual behaviour among at risk for acquired immunodeficiency syndrome (AIDS). *Journal of Personality and Social Psychology*, 63, 460–473.

Temoshok, L. (1987) Personality, coping style, emotion and cancer: towards an integrative model. *Social Science and Medicine*, 20, 833–840.

Tiffany, S.T., Conklin, C.A., Shiffman, S. and Clayton, R.R. (2004) What can dependence theories tell us about assessing the emergence of tobacco dependence? *Addiction*, 99, 78–86.

Townsend, P. and Davidson, N. (1982) *Inequalities in Health: the Black Report*. London: Penguin.

Trafimow, D., Sheeran, P., Conner, M. and Findlay, K.A. (2002) Evidence that perceived behavioural control is a mulitidimensional construct: perceived control and perceived difficulty. *British Journal of Social Psychology*, 41, 101–121.

Uitterhoeve, R.J., Vernooy, M., Litjens, M., Potting, K., Bensing, J., De Mulder, P. and van Achterberg, T. (2004) Psychosocial interventions for patients with advanced cancer – a systematic review of the literature. *British Journal of Cancer*, 91, 1050–1062.

Umeh, K. and Rogan-Gibson, J. (2001) Perceptions of threat, benefits and barriers in breast self-examination amongst asymptomatic women. *British Journal of Health Psychology*, 6, 362–372.

van Empelen, P., Kok, G., van Kesteren, N.M., van den Borne, B., Bos, A.E. and Schaalma, H.P. (2003) Effective methods to change sex-risk among drug users: a review of psychosocial interventions. *Social Science and Medicine*, 57, 1593–1608.

van der Plight, J. (1998) Perceived risk and vulnerability as predictors of precautionary behaviour. *British Journal of Health Psychology*, 3, 1–14.

Verplanken, B. (2005) Habits and implementation intentions. In J. Kerr, R. Weikunat and M. Moretti (eds), *The ABC of Behavioural Change*. Oxford: Elsevier Science. pp. 99–109.

Verplanken, B. and Aarts, H. (1999) Habit, attitude and planned behaviour: is habit an empty construct or an interesting case of goal-directed authomaticity? *European Review of Social Psychology*, 19, 101–134.

Verplanken, B. and Orbell, S. (2003) Reflections on past behaviour: a self-report index of habit strength. *Journal of Applied Social Psychology*, 33, 1313–1330.

Vitetta, L., Anton, B., Cortizo, F. and Sali, A. (2005) Mind-body medicine: stress and its impact on overall health and longevity. *Annals of the New York Academy of Sciences*, 1057, 492–505.

Vögele, C. (1998) Serum lipid concentrations, hostility and cardiovascular reactions to mental stress. *International Journal of Psychophysiology*, 28, 167–179.

Wallston, K.A. (1992) Hocus-pocus, the focus isn't strictly on locus: Rotter's social learning theory modified for health. *Cognitive Therapy and Research*, 16, 183–199.

Wallston, K. A. (1997) Perceived control and health behaviour. In A. Baum, S. Newman, J. Weinman, R. West and C. McManus (eds), *Cambridge Handbook of Psychology, Health and Medicine*. Cambridge: Cambridge University Press. pp. 151–154.

Wallston, K.A., Stein, M.J. and Smith, C.A. (1994) Form C of the MHLC scales: a condition-specific measure of locus of control. *Journal of Personality Assessment*, 63, 534–553.

Wallston, K.A., Wallston, B.S. and DeVellis, R. (1978) Development of the Multidimensional Health Locus of Control (MHLC) scales. *Health Education Monographs*, 6, 160–170.

Waters, A. J., Shiffman, S., Sayette, M. A., Paty, J. A., Gwaltney, C. J. and Balabanis, M. H. (2003) Attentional bias predicts outcome in smoking cessation. *Health Psychology*, 22, 378–387.

Watson, D. and Clark, L.A. (1984) Negative affectivity: the disposition to experience aversive emotional states. *Psychological Bulletin*, 96, 465–490.

Wdowik, M.J., Kendall, P.A., Harris, M.A. and Auld, G. (2001) Expanded health belief model predicts diabetes self-management in college students. *Journal of Nutrition Education*, 33, 17–23.

Webb, T.L. and Sheeran, P. (2004) Identifying good opportunities to act: implementation intentions and cue discrimination. *European Journal of Social Psychology*, 34, 407–419.

Webb, T.L. and Sheeran, P. (2006) Does changing behavioral intentions engender behavior change? A meta-analysis of the experimental evidence. *Psychological Bulletin*, 132, 249–268.

Weinman, J. (1987) *An Outline of Psychology as Applied to Medicine*. London: J. Wright.

Weinman, J., Petrie, K.J. and Moss-Morris, R. (1996) The Illness Perception Questionnaire: a new method for assessing the cognitive representation of illness. *Psychology and Health*, 11, 431–445.

Weinstein, N.D. (1980) Unrealistic optimism about future life events. *Journal of Personality and Social Psychology*, 39, 806–820.

Weinstein, N.D. (1988) The precaution adoption process. *Health Psychology*, 7, 355–386.

Weinstein, N.D. (1989) Optimistic biases about personal risks. *Science*, 246, 1232–1233.

Weinstein, N.D. and Klein, W.M. (1995) Resistance of personal risk perceptions to debiasing interventions. *Health Psychology*, 14, 132–140.

Weinstein, N.D., Lyon, J.E., Sandman, P.M. and Cuite, C.L. (1998) Experimental evidence for stages of health behaviour change: the precaution adoption process model applied to home radon testing. *Health Psychology*, 17, 445–453.

Weinstein, N.D. and Sandman, P.M. (1992) A model for the precaution adoption process: evidence from home radon testing. *Health Psychology*, 11, 170–180.

Weinstein, N.D. and Sandman, P.M. (2002) Reducing the risks of exposure to radon gas: an application of the precaution adoption process model. In D.R. Rutter and L. Quine (eds), *Changing Health Behaviour*. Buckingham: Open University Press. pp. 66–86.

Welkenhuysen, M., Evers-Kiebooms, G., Decruiyenaere, M. and van den Berghe, H. (1996) Unrealistic optimism and genetic risk. *Psychology and Health*, 4, 479–492.

Wetherell, M. (1997) Linguistic repertoires and literary criticism: new direction for a social psychology of gender. In M. Gergen and S. Davis (eds), *Towards a New Psychology of Gender: A Reader*. London: Routledge. pp. 149–167.

Whalen, C.K., Henker, B., O'Neil, R., Hollingshead, J., Holman, A. and Moore, B. (1994) Optimism in children's judgments of health and environmental risks. *Health Psychology*, 13, 319–325.

Whitmarsh, A., Koutanji, M. and Sidell, K. (2003) Illness perceptions, mood and coping in predicting attendance at cardiac rehabilitation. *British Journal of Health Psychology*, 8, 209–221.

Wiers, R.W., Cox, W.M., Field, M., Fadardi, J.S., Palfai, T.P., Schoenmakers, T. and Stacy, A.W. (2006) The search for new ways to change alcohol-related cognitions in heavy drinkers. *Alcoholism: Clinical and Experimental Research*, 30, 320–321.

Williams, K.E. and Bond, M.J. (2002) The roles of self-efficacy, outcome expectancies and social support in the self-care behaviours of diabetics. *Psychology, Health and Medicine*, 7, 112–141.

Williamson, L.M., Hart, G.J., Flowers, P., Frankis, J.S. and Der, G.J. (2001) The Gay Men's Task Force: the impact of peer education on the sexual health behaviour of homosexual men in Glasgow. *Sexually Transmitted Infections*, 77, 427–432.

Willig, C. (1998) Constructions of sexual activity and their implications for sexual practice. *Journal of Health Psychology*, 3, 383–392.

Willig, C. (2004) Discourse analysis and health psychology. In M. Murray (ed.), *Critical Health Psychology*. London: Palgrave. pp. 155–170.

Witte, K. (1992) Putting the fear back into fear appeals: the extended parallel process model. *Communication Monographs*, 59, 329–349.

World Health Organization (2002) *The World Health Report 2002: Reducing Risks, Promoting Healthy Life*. Geneva: WHO.

Yabroff, K.R and Mandelblatt, J.S. (1999) Interventions targeted towards patients to increase mammography use. *Cancer Epidemiological Biomarkers and Prevention*, 8, 749–757.

Yzer, M., Fisher, J.D., Bakker, A.B., Siero, F. and Misovich, S.J. (1998) The effects of information about AIDS risk and self-efficacy on women's intention to engage in AIDS-preventive behaviour. *Journal of Applied Social Psychology*, 28, 1837–1852.

INDEX